from this GENERATION for ever

VOLUME 2: PRESERVATION

A Study of God's Promise to Preserve His Word

Bryan C. Ross

Copyright © 2023, Bryan C. Ross

From This Generation For Ever: A Study of God's Promise to Preserve His Word
Volume 2: Preservation

All Scriptures are quoted from the King James Version.

ISBN: 978-1-945774-98-0

Trust House Publishers
P.O. Box 3181
Taos, NM 87571 USA
www.trusthousepublishers.com

Ordering Information: Quantity sales. Special discounts are available on quantity purchases by churches, associations, and others. For details, contact the publisher at the address above.

Orders by U.S. trade bookstores and wholesalers. Please contact the publisher.

2 3 4 5 6 7 8 9 1

The following notes were taught to the saints of Grace Life Bible Church in Grand Rapids, MI between September 11, 2016, and May 14, 2017. The purpose of this project has been to set forth our belief that the King James Bible is God's Word for English speaking people. Our goal has been to enunciate a position on the final authority of the King James Bible that is scriptural, reasonable, factual, and historically accurate. The notes presented herein are the edited course notes that were distributed to participants when the lessons were originally taught. As of the publiciaton of the present volume the class is still being taught. To access the video and MP3 audio for these Lessons please go to the online classroom at bit.do/preservationproject or by visiting the School of Theology page on the Grace Life Bible Church website.

I would like to thank Sylvia and Mike Erspamer for their assistance every week in proofreading the notes. Also, to Amy Stuart for proofreading the manuscript. Many thanks are also in order to the members of the Adult Sunday School class at Grace Life Bible Church. Without your interest and support this class would not have been possible.

TABLE OF CONTENTS

LESSON 28 Introduction to Preservation | **11**

LESSON 29 Introduction to Preservation, Part 2 | **21**

LESSON 30 Various Views of Preservation | **33**

LESSON 31 Preservation: Examining the Relevant Passages, Psalm 12:6-7 | **45**

LESSON 32 Preservation: Examining the Relevant Passages, Psalm 12:6-7, Part 2 | **57**

LESSON 33 Preservation: Examining the Relevant Passages, Psalm 119 | **69**

LESSON 34 Preservation: Examining the Relevant Passages, Isaiah 30:8 | **79**

LESSON 35 Preservation: Examining the Relevant Passages, Isaiah 40:8 & I Peter 1:23-25 | **87**

LESSON 36 Preservation: Examining the Relevant Passages, Matthew 4:4 | **99**

LESSON 37 Preservation: Examining the Relevant Passages, Matthew 4:4, Part 2 | **111**

LESSON 38	Preservation: Examining the Relevant Passages, Matthew 24:35	**121**
LESSON 39	Preservation: Faith in the Promise of God	**133**
LESSON 40	Why Preservation Matters	**149**
LESSON 41	Preservation: the Corollary of Inspiration	**171**
LESSON 42	Preservation: the Corollary of Inspiration, Part 2	**187**
LESSON 43	Passages Proving Plenary Preservation is Presumptuous	**205**
LESSON 44	Jot and Tittle Preservation, Matthew 5:17-18	**227**
LESSON 45	Jot and Tittle Preservation, Matthew 5:17-18, Part 2	**241**
LESSON 46	Final Thoughts on the Corollary and the Extent of Preservation	**253**
LESSON 47	The Method of Preservation: Providential or Miraculous?	**263**
LESSON 48	The Process of Preservation: The Multiplicity of Copies	**281**

LESSON 49	The Process of Preservation: The Multiplicity of Copies, Part 2 | **291**
LESSON 50	The Process of Preservation: The People of Preservation in the Old Testament | **299**
LESSON 51	The Process of Preservation: The People of Preservation in the Old Testament, Part 2 | **309**
LESSON 52	The Process of Preservation: Preservation and the New Testament | **317**
LESSON 53	The Process of Preservation: The Preservation of the New Testament, Part 2 | **327**
LESSON 54	The Process of Preservation: Simultaneous Nature of Preservation and Corruption | **337**
LESSON 55	The Process of Preservation: The Question of Access and Availability | **353**
LESSON 56	Concluding Thoughts on Preservation | **367**

INTRODUCTION TO PRESERVATION

INTRODUCTION

- Since the completion of Lesson 27, I have been reading and studying in preparation for the resumption of class. The bulk of my reading over the last four and a half months has been focused on the doctrine of preservation. In the interest of full transparency, I have read a host of books or portions thereof as well as essays and articles in theological journals. My reading has traversed both sides of the preservation controversy, and I included the titles listed in the Summer 2016 Reading List on page 8.

- During our intermission I also wrote a paper titled *The King James Bible in America: An Orthographic, Historical, and Textual Investigation.* This paper is currently undergoing a peer review by a group of pastors and Bible teachers. In September 2019 this paper was published by Dispensational Publishing House and can be order directly form the publisher at the following address:

    o https://dispensationalpublishing.com/product/the-king-james-bible-in-america/

- Much of what I read was very challenging to my previous thinking on the topic of preservation. More than once during the past four and a half months I contemplated giving up and just ending the class. As the reading list demonstrates there are scholarly men with high academic credentials on both sides of this issue. All of this just highlights even more our need to base our thinking on this topic upon God's word, not mere human opinion.

- I am still in the process of working through how to explain where I am at on these issues. I am aware that doing this in real time, in front of a live audience, might expose me to criticism as I work through the limitations of terminology. Here is what I know; even within the King James Camp there is no universally agreed upon viewpoint to which everyone subscribes. There are many sub-views that are arrived at via various means and for a variety of reasons. There is a tendency exhibited by some to consider those with nuanced or slightly different views as not being "King James enough." All I am asking for is a fair hearing before one decides to brand me one way or the other.

REVIEW

- After dealing with some preliminary issues (Lessons 1-10), the main objective of our first term was to set forth a clear understanding of the doctrine of inspiration. In doing so, we considered the following:

    o Various Theories of Inspiration (Lesson 11)

    o Potential Pitfalls of the Plenary Position (Lesson 12)

    o Passages Proving the Plenary Position (Lesson 13)

    o Divine Dictation as the Mechanism of Inspiration? (Lessons 14-17)

    o God's Design in Inspiration: Equality Between the Living and Written Word (Lesson 18)

    o The Living Word's Attitude Toward the Written Word (Lesson 19)

    o The New Testament Writer's Attitude Toward the Written Word (Lesson 20)

    o Internal Evidence of Inspiration: Undesigned Coincidences (Lessons 21-22)

    o Internal Evidence of Inspiration: Fulfilled Prophecy (Lesson 23)

    o External Evidence of Inspiration: The Historicity of the Old Testament (Lesson 24)

    o External Evidence of Inspiration: The Historicity of the New Testament (Lesson 25)

    o External Evidence of Inspiration: The Transmission of the Text (Lesson 26)

    o Disclaimers Regarding the Limitations of Inspiration (Lesson 27)

- In Lesson 2, I introduced you to the following set of presuppositions that we used to guide our study of inspiration:

  o God exists. (Psalm 14:1)

  o God has magnified His word above His own name. (Psalms 138:2)

  o God's word is eternally settled in heaven. (Psalms 119:89)

  o God, through the process of inspiration, has communicated His word to mankind. (I Timothy 3:16 & II Peter 1:21)

  o God's words were written down so that they could be made eternally available to men. (Isaiah 30:8, I Peter 1:23)

  o God promised to preserve that which He inspired. (Psalms 12:6-7)

- Generally speaking, the first five of these presuppositions are not in dispute among leading Evangelical and Fundamentalist theologians. However, the same could certainly not be said for the sixth presupposition regarding preservation. Much ink has been spilt debating this doctrine. It is to understand the sixth presupposition i.e., the doctrine of preservation, that we will devote the majority of our time in this section of the class.

- Introductory Lessons 3 and 4 as well as 8 through 10 did touch upon preservation, perhaps a bit prematurely, but they lack the details we will begin covering in this Lesson. By way of review, we observed the following basic points about preservation in these early lessons:

  o Preservation is the Bible's claim for itself. God promised to preserve that which He inspired.

  o God did not see fit to accomplish His fundamental promise of preservation by preserving the original autographs. This is evident because had He chosen to accomplish preservation in this fashion, we would possess the originals today.

  o To accomplish the preservation of His word, God did not preserve it in a state of *"verbatim identicality"* but in a state of "pureness."

- There are substantive differences in meaning between the *TR* and the Critical Text that impact the accuracy of the text, some of which impact doctrine.

- The goal of these early lessons *was not* to set forth a fully developed doctrine of preservation. One must first fully appreciate the doctrine of inspiration before being able to fully grasp the doctrine of preservation in its fullness. Put another way, if one does not accurately understand inspiration, he will struggle to understand what is being preserved and how to scripturally identify the process.

TAKING STOCK OF THE FACTS

- Fact 1 — the original autographs are not extant i.e., they no longer exist.

- Fact 2 — no two Greek manuscripts are exactly the same.
  - Alexandrian manuscripts (Codex Sinaiticus) and B (Codex Vaticanus), the two so-called oldest and best, differ with each other in over 3,000 places in the gospels alone.
  - The manuscripts comprising the Alexandrian Text Type differ from those comprising the Byzantine Text Type.
  - No two Byzantine manuscripts read exactly the same.

- Fact 3 — no two printed editions of the Greek New Testament are exactly the same.
  - Editions of the TR are not exactly the same.
  - The TR differs from the Critical Text.

- - Critical Text editions are not exactly the same.
    - United Bible Society
    - Nestle-Aland
- Fact 4 — no two editions of the King James Bible are exactly the same.
- Fact 5 — the King James differs from modern versions.
- Fact 6 — no two modern versions read exactly the same.
- Summary Statement:
  - "If the preservation of the Word of God depends upon exact preservation of the words of the original documents, then the situation is dire. No two manuscripts contain exactly the same words. No two editions of the Masoretic Text contain exactly the same words. No two editions of the *Textus Receptus* contain exactly the same words. No two modifications of the King James Version contain exactly the same words and the Bible nowhere tells us which edition, if any, does contain the exact words of the originals. These are not speculations, these are plain facts." (Bauder, 155)
- All of this raises serious questions as to the extent and means by which preservation was accomplished. Some, as we will see in the coming weeks, go so far as to say that there is no such thing as preservation i.e., it is a contrived doctrine to support King James Onlyism.
- What is clear is this, demanding "exact sameness" or "*verbatim identicality* of wording" as your standard of preservation reaches beyond the historical and textual facts and is ultimately unhelpful and detrimental to one's position. Yet, this is exactly what many King James Only advocates argue for when they hold to "plenary preservation" or "identical preservation." Opponents of the King James are more than happy to allow King James advocates to adopt this standard as their burden of proof because they know that "*verbatim*" or "Xerox" preservation cannot be sustained in light of the facts.

- The following points are inescapable:
  - God promised to preserve His word.
    - Psalms 12:6-7; 105:5; 119:89, 111, 152, 160; Isaiah 30:8; 40:8; Matthew 24:35; I Peter 1:23-25
  - God did not see fit to preserve His word by preserving the originals.
    - This is self-evident because the originals no longer exist.
  - God did not supernaturally over-take the pen of every scribe, copyist, or typesetter who ever handled the text to ensure that no differences of any kind entered the text.
    - Differences exist at every level of this discussion.
  - If the standard for preservation is "plenary," "pristine", or "*verbatim*" identicality, why did God not just preserve the originals and thereby remove all doubt?

- So how do we make sense of all of this? One could adopt a completely humanistic or naturalistic approach and try to reason through the conundrum based on human viewpoint alone. Or one can look to God's word for guidance and insight into how to think about the problem, just as we did in our investigation of inspiration. I believe that we should allow the Holy Spirit to instruct us how to think about the issue. When in doubt, the viewpoint of faith is always best.

- This brings us back to the end of Lesson 27 (See Volume 1). Many encounter problems studying manuscript evidence/textual criticism because they approach the subject from the vantage point of human viewpoint. In other words, the subject is broached with a lack of thorough understanding of the fundamental underlying doctrines.

- As we have seen through our study of inspiration, the Bible is unlike any other book and should be approached accordingly. Once again, Dr. Edward F. Hills pointed this out in his 1956 book *The King James Version Defended*.

- o "The Christian Church has long confessed that the books of the New Testament, as well as those of the Old, are divine Scriptures, written under the inspiration of the Holy Spirit. ". . Since the doctrine of divine inspiration of the New Testament has, in all ages, stimulated the copying of these sacred books, it is evident that this doctrine is important for the history of the New Testament text, no matter whether it be a true doctrine or only a belief of the Christian Church. But what if it be true? What if the original New Testament manuscripts actually were inspired of God? If the doctrine of divine inspiration of the New Testament is a true doctrine, then New Testament textual criticism is different from the textual criticism of ordinary books." (Hills, 1-2)

- o "Thus there are two methods of New Testament textual criticism; the consistently Christian method and the naturalistic method. These two methods deal with the same materials, the same Greek manuscripts, and the same translations and biblical quotations, but they interpret the materials very differently. The consistently Christian method interprets the materials of New Testament textual criticism in accordance with the doctrines of the divine inspiration and providential preservation of the Scriptures. The naturalistic method interprets these same materials in accordance with its own doctrine that the New Testament is nothing more than a human book." (Hills, 3)

- What does Hills mean when he uses the phrase "naturalistic method" in these quotes? He is referring to the methodology of "naturalism" or the "philosophical viewpoint according to which everything arises from natural properties and causes, and supernatural or spiritual explanations are excluded or discounted." (Google Definition)

- Drs. Westcott and Hort, in the introduction to The New Testament in the Original Greek, started their task with the presupposition that the Bible is to be treated like any other book.

    - o "The principles of criticism explained in the foregoing section hold good for all ancient texts preserved in a plurality of documents.

> In dealing with the text of the New Testament no new principle whatever is needed or legitimate. (Westcott and Hort, 73)

- This presupposition is no doubt a result of their low view of inspiration. When speaking about "primitive corruption" in the text, Dr. Hort states:

    o "Little is gained by speculating as to the precise point at which such corruptions came in. They may be due to the original writer, or his amanuensis if wrote from dictation, or they may be due to one of the earliest transcribers." (Westcott and Hort, 280-281)

- On this point Hort stands in opposition to modern evangelical scholarship in that he allows for "corruption" to have entered the text via the "original writer." Such a position explains why Hort is reluctant to ascribe infallibility to the text in any form. In a letter addressed to J.B. Lightfoot dated May 1, 1860, Hort stated in part:

    o "I am convinced that any view of the Gospels, which distinctly and consistently recognizes for them a natural and historical origin (whether under a special Divine superintendence or not) and assumes that they did not drop down ready-made from heaven, must and will be 'startling' to an immense portion of educated English people. But so far, at least, Westcott and I are perfectly agreed, and I confess I had hoped that you (Lightfoot) would assent. . . If you make a decided conviction of the absolute infallibility of the N.T. practically a *sine quo non* for co-operation, I fear I could not join you, even if you were willing to forget your fears about the origin of the Gospels. I am most anxious to find the N.T. infallible, and have a strong sense of the Divine purpose guiding all its parts; but I cannot see how the exact limits of such guidance can be ascertained except by unbiased a posterior criticism. . . (Regarding the question of "Providence" in Biblical Hort writes) Most strongly I recognize it; but I am not prepared to say that it necessarily involves absolute infallibility." (Hort, 419-421)

- This is the type of textual criticism that Dr. Hills is referring to when he talks about the "naturalistic method." He is speaking about an approach to the scriptures that doubts their supernatural origin, doubts their infallibility even in the original autographs, and treats the Bible as though it were like any other book. Such was the approach of Drs. Westcott and Hort.

WORKS CITED

Bauder, Kevin T. "An Appeal to Scripture" in *One Bible Only? Examining the Exclusive Claims for the King James Bible*. Grand Rapids, MI: Kregel Publications, 2001.

Hills, Edward F. *The King James Version Defended*. Des Moines, IA: Christian Research Press, 1956.

Hort, Fenton John Anthony. *Life and Letters of Fenton John Anthony Hort, Vol. I*. London: Macmillian and Company LTD, 1896.

Westcott, Brooke Foss & Fenton John Anthony Hort. *The New Testament in The Original Greek*. London: Macmillian and Company LTD, 1896.

INTRODUCTION TO PRESERVATION, PART 2

INTRODUCTION

- In the previous Lesson we resumed class by reviewing some key points from Term 1 (Lessons 1-27) regarding inspiration and preservation.

  The bulk of our time in Lesson 28 was spent on "Taking Stock of the Facts" as they pertain to the textual debate and the doctrine of preservation. To accomplish this task, I provided you with some written statements as I drew the following diagram on the board:

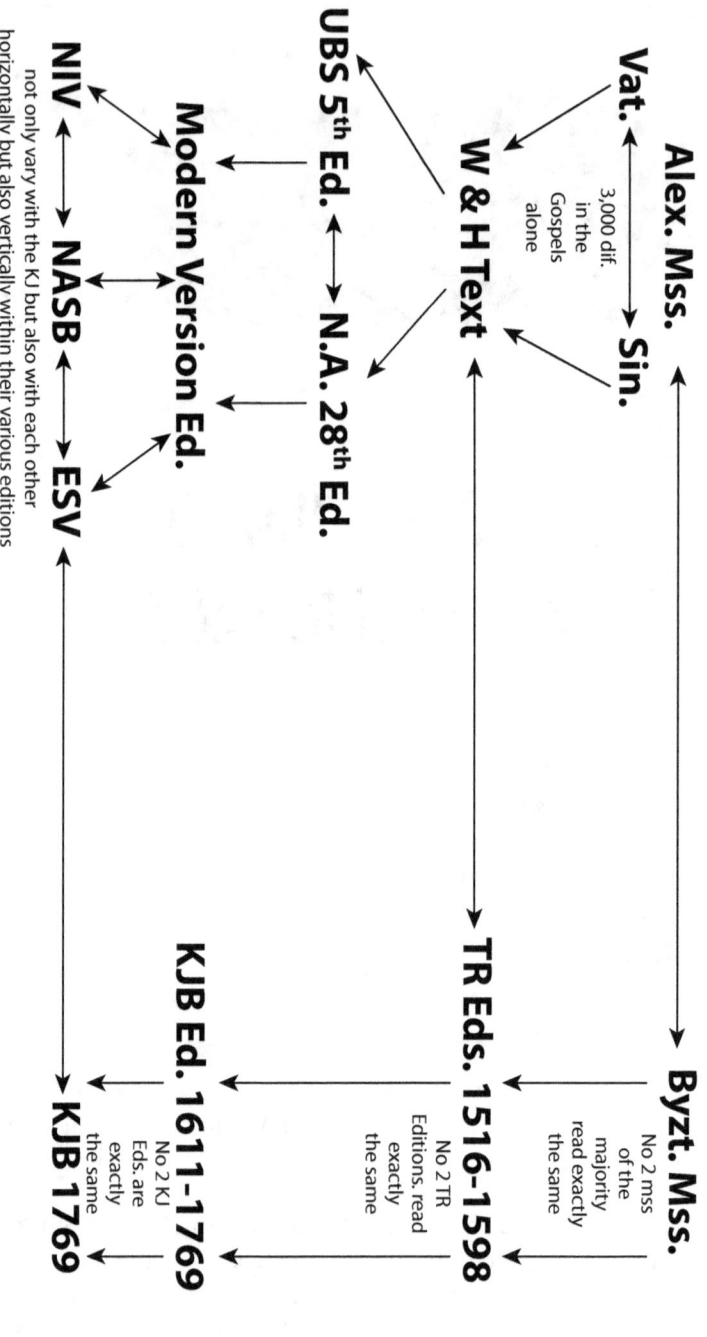

- After presenting the diagram we read the following summary statement from the pen of Kevin T. Bauder:

    o "If the preservation of the Word of God depends upon exact preservation of the words of the original documents, then the situation is dire. No two manuscripts contain exactly the same words. No two editions of the Masoretic Text contain exactly the same words. No two editions of the *Textus Receptus* contain exactly the same words. No two modifications of the King James Version contain exactly the same words and the Bible nowhere tells us which edition, if any, does contain the exact words of the originals. These are not speculations, these are plain facts." (Bauder, 155)

- From this we concluded that demanding "exact sameness" or "verbatim identicality of wording" as your standard of preservation reaches beyond the historical and textual facts and is ultimately unhelpful and detrimental to one's position. Yet, this is exactly what many King James advocates argue for when they hold to "plenary preservation" or "identical preservation." Opponents of the King James are more than happy to allow King James Only advocates to adopt this standard as their burden of proof because they know that "verbatim" or "identical" preservation cannot be sustained in light of the facts.

    o God promised to persevere His word.

    - Psalms 12:6-7; 105:5; 119:89, 111, 152, 160; Isaiah 30:8; Matthew 24:35; I Peter 1:23-25

    o God did not see fit to preserve His word by preserving the originals.

    - This is self-evident because the originals no longer exist.

    o God did not supernaturally over-take the pen of every scribe, copyist, or typesetter who ever handled the text to ensure that no differences of any kind entered the text.

    - Differences exist at every level of this discussion.

- o If the standard for preservation is "plenary," pristine", or "*verbatim*" identicality, why did God not just preserve the originals and thereby remove all doubt?

- So how do we make sense of all of this? One could adopt a completely humanistic or naturalistic approach and try to reason through the conundrum on the basis of human viewpoint alone, or, one can look to God's word for guidance and insight into how to think about the problem, just as we did in our investigation of inspiration. I believe that we should allow the Holy Spirit to instruct us how to think about the issue. When in doubt, the viewpoint of faith is always best.

  - o Drs. Westcott & Hort maintained that the Bible should be treated like any other book on account of their low view of inspiration. They maintained that corruption could have entered the text at the hands of the original writers and thereby refused to ascribe "absolute infallibility" even to the original autographs. (See Lesson 28 for supporting quotations.)

- In this Lesson, I want to finish my point regarding the book of Jeremiah and its importance in terms of framing the discussion.

USING THE BOOK OF JEREMIAH TO FRAME THE DISCUSSION

- Practically speaking, we do not need to not place more emphasis on something than God does. Please consider the following questions about Mary as an example:
  - o Was Mary the mother of Jesus?
  - o Was Mary a virgin?

- o Was Mary a perpetual virgin?
- o Was Mary the mother of God?

- Only two of these statements are true. What happens when someone embraces all four and thereby places more emphasis on Mary than God does? Practically, they wind up with a statue (idol) in their front yard.

- Likewise, we do not need to ascribe more importance to the original autographs than God does. Nor should we demand more from the doctrine of preservation than God does in His word. I want to use the book of Jeremiah to illustrate both of these points.

- Jeremiah 36:1-4 — Baruch writes from the mouth of Jeremiah the original manuscript of Jeremiah 1-36 (Original #1).

- Jeremiah 36:20-24 — Jehoiakim and Jehudi destroy the original manuscript of Jeremiah. Note that the text explicitly states in verse 24 that "they were not afraid." Don't they know that they just destroyed an original autograph?

- Jeremiah 36:27-32 — God re-inspires Jeremiah in chapters 1 through 36 and adds "many like words" to what was destroyed in the fire by Jehoiakim (Original #2).

- Jeremiah 45:1 — these additional words comprise chapters 45 through 52 at a minimum and possibly chapters 37 through 41 as well.

- Jeremiah 51:61-63 — Jeremiah writing at the bidding of God the Holy Spirit tells Seraiah to destroy Original #2 by tying a stone to it and throwing it into the Euphrates River after it is read in Babylon. God almighty orders the destruction of Original #2. Why would God do this? Didn't God know that a bunch of Fundamentalists in the 20th and 21st century would be looking for the originals?

- Daniel 9:2 — over 70 years later Daniel comes to understand, by reading the book of Jeremiah, that the captivity was supposed to last 70 years. How is that possible if Original #2 was destroyed? Copies were made prior to the captivity. Once the copies were made, God did not care what happened to the original. The original contents of Original #2 were preserved via the copying process. Daniel had access to the inspired word of God through the copy he had in front of him.

- Matthew 2:17-18 — contains a quotation from Jeremiah 31:15. First, how did Matthew have access to what Jeremiah said over 470 years (70 year captivity + 400 years of silence) later if God had not preserved His word? So, God secured the contents of the book of Jeremiah despite directing Jeremiah to have Original #2 thrown in the Euphrates River.

    o This seems to suggest that modern attempts to search for, find, and/or reconstruct the originals are out of step with how the Bible would teach you to think about things.

        - *Searching for the Original Bible* by James Price
        - *The Quest for the Original New Testament* by Philip Comfort

- Second, notice that Jeremiah 31:15 and Matthew 2:18 do not possess identical or *verbatim* wording i.e., they are not exactly the same even within the KJB.

Jeremiah 31:15	Matthew 2:18
Thus saith the LORD; A voice was heard in Ramah, lamentation, *and* bitter weeping; Rahel weeping for her children refused to be comforted for her children, because they *were* not.	In Rama was there a voice heard, lamentation, and weeping, and great mourning, Rachel weeping *for* her children, and would not be comforted, because they are not.
A voice was heard in Ramah,	In Rama was there a voice heard,
lamentation, *and* bitter weeping;	lamentation, and weeping, and <u>great mourning</u>,
Rahel weeping for her children refused to be comforted for her children,	Rachel weeping *for* her children, and would not be comforted,
because they *were* not.	because they are not.

- These facts demonstrate that demanding *"verbatim identicality"* of wording as the standard for preservation is excessive and reaches beyond how the Bible would teach you to think about the matter. Necessitating "plenary verbal preservation" or "identical preservation" demands that the words be preserved exactly as they were given under inspiration without any wording differences of any kind.

- While these two verses (Jeremiah 31:15 and Matthew 2:18) do not exhibit *verbatim* wording, they are "substantively equivalent" with each other i.e., they possess a "doctrinal equivalence." They say/teach/communicate the exact same doctrinal content without using the exact same individual words. Put a different way, they constitute a different way of saying the same thing, not a substantive difference in meaning.

- Psalms 12:6-7 — what the doctrine of preservation assures is exactly what verse 6 states, namely the preservation of a Pure Text i.e., a text that does not report information about God, His nature or character, His doctrine, His dispensational dealings with mankind, history, archeology, or science that is false. In short, God's promise to preserve His word assures the existence of a text that has not been altered in its "fundamental character" despite not being preserved in a state of "verbatim identicality."

- This understanding of preservation is in line with the definition of the word provided by Noah Webster in his *American Dictionary of the English Language* (1828):

  - "The act of preserving or keeping safe; the act of keeping from injury, destruction or decay; as the preservation of life or health; the preservation of buildings from fire or decay; the preservation of grain from insects; the preservation of fruit or plants. When a thing is kept entirely from decay, or nearly in its original state, we say it is in a high state of preservation."

- Once again, I believe that the key to untying this knot resides in recognizing the difference between 1) a different way of saying the same thing, and 2) a substantive difference in meaning.

- I believe that God preserved His word for the same reason I believe that God inspired it. Preservation is the Bible's claim for itself. The doctrine of preservation impacts how one ought to look at the textual and translational issues and ensures that we have more than just a shell of the "original Bible" as the Originals Only position maintains.

- In the coming weeks, we will begin to further elaborate on these matters.

WORKS CITED

Bauder, Kevin T. "An Appeal to Scripture" in *One Bible Only? Examining the Exclusive Claims for the King James Bible*. Grand Rapids, MI: Kregel Publications, 2001.

TAKING STOCK OF THE FACTS: EXACT SAMENESS CHART AND EXPLANATION

This appendix seeks to combine the written description provided in Lesson 28 with the representative chart produced and presented in Lesson 29. In short, the written description and the chart are designed to work in concert with each other.

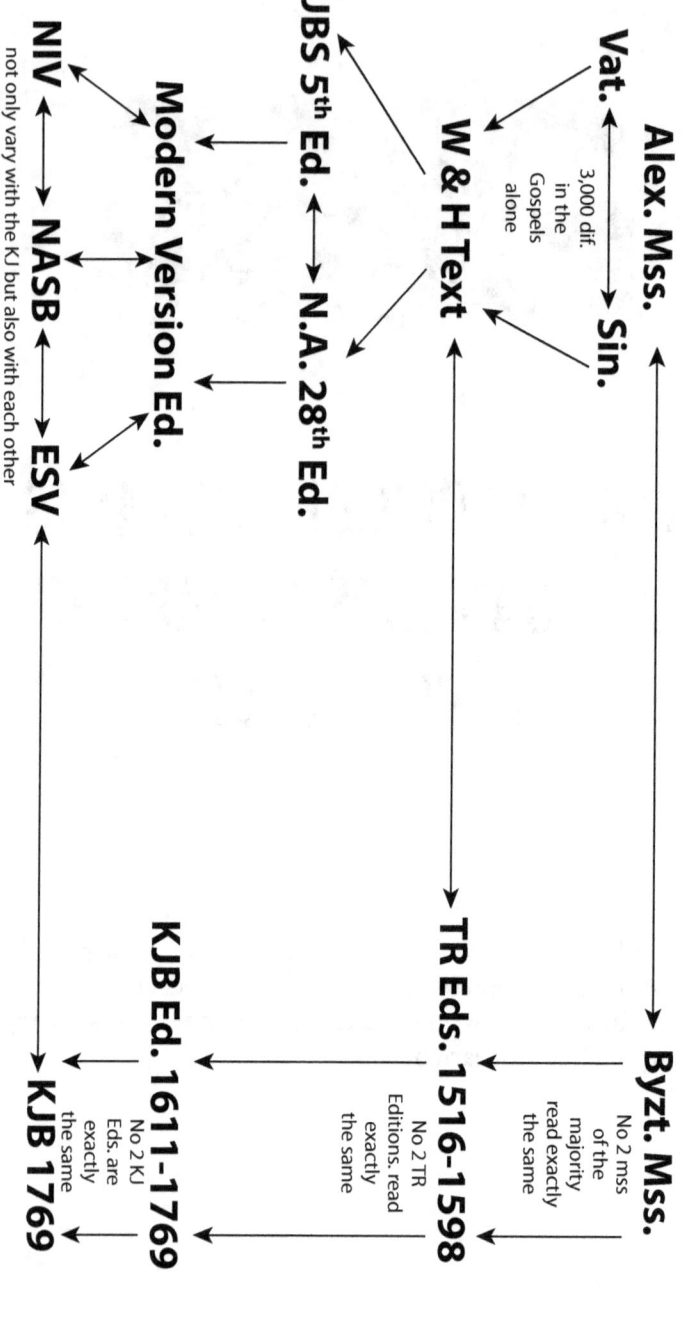

- Fact 1 — the original autographs are not extant i.e., they no longer exist.

- Fact 2 — no two Greek manuscripts are exactly the same.

    o Alexandrian manuscripts (Codex Sinaiticus) and B (Codex Vaticanus), the two so-called oldest and best, differ with each other in over 3,000 places in the gospels alone.

    o The manuscripts comprising the Alexandrian Text Type differ from those comprising the Byzantine Text Type.

    o No two Byzantine manuscripts read exactly the same.

- Fact 3 — no two printed editions of the Greek New Testament are exactly the same.

    o Editions of the TR are not exactly the same.

    o The TR differs from the Critical Text.

    o Critical Text editions are not exactly the same.

    - United Bible Society 5th Edition

    - Nestle-Aland 28th Edition

- Fact 4 — no two editions of the King James Bible are exactly the same.

- Fact 5 — the King James differs from modern versions.

- Fact 6 — no two modern versions read exactly the same.

Summary Statement:

  o "If the preservation of the Word of God depends upon exact preservation of the words of the original documents, then the situation is dire. No two manuscripts contain exactly the same words. No two editions of the Masoretic Text contain exactly the same words. No two editions of the *Textus Receptus* contain exactly the same words. No two modifications of the King

James Version contain exactly the same words and the Bible nowhere tells us which edition, if any, does contain the exact words of the originals. These are not speculations, these are plain facts." (Bauder, 155)

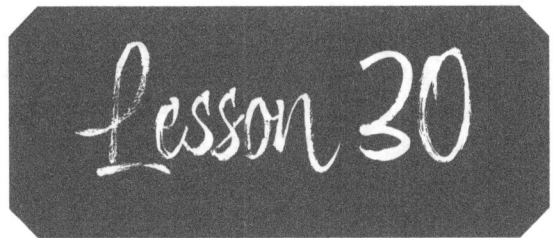

VARIOUS VIEWS OF PRESERVATION

INTRODUCTION

- In Lesson 28, we resumed class by looking at some introductory things related to preservation. After laying out six indisputable facts and discussing their implications, we used the book of Jeremiah as a case study to teach us how to think through these issues.

- In this lesson, I want to use what we learned last week as a jumping off point to discuss the various views of preservation that have been articulated by Evangelical and Fundamentalist theologians.

PRESERVATION OR RESTORATION: THE CORE ISSUE

- In Lesson 8, Understanding Basic Terminology: Preservation (11/15/15), we discussed some basic information regarding preservation from the pen of Dr. R.B. Ouellette the Pastor of First Baptist Church in Bridgeport, Michigan in his book *A More Sure Word: Which Bible Can You Trust?*. Dr. Ouellette described the relationship between inspiration and preservation as follows:

    o "... inspiration was completed in the past, preservation began in the past and carries through today..." (Ouellette, 34)

- Dr. Ouellette acknowledged that preservation is a hotly debated topic in our day. Likewise, he shared some thoughts as to why he believed that to be the case.

    o "There are seminaries that exist today that seem to 'explain away' every verse that teaches preservation. I have a problem with some who feel that verses or doctrine must be 'explained away'. I prefer to read the Bible and understand it literally. When God says His word will last forever, that it will last for a thousand generations, I believe that means God will preserve His word forever.

    In the Bible, the writers had no problem quoting Scripture that had been preserved up to that time. Peter quotes Isaiah 40 (I Peter 1:23-25); Paul quotes extensively from the Old Testament in Romans 9-11. Each time a New Testament writer quotes from the Old Testament, he is demonstrating that God has been able to preserve His word. Preservation is highly debated today because ultimately, the preservation issue will decide the translation issue — and preservation is completely a matter of faith in God's power." (Ouellette, 33)

Elsewhere, Ouellette states the following regarding Matthew 24:35, Psalms 119:60, and Psalms 119:89:

- o "It sounds to me as though God is teaching us a doctrine of preservation. The Scriptures clearly teach that even if Heaven and Earth were to pass away, the words would not. We are clearly taught that the righteous judgements of God endure forever, and that His Word has been forever settled in Heaven." (Ouellette, 47)

Dr. Ouellette cites statements issued by Detroit Baptist Theological Seminary (DBTS) and Gordon Fee in his book *The Textual Criticism of the New Testament* as a case in point of the propensity that exists within Christian academia to "explain away the clear teaching of Scripture" with respect to preservation. He writes in part,

- o ". . . issues related to the biblical text are matters of faith—regardless of which side of the issue one takes. Textual scholarship should not operate solely upon scientific principles as though there was nothing divine about the origin of our Bible. The Bible does have something to say about its own preservation, thus necessitating a doctrine of preservation." (Ouellette, 52)

- In a later chapter, Ouellette summarizes his thoughts regarding preservation with the following statement,
  - o "Those who advocate the Westcott and Hort position (i.e., the Critical Text) always have trouble with the preservation issue because it negates their practice. In the question of Bible translations, one either has a "preserved" Bible or a "restored, reconstructed" Bible." (Ouellette, 83)

- This is an important central question:
  - o Do we have a preserved word or a restored, reconstructed word?
    - Jeremiah 51:61-63 — should we be trying to "reconstruct" what God ordered to be destroyed? Is it even possible to do so?

- King James Only advocate Floyd Nolan Jones states the following regarding this question in his book *Which Version is the Bible?*:

    - "The uncompromising stand is taken herein that God gave us His pure Word in the original autographs, and that He preserved it in its pure form unto this day—and will continue so doing forever. Indeed preservation is the only issue separating the Biblicist from other professing Christians in this matter; yet, the traditional viewpoint has always been that God not only gave mankind His pure word but that He also assumed the oversight of its preservation as well. Over the years, this position has deteriorated and the contemporary view is that God has not protected the Scriptures, that they are not available in a pure form, and that this necessitates their recovery by reconstructing them from the Greek manuscripts which have survived today." (Jones, 3-4)

- Elsewhere, speaking about contemporary scholarship Jones states,

    - "They have altered the crucial doctrine of preservation to that of restoration—and most text critics do not believe that such restoration is even any longer possible. . . Is it reasonable that God gave man His pure infallible Word and then allowed it to become so corrupted over time that He (we) was left to call and rely upon unregenerate men to restore it?" (Jones, 19-20)

- David W. Cloud concurs with both Ouellette and Jones when he writes:

    - "The doctrine of biblical preservation lies at the very heart of the Bible text debate. The Bible cannot be treated as any other book. It is God's Word. God gave it and God has promised to preserve it. The underlying thesis, though, of modern textual criticism is that the Bible became corrupted through the centuries and it is the task of textual criticism to restore it in its original purity." (Cloud, 101)

- The importance of this central question (Preservation or Restoration?) has not been lost on modern version advocates. As we saw in Lesson 8, standard Systematic Theology books have largely ignored any discussion of preservation. The same, however, could not be said for theological journals and standalone works. It is to these works that we will now turn our attention in an effort to understand the various views of preservation that have been enunciated.

VIEWS ON PRESERVATION

- To frame this discussion, we will use Professor William W. Combs' article titled "The Preservation of Scripture" from the Fall 2000 issue of the *Detroit Baptist Seminary Journal*. In seeking to outline the variety of viewpoints regarding preservation, Combs states the following:
    - "The views of evangelical Christians who are currently engaged in the present debate about preservation can be classified a number of ways. At the most fundamental level, one can make a twofold division: 1) those who deny the Scriptures teach any doctrine of preservation and 2) those who affirm there is a doctrine of preservation taught by the Scriptures either directly or indirectly. However, a threefold division is more helpful since those in group 2, who affirm a doctrine of preservation, are themselves sharply divided as to what that doctrine teaches. On the one side are those who believe that the Scriptures have been preserved in the totality of the biblical manuscripts (Hebrew, Aramaic, and Greek), and on the other side, are those who believe that the Scriptures have only been accurately preserved in the KJV/TR/MT tradition—that any other textual tradition is corrupt." (Combs, 6)

- According to Combs, there are essentially three positions with respect to the doctrine of preservation.

    o View 1 — Denial of a Doctrine of Preservation

    o View 2 — Preservation in the KJV/TR/MT Tradition

    o View 3 — Preservation in the Totality of Manuscripts

- Before summarizing each of the three positions, Combs offers the following general words of caution:

    o "Right at the onset, we must distinguish between belief in a doctrine of preservation and simply, belief in preservation. This is crucial in understanding exactly what those in group 1 are denying. To my knowledge, no one in that group denies the preservation of Scripture, that is, that the books of the Old and New Testaments have been substantially preserved to our day. But they do deny that Scripture anywhere promises, either directly or indirectly, its own preservation—a doctrine of preservation. That is, they can speak of the preservation of Scripture because it is a historical reality, but it is not a theological necessity... Those in group 2, who affirm a doctrine of preservation, also believe that the historical evidence demonstrates the preservation of Scripture, but add that this preservation is a theological necessity—Scripture must be preserved because Scripture itself promises its own preservation." (Combs, 6-7)

- With these caveats in mind, let's take a closer look at each of the three views identified by Combs.

View 1 – Denial of a Doctrine of Preservation

- The two most outspoken proponents of this view are Daniel B. Wallace author of "Inspiration, Preservation, and New Testament

Textual Criticism" in *Grace Theological Journal* (Spring 1991) and W. Edward Glenny author of "The Preservation of Scripture" found in *The Bible Version Debate: The Perspective of Central Baptist Theological Seminary*.

- Regarding the origin of their "novel" view, Combs states:
  - "Though it is impossible to prove that most evangelical Christians have always affirmed a doctrine of preservation, the position of Wallace and Glenny appears to be a rather novel one. It is clearly the rise of the KJV/TR position that they are seeking to refute—a preservation that hints at, and often openly declares, the prefect preservation of the text of Scripture. But in refuting the extreme view, they have eliminated any vestige of the preservation of Scripture as a doctrine." (Combs, 7)

- After surveying the "Biblical Problems" with the notion of preservation, Glenny declares:
  - "We do not have a promise in God's Word that he will preserve it, let alone details about how He will preserve it. . . not only does no verse in Scripture explain how God will preserve His Word, but there is no statement in Scripture from which one can establish the doctrine of preservation of the text of scripture." (Glenny, 945-95)

- So according to the view articulated by Wallace and Glenny, preservation in a general sense is a historical reality but not a scriptural necessity. In seeking to explain their position, Combs states:
  - "Whatever has been preserved, whether it is the Bible or, for instance Julius Caesar's *Commentaries on the Galliac War*, has been preserved because God is in control of the universe. Any ancient document that is extant today owes its present existence to God's preservation. So we can say that all the works of ancient authors in existence today have been "providentially preserved." But again, this does not necessarily imply a doctrine of preservation—that God must preserve. God did not have to

preserve Caesar's *Commentaries* . . . A doctrine of preservation of the Scriptures says that they must be preserved—that they cannot have perished." (Combs, 8)

- On this view there is no distinction made between the preservation of Paul or Caesar. Wallace and Glenny put forth the following two arguments against the doctrine of preservation:

  o "First, preservation is not a necessary corollary of inspiration; that is, while inspiration is a true doctrine, there is nothing in the doctrine itself that demands that what God inspired He was bound to preserve. Second, the biblical texts that are used to support a doctrine of preservation have been misrepresented, and, in fact, do not teach such a doctrine." (Combs, 8)

View 2 – Preservation in the KJV/TR/MT Tradition

- The following are just some summary statements regarding this view of preservation as summarized by Combs:

  o "Although this doctrine receives greater emphasis and is more fundamental in the KJB/TR position, as we noted earlier, the preservation arguments also show up in most formulations of the MT position. This distinguishing factor in this expression of the doctrine of preservation is the notion that God has only accurately preserved the Scriptures in a particular translation (KJV) and printed Greek text (TR) or in a particular manuscript tradition (Byzantine). Other translations of the Bible and other Greek texts are corrupt to such a degree that they generally cannot be called the Word of God." (Combs, 8)

- Combs accurately identifies that advocates of this position tend to utilize the term "providential" as a descriptor for how preservation occurred.

    - "This view of preservation is often described by its supporters as nothing more than providential preservation. When, for example, opponents charge that those who hold this view actually believe in a continuing miracle of inspiration, advocates commonly protest that that is not their position. . .they, we are told, believe in providential preservation. However, one gets the impression from their discussions that for the advocates of this viewpoint the word providential has taken on an unusual meaning, that providential preservation places the preservation of the Scriptures on a different level than other works." (Combs, 9)

- Lastly, in his summary of this type of preservation, Combs addresses the issue of public availability throughout history and the importance of the TR.

    - "Finally, preservation means that the biblical text has always been publicly available throughout the history of the church. Hills says, "It must be that down through the centuries God has exercised a special, providential control over the copying of the Scriptures and the preservation and use of the copies, so that trustworthy representatives of the original text have been available to God's people in every age." These last two points are quite important because they are used to rule out immediately any printed Greek text or version that is not based on the TR. Only the TR, we are told, displays the kind of "perfect" preservation that Scripture promises for itself, and the only Greek text available throughout all of church history, according this view, has been the TR. Any printed text or version not based upon the TR must therefore be of necessity corrupt—not worthy of the title, "the Word of God." (Combs, 11)

- Another name for this viewpoint might be "perfect," "identical," or "*verbatim*" preservation. *Thou Shalt Keep Them: A Biblical Theology of the Perfect Preservation of Scripture* edited by Kent Brandenburg stands out as a primary example of this viewpoint. Generally, supporters of this view demand "exact sameness" or "identical wording" as their standard of preservation. Therefore, "perfect" according to this view means "*verbatim*" wording without any differences of any kind.

- Consequently, I would consider my personal views on preservation to be a nuanced version of the TR position on the matter.

View 3 – Preservation in the Totality of Manuscripts

- This view holds that God has preserved His word in the totality of available manuscript witnesses. Supporters of this position acknowledge and affirm "that a doctrine of preservation is taught in Scripture." However, they have rejected the view that "preservation is restricted to just a single text-type (e.g., Byzantine Text), printed text (e.g., TR), or version (e.g., KJV)." (Combs, 11)

- The following statement from Detroit Baptist Theological Seminary is emblematic of this position:
    - "While the Bible clearly teaches the ultimate indestructibility of the verbal revelation of God (Matthew 25:34; I Peter 1:25), it does not tell how and where the written manuscript lineage of that Word is preserved. We believe that God has providentially preserved His word in the many manuscripts, fragments, versions, translations, and copies of the Scripture that are available, and that by diligent study, comparison, and correlation, the original text (words) can be ascertained." (Quoted by Combs, 11)

- According to this view, the original text needs to be ascertained i.e., determined in order that it might be "reconstructed" or "restored" from the mass of preserved manuscripts. James R. White is representative of this position in *The King James Only Controversy* when he states:

  - "But the tenacity of the New Testament text, while forcing us to deal with textual variants, also provides us with assurance that our work is not in vain. One of those variant readings is indeed the original. We are called to invest our energies in **discovering** which one it is." (White, 48)

- Advocates of this view, like the previous one, generally see a connection between inspiration and preservation. The difference lies in how far they extend the connection. Supporters of the KJV/TR position restrict the relationship between inspiration and preservation to the KJV, TR, or MT only. In contrast, proponents of the Totality of Manuscripts position do not.

- Given the parameters of this position, it is obvious that it does not require that the preserved text be available to God's people at all times.

CONCLUSION

- In the next Lesson we will begin a study of the Biblical data to determine whether there is a doctrine of preservation taught in the Bible.

- Once we have ascertained the answer to this question, we will begin to explore other issues related to preservation such as the extant and method of preservation. These considerations will help us determine where preservation occurred.

WORKS CITED

Cloud, David W. *Myths About the Modern Bible Versions.* Oak Harbor, WA: Way of Life Literature, 1999.

Combs, William W. "The Preservation of Scripture?" in *Detroit Baptist Seminary Journal.* Fall 2000.

Glenny, W. Edward. "The Preservation of Scripture" in *The Bible Version Debate: The Perspective of Central Baptist Theological Seminary.* Minneapolis, MN: Central Baptist Theological Seminary, 1997.

Jones, Floyd Nolen. *Which Version is the Bible?* Humboldt, TN: KingsWord Press, 1989.

Ouellette, R.B. *A More Sure Word: Which Bible Can you Trust*? Lancaster, CA: Striving Together Publications, 2008.

White, James R. *The King James Only Controversy: Can You Trust Modern Translations?* Bethany House Publishers: Minneapolis, MN: 1995.

Sunday, October 2, 2016—Grace Life School of Theology—*From This Generation For Ever*

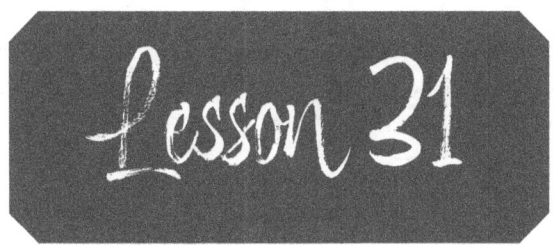

PRESERVATION: EXAMINING THE RELEVANT PASSAGES, PSALM 12:6-7

INTRODUCTION

- In Lesson 30 we surveyed the following three views of preservation.
    - View 1 — Denial of a Doctrine of Preservation
    - View 2 — Preservation in the KJV/TR/MT Tradition
    - View 3 — Preservation in the Totality of Manuscripts

- Views 2 and 3 maintain that the scriptures do teach a doctrine of preservation, i.e., they hold that preservation is the Bible's claim for itself. However, they disagree in the particulars regarding how and where preservation occurred.

- Meanwhile the first view denies the existence of any formal doctrine of preservation, i.e., it asserts that the scriptures *do not* claim their own preservation.

- Consequently, the first order of business in a study of preservation is to survey the relevant passages in order to ascertain whether or not the scriptures do teach their own preservation. As we consider each passage, I will also be careful to note how views 2 and 3 might differ from each other in how they understand a particular passage.

- Once we have answered the core question of whether or not the scriptures teach their own preservation, we can then consider the extant and method of preservation which divides views 2 and 3.

PSALM 12:6-7

- Any study of preservation must begin with a consideration of Psalm 12:6-7. These verses are shrouded in controversy and are in many respects a microcosm of the entire debate regarding preservation.

- For many King James supporters Psalm 12:6-7 comprise the clearest statement of God's promise to preserve His "words" found in the entire cannon of scripture. It is from this passage that many derive their belief in the doctrine of preservation. This is due largely to the fact that the King James actually uses the word "preserve" in verse 7.

- Meanwhile, many modern version advocates view these verses as referring to something altogether different. The controversy centers on what is being preserved in this passage; God's "words" or God's people? To be clear, just because one does not hold that Psalm 12:6-7 are referring to the preservation of God's "words" does not automatically mean that they do not believe in the doctrine of preservation.

- Generally speaking, those who seek to deny that Psalm 12:6-7 is teaching the preservation of the "words" do so by utilizing grammatical and contextual arguments.

- In order to adequately discuss all the relevant aspects of this controversy, we will consider the following points regarding whether or not Psalm 12:6-7 is teaching the preservation of the "words."

    o Grammatical Arguments: Gender Discordance

    o Contextual Arguments: Preservation of the Righteous

    o Correct Exposition: Preservation of the Words

    o Extreme uses of Psalm 12:6-7 in pro-King James argumentation

Grammatical Arguments: Gender Discordance

- A consideration of how various translations render these verses in English illustrates the issue of alleged "gender discordance".

KJB	NIV	NASB	ESV
6) The words of the LORD *are* pure words: *as* silver tried in a furnace of earth, purified seven times. 7) Thou shalt keep them, O LORD, thou shalt preserve them from this generation for ever.	6) And the words of the LORD are flawless, like silver purified in a crucible, like gold refined seven times. 7) You, LORD, **will keep the needy safe and will protect us forever from the wicked,**	6) The words of the LORD are pure words; As silver tried in a furnace on the earth, refined seven times. 7) You, O LORD, will keep them; **You will preserve him from this generation forever.**	6) The words of the LORD are pure words, like silver refined in a furnace on the ground, purified seven times. 7) You, O LORD, will keep them; **you will guard us from this generation forever.**

- The NIV, NASB, and ESV all have the LORD protecting, preserving, or guarding his people "from this generation forever." This is evident from their use of the pronoun "us" (NIV and ESV) and "him" (NASB) in verse 7.

- In contrast, the King James has the LORD preserving "them" in verse 7. In order to determine what is being preserved in the King James one must look to the nearest antecedent which is found in verse 6. What is being discussed in verse 6 in all four versions? The "words of the LORD." So to what is the "them" referring to in verse 7 in the King James? To the "words of the LORD" in verse 6. So what is the King James saying that the LORD will preserve "from this generation for ever" in verse 7? The "words of the Lord" in verse 6.

- In summation, modern versions teach the eternal preservation of God's people whereas the King James is teaching the eternal preservation of the "words of the Lord." A substantive difference in meaning if ever there was one.

- The reason for the discrepancy is based upon an alleged technicality of Hebrew grammar often referred to as "gender discordance" in the relevant literature.

- Professor William W. Combs of Detroit Baptist Seminary succinctly summarizes the grammatical concerns as follows:

    - "... it is more probable that verse 7 ("Thou shalt keep them... thou shalt preserve them") is not referring to "the words of the LORD" in verse 6. That is, the antecedent of "them" in verse 7 is probably not the "words" of verse 6. The Hebrew term for "them" (twice in v. 7) is masculine, while the term for "words" is feminine. Therefore, most interpreters and versions understand the promise of preservation in verse 7 to apply to the "poor" and "needy" of verse 5." (Combs, 15)

- Professor Combs goes on to cite the NIV as an example. Please note the phenomena on the following table comparing the KJB with the NIV. A similar chart could be produced for both the NASB and the ESV.

KJB	NIV
5) For the oppression of the poor [mas.], for the sighing of the needy [mas.], now will I arise, saith the LORD; I will set *him* in safety *from him that* puffeth at him. 6) The words [fem.] of the LORD *are* pure words: *as* silver tried in a furnace of earth, purified seven times. 7) Thou shalt keep them [mas.], O LORD, thou shalt preserve them [mas.] from this generation for ever.	5) "Because the poor [mas.] are plundered and the needy [mas.] groan, I will now arise," says the LORD. "I will protect them from those who malign them." 6) And the words [fem.] of the LORD are flawless, like silver purified in a crucible, like gold refined seven times. 7) You, LORD, will keep the needy [mas.] safe and will protect us [mas.] forever from the wicked,

- In short, this argument asserts that the masculine words in verse 7 must match the masculine words in verse 5 because there must be an agreement in terms of gender. Therefore, what is being preserved in verse 7 is not the "words" from verse 6 because the Hebrew word is feminine not masculine.

- W. Edward Glenny of Central Baptist Theological Seminary concurs with Professor Combs regarding the grammar of the passage.

    o "Hebrew grammar requires that it be the righteous whom God is keeping and preserving in verse 7. The word "them" (v. 7a) is a masculine pronominal suffix and "the words" of verse 6a is feminine in gender. In the Hebrew text, verse 7b reads "You will preserve him from this generation forever." Delitzsch says the "him" refers "to the man who yearns for deliverance mentioned in the divine utterance (v. 5 in Eng.). The connection is clear in the Hebrew because these pronouns are both third masculine singular." (Glenny, 91)

- So for many expositors these arguments based upon "gender discordance" are sufficient to disqualify Psalm 12:6-7 as a passage teaching the preservation of scripture.

- As one might expect, not all expositors agree with Combs and Glenny regarding the role of "gender discordance" in establishing the correct understating/translation of Psalm 12:6-7. One such example is Dr. Thomas Strouse, who wrote an "Article Review" of Professor Combs' article on "The Preservation of Scripture" quoted above for *Sound Words from New England* in the spring of 2001.

- According to Strouse, the grammatical arguments put forth by Combs and Glenny are flawed in at least two ways.

    o "However, two important grammatical points overturn his argument. First, the rule of proximity requires "words" to be the natural, contextual antecedent for "them." Second, it is not uncommon, especially in the Psalter, for feminine plural noun synonyms for the "words" of the Lord to be the antecedent for masculine plural pronouns/pronominal suffixes, which seem to "masculinize" the verbal extension of the patriarchal God of the Old Testament. Several examples of this supposed gender difficulty occur in Psalm 119. In verse 111, the feminine plural "testimonies" is the antecedent for the masculine plural pronoun "they." Again, in three passages the feminine plural synonyms for "words" have masculine plural pronominal suffixes (vv. 129, 152, 167)." (Strouse, 2)

- In other words, it seems quite common, especially in the other Psalm dealing with God's word to exhibit the same "gender discordance" exhibited in Psalm 12:6-7. Let's consider the following examples.

Psalm 119:111

KJB	NIV	NASB	ESV
Thy testimonies [fem. pl] have I taken as an heritage for ever: for they [mas. pl] *are* the rejoicing of my heart.	Your statutes [fem. pl] are my heritage forever; they [mas. pl] are the joy of my heart.	I have inherited Your testimonies [fem. pl] forever, For they [mas. pl] are the joy of my heart.	Your testimonies [fem. pl] are my heritage forever, for they [mas. pl] are the joy of my heart.

Psalm 119:129

KJB	NIV	NASB	ESV
Your testimonies [fem. pl] are wonderful: therefore doth my soul keep them [mas. pl].	Your statutes [fem. pl] are wonderful; therefore I obey them [mas. pl].	Your testimonies [fem. pl] are wonderful; Therefore my soul observes them [mas. pl].	Your testimonies [fem. pl] are wonderful; therefore my soul keeps them [mas. pl].

Psalm 119:167

KJB	NIV	NASB	ESV
My soul hath kept thy testimonies [fem. pl]; and I love them [mas. p] exceedingly.	I obey your statutes [fem. pl], for I love them [mas. pl] greatly.	My soul keeps Your testimonies [fem. pl], And I love them [mas. pl] exceedingly.	My soul keeps your testimonies [fem. pl]; I love them [mas. pl] exceedingly.

- These verses are all talking about the word of God and exhibit the same gender discord as Psalm 12:6-7. Yet, modern versions have not seen fit to rectify the discord in these passages by translating them differently from the KJB. Therefore, it seems that proximity takes precedence over gender accord even in modern versions.

- The grammatical argument against the preservation of God's words in Psalm 12:6-7 appears to be false. The classic Hebrew Grammar book *Gesenius' Hebrew Grammar* states the following regarding "gender discordance" so called in the Hebrew text:

    o "Through a weakening in the distinction of gender, which is noticeable elsewhere and which probably passed from the colloquial language into that of literature, masculine suffixes (especially in the plural) are not infrequently used to refer to feminine substantives." (Kautzsch, 440)

Here are some other examples of so called "gender discordance" from elsewhere in the Hebrew scriptures:

- Genesis 31:9 — "Thus God hath taken away the cattle of your [masculine plural pronoun suffix—referring to Rachel and Leah] father, and given *them* to me."
  - NIV, NASB, and ESV all follow the King James.

- Genesis 32:15 — "Thirty milch camels with their [masculine plural pronoun suffix—referring to the thirty female camels] colts, forty kine, and ten bulls, twenty she asses, and ten foals."
  - NIV, NASB, and ESV all follow the King James.

- Exodus 1:21 — "And it came to pass, because the midwives [fem.] feared God, that he made them [masculine plural pronoun suffix — a reference to the midwives] houses."
  - NIV, NASB, and ESV all follow the King James.

- More recently (1990), the Hebrew grammar by Bruce K. Waltke and M. O'Conner titled *An Introduction to Biblical Hebrew Syntax* states, "The masculine pronoun is often used for a feminine antecedent." (Waltke & O'Conner, 361)

- Before offering some closing comments on this matter, I would like to consider one more occurrence of "gender discordance" from Psalm 119.

Psalm 119:152

KJB	NIV	NASB	ESV
Concerning thy testimonies [fem. pl], I have known of old that thou hast founded them [mas. pl] for ever.	Long ago I learned from your statutes [fem. pl] that you established them [mas. pl] to last forever.	Of old I have known from Your testimonies [fem. p] That You have founded them [mas. pl] forever.	Long have I known from your testimonies [fem. pl] that you have founded them [mas. pl] forever.

- Once again, we see an occurrence of "gender discordance" in a Psalm speaking about the eternal nature of the Lord's "testimonies." Yet, once again, the modern versions follow the King James and make no attempt to fix the "discord" as they did in Psalm 12:6-7.

- Above, we quoted from Professor William Combs' article "The Preservation of Scripture" in which he cited "gender discordance" in Psalm 12:5-7 as a means for arguing that the passage is not referring to the preservation of the "words" and can therefore not be used to establish a "doctrine of preservation." (Combs, 15)

- Later, in the same article, however, we find Professor Combs stating that Psalm 119:152 "appears to be a fairly direct promise of preservation." (Combs, 18). In the whole of his comments on this verse, Combs says nothing about the "gender discordance" clearly demonstrated above.

- Why would someone hold that "gender discordance" disqualifies the preservation of the "words" in one passage (Psalm 12) while, at the same time, asserting that another passage (Psalm 119:152) exhibiting the same grammatical phenomena is "a fairly direct promise of preservation"?

- If accordance in gender trumps proximity, why is the principle not applied consistently throughout the Hebrew Old Testament? Why is gender accordance all of sudden a problem in Psalm 12:6-7 when it is not in a host of other passages?

- At a minimum, it would seem that the alleged grammatical rule regarding gender agreement in the Hebrew text is selectively applied at best. Regarding the instances of "gender discordance" in Psalm 119 noted above, Dr. Thomas Strouse states:

  - "These examples show the importance of maintaining the Biblically accepted Hebrew grammar of closest antecedent and the Biblically accepted gender discordance in exception cases for theological reasons." (Strouse, "The Permanent Preservation of God's Words: Psalm12:6-7, 32").

- As demonstrated above, even modern versions adopt discordance in gender in order to adequately convey the sense in English.

- On the other end of the spectrum, grammatical arguments based on "gender discordance" demonstrate the lengths some are willing to go in their argumentation to remove the testimony of the clearest verse in the cannon regarding the preservation of scripture.

- On this point it seems that Daniel B. Wallace and W. Edward Glenny are more consistent in their total denial of a doctrine of preservation than William W. Combs. Combs holds that "gender discordance" excludes Psalm 12:6-7 from teaching the preservation of the "words" while at the same time maintaining Psalm 119:152 does while exhibiting the same grammatical realities.

- If Psalm 12:6-7 does not teach the preservation of the "words," proof must be furnished via a different line of argumentation. Grammatical arguments based upon "gender discordance" are inconsistent and unpersuasive.

- In the next Lesson we will consider arguments from the contents of Psalm 12.

WORKS CITED

Combs, William W. "The Preservation of Scripture?" in *Detroit Baptist Seminary Journal*. Fall 2000.

Glenny, W. Edward. "The Preservation of Scripture" in *The Bible Version Debate: The Perspective of Central Baptist Theological Seminary*. Minneapolis, MN: Central Baptist Theological Seminary, 1997.

Kautzsch, E. *Gesenius' Hebrew Grammar 2nd Ed.* Oxford: Clarendon Press, 1910.

Strouse, Thomas. "Article Review" in *Sound Words from New England Vol. 1, Is. 4*. Spring 2001.

Strouse, Thomas. "The Permanent Preservation of God's Words: Psalm 12:6-7" in *Thou Shalt Keep Them: A Biblical Theology of the Perfect Preservation of Scripture*. El Sobrante, CA: Pillar & Ground Publishing, 2003.

Waltke, Bruce K. and M. O'Conner. *An Introduction to Biblical Hebrew Syntax*. Eisenbrauns: Winona Lake, IN, 1990.

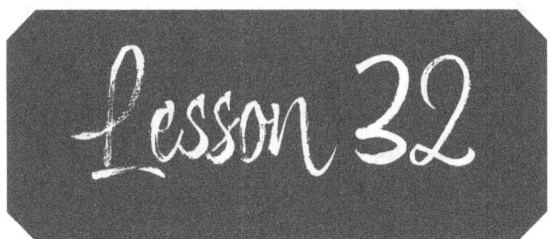

PRESERVATION: EXAMINING THE RELEVANT PASSAGES, PSALM 12:6-7 (PART 2)

INTRODUCTION

- In the previous lesson we began our investigation into whether or not the scriptures teach a formal doctrine of perseveration. Please recall the following three views laid out in Lesson 30:

    o View 1 — Denial of a Doctrine of Preservation
    o View 2 — Preservation in the KJV/TR/MT Tradition
    o View 3 — Preservation in the Totality of Manuscripts

- We commenced this process by initiating an examination of the relevant passages commonly used to teach the doctrine of preservation. Our investigation began with Psalm 12:6-7.

- By way of review, we observed the following general points about Psalm 12:6-7 in Lesson 31:

    o Many believe it to be the clearest and most important promise in the entire cannon regarding God's promise to preserve His word.

    o Controversy surrounds the passage regarding who or what is being preserved: 1) the "words" or, 2) the people i.e., "poor" and "needy" from verse 5.

    o Those who maintain that the passage is teaching the preservation of the people generally make two arguments to support their position: 1) Grammatical Arguments and 2) Contextual Arguments.

As we investigate Psalm 12, we will consider the following points:

   o Grammatical Arguments: Gender Discordance

   o Contextual Arguments: Preservation of the Righteous

   o Correct Exposition: Preservation of the Words

   o Extreme uses of Psalm 12:6-7 in pro-King James argumentation

- The bulk of Lesson 31 focused on point one; "Grammatical Arguments: Gender discordance." It was concluded that arguments based upon gender agreeance were inconsistent, irregular, and therefore inadequate for proving that Psalm 12:6-7 does not teach the preservation of the "words."

- In this lesson we want to focus our attention on points two and three; namely: "Contextual Arguments" and the "Actual Teaching" of the passage.

PSALM 12:6-7

Contextual Arguments: The Preservation of the Righteous

- For the sake of consistency, let's begin our discussion by looking at William W. Combs' essay "The Preservation of Scripture." Combs summarizes the contextual arguments as follows:

    o "David's subject in the Psalm is stated right in verse 1: "Help, LORD, for the godly man ceases to be, for the faithful disappear from among the sons of men." David is concerned about the righteous who are being oppressed by the wicked of "this generation." In the midst of this he declares his assurance that God will preserve the righteous forever. Taken in this sense, this passage has no bearing on the doctrine of preservation." (Combs, 15)

- In other words, according to Combs, the context of the passage is about the preservation of God's people not the "words" of God.

- W. Edward Glenny agrees with Combs regarding the context of Psalm 12 and offers the following expanded explanation in his essay, "The Preservation of Scripture":

    o "The psalm is an expression of David's confidence in the pure words of God. In verse 4 he prays for deliverance from the proud flatterers all around him who cannot be trusted (v. 2b). Verse 5 gives the source of David's confidence; he is assured that the Lord will deliver him from those maligning him. In verses 6-8 David declares that his confidence is in God's Word. In this context, David's expression of confidence in God's Word in verse 6 refers to his confidence in God's affirmation that He will deliver the afflicted (v. 5). Then, in verse 7, on the basis of his confidence in God's Word (vv. 5-6), David declares his assurance that God will preserve forever the righteous, who are being afflicted, by the wicked of "this generation." The pronoun "them" in verse 7 ("thou shalt keep them") does not refer to the "words" of verse 6. It refers to the "poor" and the "needy" of verse 5, and the "godly" and "faithful" men of verse 1, whom the Lord will "preserve" (v. 7b). Furthermore, in context the "generation" (v. 7) must be the wicked who are all around the psalmist and dominate his society (vv. 1-4). It would not make sense to say that God will preserve His Word from the generation of David throughout eternity. What about the generations before David? Was God not concerned about His Word then? The point of the psalm is that the godly man will never cease; the faithful will never "fail from among the children of men" (v. 1). The righteous will never disappear from the face of the earth because God will "preserve them from this generation forever" (v. 7). Verse 8 clinches the contextual arguments. It again returns to the topic of the wicked all around from whom David and future generations of the righteous will be delivered." (Glenny, 90-91)

- First, it is important to note that Glenny's contextual argument is predicated and dependent upon the grammatical argument regarding "gender discordance." We have already concluded in Lesson 31 that grammatical arguments based upon gender accordance are inconsistent and inconclusive. Consequently, since Glenny's contextual argument is so grammar dependent, I find his exposition based upon contextual consideration to be inconclusive.

- Second, to argue that since David states, "from this generation for ever" in verse 7 means that God was not concerned about the preservation of His word before David's generation, is not a sound argument and disregards a host of relevant cross references.

    o Exodus 24:4 — is Glenny saying that God did not care what happened to the words written by Moses before the time David?

    o Isaiah 30:8 — does this verse mean that God was not concerned about His word before the book of Isaiah was written?

- In Psalm 12, David is speaking from the point of view of the scriptures he is in the process of penning.

- Third, where are the relevant cross-references to support Glenny's contextual interpretation that God's people will be perpetually preserved in an earthly sense from evil doers? God's people continue to suffer many things at the hands of wicked men even in the dispensation of grace. While there are no cross-references to support the notion that God will preserve His people from evil doers, there are ample parallel passages to support the teaching that God will preserve His word "forever."

    o   Psalm 119:152, 160; Isaiah 30:8; Matthew 24:35; I Peter 1:23-25

- Combs and Glenny are not the only writers to deny that Psalm 12:6-7 is referring to the preservation of God's written word based upon grammatical and contextual arguments. Jon Rehurek's "Preservation of the Bible: Providential or Miraculous? The Biblical View" uses Combs, Glenny, and J.J. Stewart Perowne's *Commentary of Psalms: 2 Volumes in 1* to argue similarly. Rehurek concludes:

    o   ". . . this passage does not speak of the preservation of God's written Word; it only addresses the purity and trustworthiness of His words and the preservation that is being spoken of concerns the righteous men." (Rehurek, 83)

- After considering the relevant writings, it is evident that grammatical and contextual arguments are working in concert with each other by those who seek to deny that Psalm 12:6-7 are teaching the preservation of the written word.

Correct Exposition: Preservation of the Words

- Preservationist Thomas M. Strouse acknowledges that the King James rendering of Psalm 12:6-7 stands in contradiction to that of modern versions. Strouse views the passage as one of the "clearest promises" of preservation in the Old Testament.

- "Psalm 12 is a psalm of contrasts. It contrasts the Godly with the ungodly and the Words of the Lord with the words of men. The latter contrast provides the backdrop to one of the clearest promises in the OT of the preservation of God's Words." (Strouse, 29)

- Structurally, Strouse sees the psalm as one of asymmetric contrasts:

  - "The structure of the psalm is asymmetric. This structure causes the focus to be on C, God's Promises (see below). David's lament carries the reader from the need for Divine help, because of the words of the ungodly, to focus on the promises of God for deliverance, which include the permanent preservation of His Words, the antidote to the words of the ever-present wicked.

    (A) The recognition of the need for Divine help (v. 1)

    (B) The threat of the words of the ungodly (vv. 2-4)

    (C) God's promises (v. 5)

    (A') The antidote of the Words of God (vv. 6-7)

    (B') The recognition of the need for Divine help (v. 8)" (Strouse, 30)

- Without reproducing the totality of his article, Strouse draws his reader's attention to verse 5, or statement C above.

  - "The structure of the psalm focuses on the promises of God. The Lord promised that, because "of the oppression of the poor," and "of the sighing of the needy," He would "arise and set him in safety from him that puffeth at him." Since the "poor" were despoiled and the "needy" were groaning, the Lord made significant promises." (Strouse, 31)

- Psalm 12:5—notice that the protection of the "poor" and "needy" is based upon what the LORD said i.e., His words. In the near context, the psalmist has already expressed that the Lord will "arise" to help the "poor" and "needy".

- - Psalm 9:18-19—contains the Lord's promise to "arise" and protect the "poor" and "needy."
  - Psalm 10:12-14—the Lord will "arise" to help the "poor."

- The promise of hope offered in verse 5 is only as good as the Lord's ability to perform/execute His promise.

- Psalm 12:6-7 — with the promise of God in mind in verse 5, the words of the Lord are contrasted in verses 6 and 7 with the words of the ungodly in verses 2 through 4. Regarding verses 6 and 7 Strouse writes:

  - "The content of God's help was the assurance of His ever-present Words with promises of deliverance as an antidote to the words of the wicked. The psalmist reflected on this quality and endurance of the great tangible help that the Lord desires to give man — His perfect words. The quality of the Lord's Words is likened to purified silver from a refining furnace. The result of the seven-fold refining process produced one hundred percent perfect silver in the ancient world, an apt illustration for the quality of the perfect Words of the Lord. David revealed the endurance of God's Words, indicating that they would be preserved from that generation forever." (Strouse, 31)

- The expression "from this generation for ever" reflects that David is referring to the "words" of hope he has been in the process of penning. In other words, the statement applies to the words David is in the process of writing under inspiration. Attempts to argue that the verse is not teaching the preservation of God's "words" because it only mentions the current generation and nothing before David, are weak and fail to take into account how Psalm 12 fits into the book of Psalms as a whole.

- Psalm 12:8 — David concludes the psalm by recognizing his need for the Lord's help given that the wicked surround him on every side. Consequently,

- - "David recognized that the proud words of the wicked flatterers were a constant problem, but the perfect words of God will always counter man's lies." (Strouse, 31)

- Without the preservation of the "words," what hope do the poor and needy have of their foretold future deliverance? Arguing that this passage does not teach the preservation of the "words" throws the content of the Lord's promise in verse 5 into question. Not only that, as we have already pointed out, the poor and needy have not been perpetually and supernaturally kept safe from the wicked since the generation of David.

- The entire psalm is about the words of the wicked versus the words of God.

- In the end, I believe that the passage is teaching the preservation of the "words." That being said, I would disagree with Strouse that God's promise necessitates "exact sameness" or "verbatim" wording.

- *Extreme uses of Psalm 12:6-7 in pro-King James Argumentation*

- Many King James Only advocates hold either explicitly or implicitly that Psalm 12:6-7 is referring to the KJB. In other words, they have in their thinking the notion that David is speaking directly about the KJB in this passage.

- The expression "as silver tried in a furnace of earth purified seven times" at the end of verse 6 is taken to be a direct reference to the KJB. This argument is made because the KJB is the seventh translation of the *Textus Recpetus* into the English.

  - 1525 — Tyndale
  - 1535 — Coverdale
  - 1537 — Matthews
  - 1539 — Great Bible
  - 1560 — Geneva Bible
  - 1568 — Bishops Bible
  - 1611 — King James Bible

- This assertion is based upon the numerical argument that seven is the number of perfection coupled with King James having been the seventh translation of the TR into English; therefore, it is argued that the King James is "perfect." To make this argument one must make the following assumptions:

    o David is speaking about the KJB when he wrote Psalm 12.

    o All the various editions of the six earlier TR translations into English should not be counted.

- In her booklet, *The Hidden History of the English Scriptures: Given by Inspiration to All Generations* commemorating the 400th anniversary of the KJB, Gail Riplinger includes a section titled ""Purified Seven Times" Not Eight."

    o "The KJB translators would not approve of further tampering with the English Bible. . . The KJB translators did not see their translation as one in the midst of a chain of ever evolving English translations. They wanted their Bible to be one of which no one could justly say, 'It is good, except this word or that word. . .' They planned: "to make . . . out of many good ones (Wycliffe, Tyndale, Coverdale, Great, Geneva, and the Bishops') one principal good one, not justly to be expected against; that hath been our endeavor, that our mark. The translators said that their translation was "perfected." . . . The KJB translators' assertion that their edition "perfected" leaves no work left for the new version translators. The enemy is at war with the word of God." (Riplinger, 48-49)

- Gail Riplinger's comments above typify the type of reasoning regarding Psalm 12:6-7 present in much pro-King James literature and teaching.

- A less extreme view of Psalm 12:6-7 might hold that the verses in question necessitate a sevenfold refinement process in any receptor language in order for God's "perfect" word to exist in that language.

- The dictionary defines a simile as a comparison between two things using the words "like" or "as". Psalm 12:6 contains a simile to explain how pure God's "words" are. How pure are the words of God? They are as pure "as silver tried in a furnace of earth purified seven times."

- While I believe that Psalm 12:6-7 is teaching the preservation of the "words" I do not believe that the psalmist penned these verses with an early 17th century English translation in mind. Rather David is referring to the "words" he is in the process of writing in Hebrew.

- It was those Hebrew words that God preserved thereby giving the King James translators something to translate into English. This is not to say that translations cannot be part of the preservation process, it simply means that David is not referring to or speaking about the KJB in Psalm 12.

WORKS CITED

Combs, William W. "The Preservation of Scripture?" in *Detroit Baptist Seminary Journal*. Fall 2000.

Glenny, W. Edward. "The Preservation of Scripture" in *The Bible Version Debate: The Perspective of Central Baptist Theological Seminary*. Minneapolis, MN: Central Baptist Theological Seminary, 1997.

Riplinger, Gail. "The Hidden History of the English Scriptures Given By Inspiration To All Generations." Ararat, VA: AV Publications, 2010.

Rehurek, Jon. "Preservation of the Bible: Providential or Miraculous? The Biblical View" in *The Master's Seminary Journal*. Spring 2008.

Strouse, Thomas. "The Permanent Preservation of God's Words: Psalm 12:6-7" in *Thou Shalt Keep Them: A Biblical Theology of the Perfect Preservation of Scripture*. El Sobrante, CA: Pillar & Ground Publishing, 2003.

PRESERVATION: EXAMINING THE RELEVANT PASSAGES, PSALM 119

INTRODUCTION

- In Lessons 31 and 32 we commenced our study of whether or not the Bible teaches its own preservation by looking at Psalm 12:6-7. Recall from Lesson 30 that we laid out the following three views of preservation:
    - View 1 — Denial of a Doctrine of Preservation
    - View 2 — Preservation in the KJV/TR/MT Tradition
    - View 3 — Preservation in the Totality of Manuscripts

- Please remember that we are in the process of looking at passages that establish the fundamental promise of preservation before we consider the extant and location of preservation.

- In summation of Lessons 31 and 32, I presented the reasons why I believe that Psalms 12:6-7 does teach the preservation of the written word.

- In this Lesson we want to continue our examination of the relevant passages regarding preservation. We will do this by considering a cluster of verses from Psalm 119.

GENERAL COMMENTS ON PSALM 119

- Psalm 119 is the longest chapter in the entire Bible. Most commentators and Bible students acknowledge that the entire chapter is speaking about the Law or God's written word to the nation of Israel.

- Throughout the chapter a host of different yet synonymous words are used interchangeably to refer to the scriptures. Please note that the number in parenthesis indicates that number of times that the word or phrase occurs in Psalm 119.

    o Psalm 119:1 — "law of the Lord" (24x)
    o Psalm 119:2 — "testimonies" (22x)
    o Psalm 119:3 — "his ways" (6x)
    o Psalm 119:4 — "thy precepts" (21x)
    o Psalm 119:5 — " thy statutes" (22x)
    o Psalm 119:6 — "thy commandments" (21x)
    o Psalm 119:7 — "righteous judgements" (18x)
    o Psalm 119:9, 11 — "thy word" (38x)

- Virtually every verse in Psalm 119 contains a reference to the words of God. There are 176 verses in the Psalm and 172 of them contain one of the words identified above. Please bear these facts in mind as we look at a few of the verses.

PSALM 119:89

- King James advocate D.A. Waite lists this verse as one of the texts supporting the doctrine of preservation in his book, *Defending the King James Bible*. Waite reasons:
  - "God's words are not in doubt. It is permanent. It is unconfused and plain. God has settled, that means it has been preserved, kept pure. Nothing has been lost. . . Some people say, "Well, it is settled in Heaven but not on earth." But God needs it less than we do; He knows His Words. WE are the ones who need it. He is using this verse, Psalm 119:89, to show us that God has given us Words that are settled. . . It is true that God's Words' are not only preserved and settled "in heaven" but they are also preserved by Heaven's Omnipotent God." (Waite, 7-8).

- In short Waite is arguing that there is perfect archetypal Bible in heaven which mandates and necessitates a corollary Bible on earth. For Waite this archetypal Bible exists on earth via preservation. Please note that Waite's definition of "perfect" in this case assumes *verbatim* wording as the standard.

- Meanwhile, Dr. Combs of Detroit Baptist Theological Seminary views the verse as containing no direct reference to "God's written revelation" at all. Using A.A. Anderson's work *The Psalms* to buttress his argument, Combs states:
  - "It seems more likely that "your word" in verse 89 has no direct reference to God's written revelation. As Anderson notes, "thy

word . . . is probably the expression of God's all-embracing purpose and will (cf. Isaiah 40:8)." God's purpose, His will, is "firmly fixed" in heaven "beyond the reach of all disturbing causes." . . . Thus, it would appear that this verse has no direct application to the doctrine of preservation." (Combs, 17)

- Ultimately, I agree with Combs that Psalm 119:89 is not a direct promise of preservation. That being said, the assertion that "thy word" is in no way related to God's written revelation is a bit troubling. Why would the phrase "thy word" within the context of Psalm 119 not be referring to God's written revelation?

- I have used the Psalm 119:89 in this class as our third presupposition, not as a verse that directly promises preservation of God's word on earth.

    o God exists. (Psalm 14:1)

    o God has magnified His word above His own name. (Psalms 138:2)

    o God's word is eternally settled in heaven. (Psalm 119:89)

    o God, through the process of inspiration, has communicated His word to mankind. (I Timothy 3:16 & II Peter 1:21)

    o God's words were written down so that they could be made eternally available to men. (Isaiah 30:8, I Peter 1:23)

    o God promised to preserve that which He inspired. (Psalms 12:6-7)

- King James advocates are not the only ones who view Psalm 119:89 as a statement as to the eternal existence of God's written word in heaven. Combs quotes Wayne Grudem's essay "Scripture's Self-Attestation and the Problem of Formulating a Doctrine of Scripture" as follows:

    o "... a copy of words that God in heaven has permanently decided on and has subsequently caused to be committed to writing by men." (Quoted in Combs, 16)

This is precisely the way I am using the verse in the above presuppositions. The verse is referring to the written word of God in heaven but is not speaking about its preservation on earth. Other verses in Psalm 119 speak to the issue of preservation.

Galatians 3:8 — would not be possible if God's word was not eternally settled upon in heaven.

PSALM 119:111

- We already encountered this verse back in Lesson 31 when we were discussing the issue of "gender discordance" as it related to Psalm 12:6-7. Please remember that this verse exhibits the same phenomena, yet the translators of the modern versions follow the King James in giving priority to proximity over gender agreeance.

KJB	NIV	NASB	ESV
Thy testimonies [fem. pl.] have I taken as an heritage for ever: for they [mas. pl.] *are* the rejoicing of my heart.	Your statutes [fem. pl.] are my heritage forever; they [mas. pl.] are the joy of my heart.	I have inherited Your testimonies [fem. pl.] forever, for they [mas. pl.] are the joy of my heart.	Your testimonies [fem. pl.] are my heritage forever, for they [mas. pl.] are the joy of my heart.

- Regarding this verse, King James advocate D.A. Waite writes:

  o "If you take God's Testimonies as a "heritage for ever," they must be preserved if we are to keep them." (Waite, 8)

- R.B. Ouellette includes Psalm 119:111 in a list of preservation passages along with the following remarks:

- "The doctrine of preservation is based on the Bible itself. Since the Bible is to be our authority in matters of faith and practice, it is important to see what God has stated about its preservation for each generation... There are seminaries that exist today that seem to 'explain away' every verse that teaches preservation. I have a problem with some who feel that verses or doctrine must be 'explained away.' I prefer to read the Bible and understand it literally. When God says His word will last forever, that it will last for a thousand generations, I believe that means God will preserve His word forever." (Ouellette, 32-33)

- William W. Combs, Daniel B. Wallace, John Rehurek and W. Edward Glenny do not comment on this verse in their writings on preservation.

PSALM 119:152

- As we already noted in Lesson 31, Dr. Combs believes that "verse 152 appears to be a fairly direct promise of preservation," despite the "gender discordance" observable in the verse. (Combes, 18)

KJB	NIV	NASB	ESV
Concerning thy testimonies [fem. pl.], I have known of old that thou hast founded them [mas. pl.] for ever.	Long ago I learned from your statutes [fem. pl.] that you established them [mas. pl.] to last forever.	Of old I have known from Your testimonies [fem. pl.] that You have founded them [mas. pl.] forever.	Long have I known from your testimonies [fem. pl.] that you have founded them [mas. pl.] forever.

- In support of his conclusion that Psalm 119:152 is a "direct promise of preservation," Combs states:

  - "This verse would seem to offer stronger support (than Psalm 119:89) for a doctrine of preservation. The context (vv. 145-52) makes clear reference to God's written revelation in the Torah.

The Psalmist says he will observe the Lord's "statutes" (v. 145) and keep his "testimonies" (v. 146). He waits for his "words" (v. 147) and meditates in his "word" (v. 148) and asks to be revived according to the Lord's "ordinances" (v. 149). The Psalmist observed that the wicked do not obey his "law" (v. 150). Finally, he concludes in verses 151-52 . . . These "testimonies, have been founded forever," meaning as the NIV puts it, "you established them to last forever." (Combs, 18)

- In contrast, W. Edward Glenny of Central Baptist Theological Seminary denies that the verse has anything to do with preservation.

    o "In Psalm 119:152 the Psalmist states "Concerning thy testimonies, I have known of old that Thou hast founded them forever." In the previous verse he stated that God's Word is truth and verse 150 teaches that the wicked are far from God's law. In contrast to the wicked, the Psalmist is trusting in God's Word (vv. 145-149). His confidence is that God's law is not fickle, it is trustworthy and based on God's unchanging moral character. That must be the meaning of verse 152 in its context." (Glenny, 88)

- King James advocates R.B. Oullette, D.A. Waite, David Cloud, and Jack McElroy are in agreement with William W. Combs that Psalm 119:152 establishes the fundamental promise of preservation.

PSALM 119:160

- This verse is very similar to Psalm 119:152 in that it is part of the section where the Psalmist is making numerous references to the Law: "law" (v. 153), "word" (v. 154), "statutes" (v. 155), "judgments" (v. 156), "testimonies" (v. 157), "word" (v. 158), and "precepts" (v. 159).

- Because of these contextual realities, Combs concludes the following with respect to Psalm 119:160:
  - "This verse, then, like 152, would also seem to strongly imply a doctrine of preservation." (Combs, 18-19)

- Once again, W. Edward Glenny denies that Psalm 119:160 teaches a doctrine of preservation by arguing that the verse is simply speaking about the "infallibility," "absolute trustworthiness," and "dependability" of God's word. Glenny writes:
  - "The Psalmists' hope is not based on the belief that the text of God's word will remain intact centuries after he dies, nor is he concerned that he has lost part of God's Word. His confidence is in the fact that God's word is true and infallible. In contrast with those who do not keep God's Word (v. 158), he keeps it and is depending upon it to quicken him because it is true (v. 160a). Therefore, when he says, "every one of thy righteous judgements endureth forever," he must be expressing his confidence in the infallibility and absolute trustworthiness of God's Word. Every statement in God's word is dependable." (Glenny, 89)

- Regarding Psalm 119:160, D.A. Waite simply says, ""endureth forever"—that is Bible Preservation!" (Waite, 8)

OTHER PASSAGES FROM THE PSALMS

- D. A. Waite views these additional Psalms as dealing with preservation. In the interest of time and space, I have provided just the reference followed by Waite's comments on each verse.
  - Psalm 78:1-7 — "These verses certainly indicate that God intended to preserve His Words for all time." (Waite, 7)

- Psalm 105:8 — "If a "generation" is twenty years, this would be 20,000 years. If a "generation" were thirty years, it would be 30, 000 years! God wants us to clearly see His promise of Bible preservation." (Waite, 7)

WORKS CITED

Combs, William W. "The Preservation of Scripture?" in *Detroit Baptist Seminary Journal*. Fall 2000.

Glenny, W. Edward. "The Preservation of Scripture" in *The Bible Version Debate: The Perspective of Central Baptist Theological Seminary*. Minneapolis, MN: Central Baptist Theological Seminary, 1997.

Ouellette, R.B. *A More Sure Word: Which Bible Can you Trust?* Lancaster, CA: Striving Together Publications, 2008.

Waite, D.A. *Defending the King James Bible*. Collingswood, NJ: The Bible For Today Press, 2006.

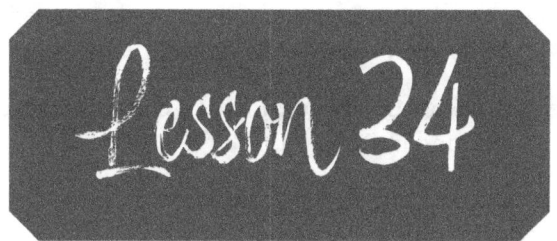

PRESERVATION: EXAMINING THE RELEVANT PASSAGES, ISAIAH 30:8

INTRODUCTION

Recall from Lesson 30 that we laid out the following three views of preservation:

- View 1 — Denial of a Doctrine of Preservation
- View 2 — Preservation in the KJV/TR/MT Tradition
- View 3 — Preservation in the Totality of Manuscripts

- Please remember that we are in the process of looking at passages that establish the fundamental promise of preservation before we consider the extant and location of preservation.

- In Lessons 31 and 32 we commenced our study of whether the Bible teaches its own preservation by looking at Psalm 12:6-7.

- Last week in Lesson 33, we considered a cluster of verses regarding preservation found in Psalm 119.

- In this lesson, I would like to consider the impact of Isaiah 30:8 upon the doctrine of preservation.

ISAIAH 30:8

- Isaiah 30:8 — "Now go, write it before them in a table, and note it in a book, that it may be for the time to come for ever and ever:"

- Much of the relevant literature on the topic of preservation does not include any discussion of this verse. In my mind this is unfortunate because this verse speaks to why God would have something written down and noted in a book. The purpose and intent of doing so is explicitly stated in verse 8, "that it may be for the time to come for ever and ever."

- This was God's motivation for any of the words He had written down under inspiration.

    o "When God talks about preserving His words, He is talking about preserving His words that are written on the page in a book." (Jordan, MSS 101—Lesson 9)

- The use of the word "book" in Isaiah 30:8 is important. The Hebrew word (*cepher*) translated "book" occurs 184 times in 174 verses in the Hebrew Old Testament. One hundred thirty-eight (138) times the King James translators rendered the word as "book" in English.

- As God progressively gave His word to Israel in "time past," the text portrays the human authors as writing a book and subsequently adding to it as more scripture is written down.

- Exodus 17:14 — God tells Moses to write it in a book for a Memorial.

- Exodus 24:4 — what did Moses write in the book? All the "words."

- Exodus 24:7—Moses reads the "book of the covenant" in verse 7. What was in the "book of the covenant"? The "words" that Moses wrote in verse 4.

- Deuteronomy 29:20-21, 27—what is "written in this book" in verse 20? The words that Moses wrote down (Exodus 24:4). Why did God want Moses to write them down? So that they would be an everlasting "memorial" (Exodus 17:14) of what God said.

- Deuteronomy 31:24-26—what was Moses writing in the book of the law? The words that God wanted Israel to remember forever. The book of the law included Genesis through Deuteronomy.

- Joshua 1:8 — after the death of Moses, Joshua emphasizes the importance of the "book of the law."

- Joshua 24:26 — Joshua is adding to the words written by Moses.

- I Samuel 10:25 — Samuel is adding to the book started by Moses and expanded by Joshua.

- I Kings 14:19 — references "the book of the chronicles of the Kings of Israel."

- II Kings 14:6 — the words written in the book of the law were still in existence at the time that II Kings was written.

- II Chronicles 24:27 — speaks of the words "written in the story of the book of the kings."

- Psalm 40:7 — the book is made up of books.

- Isaiah 34:16 — the book of the Lord.

- Jeremiah 30:2 — Jeremiah is told to write the words in a book.

- Jeremiah 36:2, 8, 11, 32; 51:60 — recall that Daniel came to understand by books that the Babylonian captivity would last seventy years. One of the books that Daniel read was the book of Jeremiah. So, Daniel had access to what was written down despite not possessing the original manuscript. Therefore, God wanted His word noted in a book so that it could be "for ever and ever."

- Isaiah 59:20 — is a reference to the Second Coming of Christ.

    o Romans 11:26-27 — Paul quotes Isaiah 59:20 as a reference to the Second Coming of Christ and the salvation of Israel when Christ comes back at the Second Advent.

- Isaiah 59:21 — "As for me, this *is* my covenant with them, saith the LORD; My spirit that *is* upon thee, and my words which I have put in thy mouth, shall not depart out of thy mouth, nor out of the mouth of thy seed, nor out of the mouth of thy seed's seed, saith the LORD, from henceforth and for ever."

- Regarding the implications of Isaiah 59:20 on the doctrine of preservation, Brother Jordan stated the following in Grace School of the Bible:

    o "He is talking about the people in the millennium. They have the word that God put in their mouth back in Isaiah (the Old Testament) and He says, "Even after the millennium, my word is still going to last forever and ever."

    "Folks, if the millennium is 2000 AD plus and Isaiah is 700 BC, you have preservation for 2700 years right there demanded in the text in order to meet the qualifications of the text. God said, "I put the words in your mouth (Isaiah) and wrote them down in a book to be there for ever, and they will be available at the Second Advent of Christ, and they will even continue after that." That is preservation."

    "If I can demonstrate, in the bible, that in the millennium God says His word is going to be present, then I can sure demonstrate the fact that it is somewhere in the dispensation of grace. If God will have His word in the millennium, He is going to preserve it through the time before the millennium." (Jordan, MSS 101—Lesson 9)

- Isaiah 29:18-19 — "And in that day [the millennium] shall the deaf hear the words of the book, and the eyes of the blind shall see out of obscurity, and out of darkness. The meek also shall increase *their* joy in the LORD, and the poor among men shall rejoice in the Holy One of Israel."

- "In that Kingdom, when the deaf hear, they will hear the words of the Bible that Isaiah is told to write down. God is going to preserve that book. That is the doctrine of preservation; that is God's promise to preserve his word." (Jordan, MSS 101—Lesson 9)

- Isaiah 30:8 — God told Isaiah to write His words in a book so that they would be available for the deaf to hear read to them in the millennium. Regarding those who deny the doctrine of preservation Brother Jordan stated:

    o "When you are studying preservation, you are not studying a figment of some fellow's imagination who just likes to run off at the mouth without studying.

    There are a lot of real simple people in the world who believe in the preservation of the scripture. They believe that they have the preserved word of God, but they do not have all of that fancy scholarship and information. They just have faith to believe that God Almighty has preserved His word.

    I want you to remember this, *any believer that you meet that does not believe in the issue of preservation has been taught not to believe it.*" (Jordan, MSS 101—Lesson 9)

- Despite the lack of discussion of Isaiah 30:8 in the scholarly literature, there is strong scriptural evidence that the verse does help establish the Biblical doctrine of the preservation of God's written word.

PRACTICAL REASONS FOR WRITING A BOOK

- The following is a list of practical reasons, covered in Grace School of the Bible for why God wrote and preserved a book.

To preserve the original revelation.

- "Can you imagine how confusing and sloppy it would get if you were just passing on oral communication? If you get a line of people and whisper something in someone's ear at the beginning of the line and then he whispers it into the next person's ear and so on, by the time it reaches the last person, it will be something entirely different.

  Now can you imagine how it would go if you had oral tradition to keep passing down the word of God? You never would know if you had it right or not.

  God wanted His revelation preserved in a book." (Jordan, MSS 101—Lesson 8)

A written text groups all the material together.

- "You can get all the material together under one cover. It would be horrible if you had to hunt around for people who had bits and pieces of the oral communication... With the written text, you can get it all in one book." (Jordan, MSS 101—Lesson 8)

A written text is independent of the speaker and the writer.

- "In Jeremiah 36, Jeremiah is in jail. He writes the thing down and gives it to his secretary and says, "Go read it to the king." It is independent of him.

  Paul says in 2 Timothy 2:9 – "Wherein I suffer trouble, as an evil doer, even unto bonds; but the word of God is not bound." He said, "They have me in jail like a criminal, but the word of God is not bound."

  They wrote it down and sent it out. It is independent regardless of what happens to the speaker." (Jordan, MSS 101—Lesson 8)

The written text is mobile.

- "It transcends the life and times of the writers and the students. It is mobile." (Jordan, MSS 101 — Lesson 8)

The written text makes everybody responsible.

- "Luke 16:29 – "They have Moses and the prophets; let them hear them."

  You have the book, so you have the revelation that you need." (Jordan, MSS 101—Lesson 8)

WORKS CITED

Jordan, Richard. *Manuscript Evidence 101, Lesson 8*. Chicago, IL: Grace School of the Bible.

Jordan, Richard. *Manuscript Evidence 101, Lesson 9*. Chicago, IL: Grace School of the Bible.

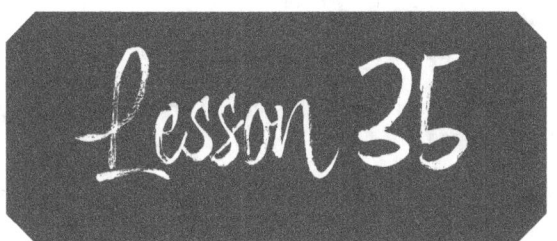

PRESERVATION: EXAMINING THE RELEVANT PASSAGES, ISAIAH 40:8 & I PETER 1:23-25

INTRODUCTION

- Recall from Lesson 30 that we laid out the following three views of preservation:

    o View 1 — Denial of a Doctrine of Preservation

    o View 2 — Preservation in the KJV/TR/MT Tradition

    o View 3 — Preservation in the Totality of Manuscripts

- Please remember that we are in the process of looking at passages that establish the fundamental promise of preservation before we consider the extant and location of preservation.

- In Lessons 31 and 32 we commenced our consideration of whether the Bible teaches its own preservation by looking at Psalm 12:6-7.

- In Lesson 33, we studied a cluster of verses regarding preservation found in Psalm 119.

- Last week in Lesson 34, we considered the impact of Isaiah 30:8 upon the doctrine of preservation.

- In this Lesson, we study the impact of Isaiah 40:8 and its New Testament cross-reference I Peter 1:23-25 upon the doctrine of preservation.

ISAIAH 40:8

- Isaiah 40:8 — "The grass withereth, the flower fadeth: but the word of our God shall stand for ever."

- This verse has attracted more attention in scholarly literature than has Isaiah 30:8.

- Remaining true to his non-preservationist stance, Dr. W. Edward Glenny sees the verse as a general statement of the infallibility of God's promise to deliver Israel from their captivity.

    o "This OT context speaks of the infallibility of God's promise to deliver His people from their captivity in Babylon. His promises will come to pass. Second . . . it is speaking of the infallibility and incorruptible nature of the Word of God not of the preservation of the text of Scripture." (Glenny, 89-90)

- To bolster his position, Glenny quotes Grudem's commentary on I Peter:

  - ". . . the Isaiah passage is a statement about the character of God's words generally, without reference to any particular form in which they occur." (Glenny, 90)

- Taking the middle of the road position once again is Dr. William W. Combs of Detroit Baptist Seminary. Not willing to go as far as Glenny (see above) or Strouse (see below), Combs concludes that Isaiah 40:8 "should not be pressed to affirm a specific and direct promise of the preservation of God's written revelation. Instead, it may have a more indirect application to the doctrine." (Combs, 20)

- Combs reasons as follows to support his conclusion:

  - "In this verse we are again faced with the problem of identifying "the word of our God," as well as the meaning of "stands forever." The Hebrew word for "stands" (μWq) when it is used figuratively can have the ideas of "fixed," "confirmed," "established," "endure," and according to BDB in this verse the particular sense is "be fulfilled." BDB also suggests parallels with Isaiah 14:24, "The LORD of hosts has sworn saying, 'Surely, just as I have intended so it has happened, and just as I have planned so it will stand,'" and Isaiah 46:10, "Declaring the end from the beginning, And from ancient times things which have not been done, Saying, 'My purpose will be established, And I will accomplish all My good pleasure.'" Thus, the idea would be that "the word of our God stands forever" in the sense that it will "be fulfilled." However, commentators universally understand the emphasis to be more that of "permanence"— the permanence of God's word in contrast to "the grass" and "the flowers." Moyer says that in verses 6–8 "the message is the contrast between human transience and divine permanence, designed to affirm that what the Lord promises he will most surely keep and perform." Thus, Isaiah says that the plans and purposes of the nations will fail, "but the word of our God stands forever"—his plans are fixed, established, permanent; they cannot be "annulled by the passage of time." Alexander suggests that "there is a tacit antithesis between the word of God and man; what man says is uncertain and precarious, what God says cannot fail." What God says, his word, cannot be changed; it is immutable." (Combs, 19-20)

- In summation, Combs views the verse as being more about the immutability of God's word than its preservation.

- In his essay, "Preservation of the Bible: Providential or Miraculous? The Biblical View?" Jon Rehurek comments on Isaiah 40:8 in a section titled *Infallibility Texts*. Rehurek, like Combes, sees the passages as indirectly applying to the doctrine of preservation.

  o "The promises of God are sure and reliable. Once again, the focus is on the abiding truthfulness of the words of the Lord; whereas men fail, the words will never fail. And, even more specifically, the text emphasizes that important truth. Oswalt says, "Whatever may lie ahead for the Israelites, they may know that God's word of promise will not fail them." This may apply indirectly to the preservation of the written word of God, but it is not the direct meaning of the statements of Isaiah. In comparison to the frailty of flowers and grass, the promises of God "stand forever," firmly established, unshakeable, immovable, and unfailing. "Stands" has the idea of being "fixed," "confirmed," "established," "enduring," and in this verse, means "be fulfilled." … Because the focus is on the permanence of God's promises (v. 8), this certainly has application to the written words of God, albeit indirectly and by implication." (Rehurek, 84-85)

- Preservationist Dr. Thomas Strouse comments on the verse in The *Locus Classicus Passages* section of his essay titled "The Translation Model Predicted by Scripture." Regarding Isaiah 40:8, Strouse states:

  o "Isaiah contrasted the frailty of man with the permanence of God's Word when he uttered, "the grass, withereth, the flower fadeth: but the word of our God shall stand for ever" (40:8; cf. v. 7). Surely Isaiah alluded to the very words which he preached and ultimately inscripturated in his book. Isaiah could write

(8:1), was commanded to write (30:8), and did write (34:16). Isaiah taught the perfect, verbal, plenary permanence of Scripture." (Strouse in *Thou Shalt Keep Them*, 245)

- Donald L. Brake includes a discussion of Isaiah 40:8 as "direct biblical evidence" of preservation in his essay "The Preservation of Scriptures." Brake writes:

  o "Isaiah 40:8 adds the thought of endurance to the concept of the stability of the Word... Isaiah 40 begins the third major section of the prophecy of Isaiah. It has as its general theme the idea of comfort while awaiting deliverance. In verses 1 through 11, Isaiah tells the nation of the endurance of God's Word, which becomes a source of comfort. The theme of verses 1 through 11 is the proclamation of the perishable nature of all flesh and the imperishable nature of the Word of God, ... What comes out of man's mouth is uncertain and temporary, but what God speaks is as eternal as his very character." (Brake in *Counterfeit or Genuine*, 182)

- Dr. David H. Sorenson states the following regarding Isaiah 40:8 in his book *Touch Not the Unclean Things: The Text Issue and Separation*:

  o "Isaiah 40:8 says (quotes the verse) ...The word translated as "shall stand" also has the sense to be established or to persist. The prophet, in essence, wrote that God's Word will persist forever." (Sorenson, 54)

- Preservationists Jack McElroy, Dr. Jack A. Moorman, and Dr. Thomas Holland all include Isaiah 40:8 in their respective lists of verses that teach the preservation of scripture. Dr. David Cloud states the following regarding Isaiah 40:8 and Isaiah 59:21 (see discussion in Lesson 34) in his book *Myths About the Modern Bible Versions*:

- o "Isaiah adds his "amen" to the doctrine of preservation. According to Isaiah 59:21, it is the very words of God which will be preserved. Note the preservation of God's Word is connected with its usage among believing people. The Scriptures will be preserved by use, not disuse." (Cloud, 108)

I PETER 1:23-25

- I Peter 1:23-25 — "Being born again, not of corruptible seed, but of incorruptible, by the word of God, which liveth and abideth for ever. For all flesh is as grass, and all the glory of man as the flower of grass. The grass withereth, and the flower thereof falleth away: But the word of the Lord endureth for ever. And this is the word which by the gospel is preached unto you."

- Given that Peter quotes Isaiah 40:8 in I Peter 1:23-25, it made sense to insert our discussion of the passage into the reworked notes for this lesson. Regarding I Peter 1:23-25, preservationist D.A. Waite states:

- "That is a reference to Bible preservation, isn't it? The Word of God is incorruptible. Strong defines his words as follows:

  - o "862. *apthartos* (ä-*fthär-tos*) from 1 (as a negative particle) and derivative of 5351; undecaying (in essence or continuance): not (in, un-)corruptible, immortal."

  God's words cannot be corrupted, corroded, decayed like our bodies. When we die and are put into the earth, our bodies see corruption. They are decayed and vanish away into dust, but the Words of God are incorruptible. They live and abide forever. That is a promise of God's preservation. The illustration of that is given in verse 24: (quotes verses 24-25)

This teaches preservation, the opposite of what happens to the flower or the grass. You know full well what happens to pretty flowers when it begins to snow. They perish. They go away. The Words of God do not go away. They do not perish. They endure." (Waite, 14)

- Please recall from above that Dr. William W. Combs does not believe that Isaiah 40:8 does not "affirm a specific and direct promise of the preservation of God's written revelation." Rather Combes views the verse as having a more "indirect application to the doctrine." Consequently, Combs does not view Peter's citation of Isaiah to be affirming a doctrine of preservation either.

    o "But does this verse directly teach that God's written revelation is "imperishable"; in other words, does it directly affirm a doctrine of preservation? There are several problems with that interpretation. First, it is not certain that the phrase "living and enduring' in verse 12 modifies "word." A case can be made that it modifies God — "through the word of the living and enduring God (marginal reading of the NRSV and the NEB)." The same two participles are applied to God in Daniel 6:27 (LXX). However, it must be admitted that this reading is rejected by most commentators. Second, Peter is quoting Isaiah 40:8 in verses 24 and 25, and we have already noted that his text is probably not a direct promise of the preservation of Scripture. Third, it is not clear that Peter's reference to the word of God in verse 23 and the "word which was preached" in verse 25 is a reference to Scripture. As was previously explained, in the New Testament the "word of God," more often than not, has reference to the gospel message, rather than God's special written revelation. Finally, the passage in Peter ends with the words: "And this is the word which was preached to you." This would seem to indicate that Peter's emphasis though has been on the gospel message as proclaimed to his readers, not on God's written revelation. That gospel message may have included references to God's Word written, but it does not appear that this is Peter's primary emphasis. Therefore, any reference to the preservation of Scriptures in these passages is probably indirect at best." (Combs, 25-26)

- So, Comb's first reason that I Peter 1:23-25 is not teaching preservation is on account of a technicality regarding what the phrase "living and enduring" refers to; a point upon which he admits that "most commentators" reject. His second, reason follows from his teaching that Isaiah 40:8 is not a "direct" promise of preservation. Thirdly, he wants his readers to embrace the notion that the phrase "word of God" refers primarily to the "gospel message" and not "God's special written revelation." Personally, I find none of this reasoning compelling to say the least.

- Like Waite, preservationist Gary La More views I Peter 1:23-25 as clearly establishing a doctrine of preservation. La More is the author of Chapter Seven of *Thou Shalt Keep Them: A Biblical Theology of the Perfect Preservation of Scripture* titled, "Words Which Abide Forever: 1 Peter 1:23-25." In this chapter La More states the following with respect to I Peter 1:23-25:

    o "Verses 23-25 of 1 Peter 1 reveal to the reader that God has provided for him the vehicle of his salvation. The purifying of the soul in v. 22 that results in the holiness of vv. 15, 16 comes because of the regeneration experience that is described in v. 23 as: "Being born again, not of (ἐκ, ek, "out of," "from") corruptible seed, but of incorruptible, by (διά, dia, "through," "by means of") the word of God, which liveth and abideth forever." So, how does this regeneration come about? It comes about by the Divine Word. The Divine Word is the incorruptible seed which liveth and abideth forever. This Divine Word is the means God uses to impart new life in an unbeliever (cf. Rom. 10:17; Jas. 1:18). Moreover, Peter's emphasis on the fact that the Word of God is living (cf. Heb. 4:12) suggests its power—unlike that of any merely human words—to generate new life in Christ. . .

    Therefore, in order to be regenerated, a man must have a Divine Word that is living and abiding forever. Without a living and abiding Word being preserved continuously by God, the believer would not have what he needs to be born again. God has promised perpetuity to His Word because He knows that without it there would be no hope of eternal salvation. An eternal God has given an eternal Word that results in an eternal salvation.

In verses 24 and 25, God refers to Isaiah 40:6-8 and contrasts the perishable nature of the flesh with the eternal viability of the Word of God. The saints, with all the blessings of verses 3 through 13, are born from above of imperishable seed (verse 23). All else, all unregenerated flesh on earth, however affluent and currently powerful and prestigious, is like grass—perishable. The flower that stems from it is destined to fade and fall.

Corruptible seed, standing in sharp contrast with incorruptible, must exist somewhere. The words of men are corrupt and corruptible seed, including words of men posing as words of god. This passage explicitly teaches that Scripture is categorically incorruptible seed. . .

In contrast to the corruptible seed, the Word of God, which gave life to the believer is eternal. The "but" of verse 25 is adversative. Without a doubt, earthly glory fades (see verse 24) but the word of God abides forever (v. 25)." (La More in *Thou Shalt Keep Them*, 70-71)

- Regarding the question of whether I Peter 1:23-25 is simply referring to the preached gospel as Combs suggested or the written Word of God, La More writes:

  o "The gospel message proclaimed was preached using His Word (*rhama*). The Word that abides forever in v. 23 is (present tense) the Word (the Gospel text) that is preached (v. 25), equating the two (*logos* in v. 23 and *rhama* in v. 25). The Old Testament was used, for the Gospel was "per the Scriptures" (I Corinthians 15:2, 3), so this passage does apply to the written Word of God (and not merely to the oral Word). Since this Word was the text of the Old Testament, no Old Testament passages were lost at the time of I Peter. The teaching here is that the Word that believers preach on earth is eternal. Believers preach the whole counsel of God's Word (Acts 20:27), therefore, every Word must be available." (La More in *Thou Shalt Keep Them*, 72)

- While I take exception with some of La More's exposition on dispensational grounds, his core message appears sound. I Peter 1:23-25 does teach the preservation of God's word.

OTHER OLD TESTAMENT PASSAGES

- Besides Psalms 12:6-7, Psalms 119:89, 111, 152, 160 as well as Isaiah 30:8; 40:8, there are other Old Testament passages that some preservationists have identified as having an impact upon the doctrine of preservation. Some of these include the following:
    - Proverbs 22:20-21 — "Here is a clear statement by the Lord that He has given us things in WRITING so that we might have "certainty" about them. The only way we can have that certainty today is for God to have preserved every one of His "words of truth." This truly is a promise of Bible preservation." (Waite, 8)
    - Ecclesiastes 3:14 — "If God has done anything or given us anything, it is perfect. He has given us His words, therefore His Words are perfect. We can't add to it or take away from it. It has been **preserved exactly**." (Waite, 8)

- Please note that Waite's standard of preservation as well as the one set forth by Strouse, and McElroy is none other than "verbatim identicality." It is on this point, i.e., the extent of preservation, that I would disagree with these brothers.

CONCLUSION

- Only an extreme position that seeks to deny any doctrine of preservation advanced by Drs. Wallace and Glenny sees Isaiah 40:8 and its sister passage I Peter 1:23-25 as having no bearing upon the preservation of scripture. Even moderates such as Combs and Rehurek acknowledge the verses' application to the doctrine of preservation even if it is just indirect.

- These two verses from Isaiah (30:8; 40:8) stand out as clear internal witnesses to Biblical doctrine and promise of preservation. Preservation is a Biblical doctrine that cannot be ignored, swept under the rug, or explained away. The cumulative force of the relevant passages are clear and irrefutable; God has promised to preserve His word.

WORKS CITED

Brake, Donald L. "The Preservation of Scripture" in *Counterfeit or Genuine*. Grand Rapids, MI: Grand Rapids International Publications, 1975.

Cloud, David W. *Myths About the Modern Bible Versions*. Oak Harbor, WA: Way of Life Literature, 1999.

Combs, William W. "The Preservation of Scripture?" in *Detroit Baptist Seminary Journal*. Fall 2000.

Glenny, W. Edward. "The Preservation of Scripture" in *The Bible Version Debate: The Perspective of Central Baptist Theological Seminary*. Minneapolis, MN: Central Baptist Theological Seminary, 1997.

La More, Gary. "Words Which Aide Forever" in *Thou Shalt Keep Them: A Biblical Theology of the Perfect Preservation of Scripture.* El Sobrante, CA: Pillar & Ground Publishing, 2003.

Rehurek, Jon. "Preservation of the Bible: Providential or Miraculous? The Biblical View" in *The Master's Seminary Journal.* Spring 2008.

Sorenson, David H. *Touch Not the Unclean Thing: The Text Issue and Separation.* Duluth, MN: Northstar Baptist Ministries, 2001.

Strouse, Thomas. "The Permanent Preservation of God's Words: Psalm 12:6-7" in *Thou Shalt Keep Them: A Biblical Theology of the Perfect Preservation of Scripture.* El Sobrante, CA: Pillar & Ground Publishing, 2003.

Waite, D.A. *Defending the King James Bible.* Collingswood, NJ: The Bible For Today Press, 2006.

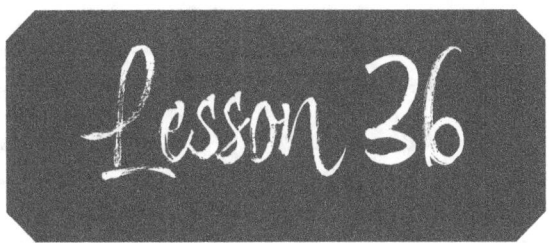

PRESERVATION: EXAMINING THE RELEVANT PASSAGES, MATTHEW 4:4

INTRODUCTION

Recall from Lesson 30 that we laid out the following three views of preservation.

- o View 1 — Denial of a Doctrine of Preservation
- o View 2 — Preservation in the KJV/TR/MT Tradition
- o View 3 — Preservation in the Totality of Manuscripts

- Please remember that we are in the process of studying the relevant passages that establish the fundamental promise of preservation. This is an important first step before we consider the extant and location of preservation.

- In Lessons 31 and 32 we commenced our study of whether or not the Bible teaches its own preservation by looking at Psalm 12:6-7.

- In Lesson 33, we considered a cluster of verses regarding preservation found in Psalm 119. Lesson 34 covered the impact of Isaiah 30:8 upon the doctrine of preservation. Meanwhile, Lesson 35 considered how Isaiah 40:8 and its cross-reference I Peter 1:23-25 help establish the doctrine of preservation.

- In this lesson, I would like to begin a consideration of the relevant New Testament texts regarding preservation beginning with Matthew 4:4.

MATTHEW 4:4

- Much of the relevant writings on both sides of the preservation debate leave out any discussion of Matthew 4:4. Those who deny that the scriptures teach a formal doctrine of preservation (View 1) such as Drs. Daniel Wallace and W. Edward Glenny do not comment on the verse in their writings. Likewise, those who accept a more limited notion of preservation (View 3) such as Dr. William W. Combs and Jon Rehurek do not include any discussion of the verse in their essays on the topic.

- Even much of the pro-King James literature (View 2) fails to note the potential impact of Matthew 4:4 upon the doctrine of preservation. The verse is frequently noted in lists of verses viewed to support the doctrine of preservation but little if any explanation is ever offered.

- Two notable exceptions are Drs. Thomas M. Strouse and D.A. Waite. Dr. Waite's *Defending the King James Bible* contains an entire page and a half explanation of the verse's impact upon the doctrine of preservation. Meanwhile, Dr. Strouse devoted an entire chapter of *Thou Shalt Keep Them: A Biblical Theology of the Perfect Preservation of Scripture* to an exposition of Matthew 4:4 as it relates to the doctrine of preservation.

- Given that these two writings are the most thorough explanations of the verse in terms of its impact upon the doctrine of preservation, we will survey the comments made by Waite and Strouse below. Thirdly, we will consider the issue of "exact sameness" as it relates to Matthew 4:4 and the overall promise of preservation. Lastly, next week in Lesson 37, we will discuss the importance of the Perfect Passive tense upon the proper exposition of the text. Our discussion of Matthew 4:4 will be organized as follows:

  o D.A. Waite on Matthew 4:4

  o Thomas M. Strouse on Matthew 4:4

  o Matthew 4:4 and the Challenge of "Exact Sameness"

  o Impact on the Perfect Passive Tense (Lesson 37)

- *D.A. Waite on Matthew 4:4*

- Waite's comments on Matthew 4:4 are broken up into two sections: 1) general comments, and, 2) a discussion of the impact of the prefect tense on the phrase "it is written." Below we will discuss Waite's comments on the impact of the perfect tense. In this section, I would just like to note the nature of Waite's general comments. Waite writes:

  o "When Jesus said, "It is written," that referred to the Old Testament. . . How can a man or woman live by every word of God that proceeds out of the mouth of God unless God has preserved these Words to listen to? It is impossible. And you and I who speak English and may not know Greek or Hebrew, how will we know God's Words unless He has preserved it to the present day, and then we have it accurately and faithfully translated into English. What the Lord Jesus Christ was telling Satan was that the Old Testament has been preserved. He is quoting from Deuteronomy. The Old Testament had been preserved right down until His day and man should live by those very Words. That is a number of years, about 1500 years from Moses until Jesus's day. He kept, guarded, and preserved "EVERY WORD."" (Waite, 9)

- Waite's fundamental point is that Jesus could not quote Deuteronomy 8:3 in refutation of the Adversary's assault unless God's word had been preserved. Mankind had access to the words of God 1500 years after they were written by Moses. This seems like strong scriptural evidence of preservation.

- *Thomas M. Strouse on Matthew 4:4*

- Strouse's comments on Matthew 4:4 are far more extensive and wide ranging than the explanation offered above by Waite. Strouse expounds upon every phrase of Matthew 4:4 into its own section. The following is Strouse's breakdown of the verse:

- Inspiration — "Proceedeth Out of the Mouth of God"

    o Authority — "Man Shall Live"

    o Availability — "By Every Word"

    o Preservation — "It Is Written"

- Strouse states the following in his introductory remarks:

    o "Satan tempted the Lord Jesus Christ early in His ministry (Mt. 4:1-11). The Lord answered the tempter with three references from Deuteronomy (8:3, 6:13, and 6:16, respectively). The first answer is significant. He stated, "It is written, Man shall not live by bread alone, but by every word that proceedeth out of the mouth of God (v. 4, cited from Dt. 8:3). This response summarizes the Lord's Bibliology.

    He affirmed the doctrine of verbal, plenary inspiration of the autographa by stating the source of Scripture—"proceedeth out of the mouth of God."

> He affirmed the authority of the written Scripture, and consequently its infallibility and inerrancy, by upholding it as a standard by which — "man shall . . . live."
>
> He affirmed the availability of Scripture since He declared His personal access and implied mankind's general access to God's Words — "by every word."
>
> He affirmed the doctrine of verbal, plenary preservation of Scripture by the expression — "It is written."
>
> . . . The living word (Christ) validated His written Words since He believed He had the verbal, plenary Old Testament (OT) Words intact in His day. The purpose of this chapter is to examine in detail the Lord's claims about the full and complete text of the Hebrew OT available in His day." (Strouse in *Thou Shalt Keep Them*, 35)

- In short, the Lord Jesus Christ believed in and affirmed the preservation of the Old Testament. According to Strouse, the Lord's Bibliology includes the belief in: 1) plenary verbal inspiration, 2) the infallibility and inerrancy of scripture, 3) the availability and personal access of scripture, and 4) the plenary preservation of scripture.

- I will comment upon Strouse's fourth point in the section below on Matthew 4:4 and the Challenge of "*Verbatim Identicality*."

- In footnote number 27, Strouse offers the following important insight:

  - "Although the Lord Jesus could have rebuked Satan with the power of His own personal authority (cf. Mt. 16:23), Christ submitted His personal authority to the written Scripture, and chose to rebuke His chief adversary with the highest authority— the written Words of God (Psalm. 138:2)." (Strouse in *Thou Shalt Keep Them*, 35)

- In this footnote Strouse, points out the complete reliance upon and confidence that the Lord Jesus Christ had in the written word of God during his earthly ministry.

- Given the fact that Strouse's essay is extensive and exceeds the topical limitations of this lesson we will limit our discussion of his comments to only those portions that deal directly with the topic of preservation. In the section titled "Preservation—"It Is Written"", Strouse states the following regarding preservation:

    o "The passage at hand utilizes the expression "it is written" four times (vv. 4, 6, 7, 10). The Lord submitted Himself to the written OT Scriptures in response to Satan's temptations and claimed the preservation of three passages (Dt. 8:3, 6:16, and 6:13) for His defense (cf. Eph. 6:17). Satan was forced to submit himself to the written Scripture and even declared the preservation of Psalm. 91:11-12 (v. 6) with "it is written" . . . Christ declared that the Hebrew text Dt. 8:3, was still intact, including the consonants and vowels, up to His day." (Strouse in *Thou Shalt Keep Them*, 38)

- In pointing out that Satan quotes Psalm 91:11-13 in Matthew 4:6, Strouse raises a fascinating point. Even the Adversary believes in the doctrine of preservation. How can the adversary believe in the doctrine of preservation while many within Christian academia do not? Satan's ability to quote Psalm 91 to the Lord Jesus Christ during his earthly ministry means that God's words were preserved from the time of David forever just as Psalm 12:6-7 in the KJB assert.

- Strouse points out that God incarnate in the person of Jesus Christ was consistent in both belief and practice with what was promised in the Old Testament cannon.

    o "The incarnate God in the person of Jesus Christ was consistent in His belief and practice since He submitted Himself to the perfectly preserved inscripturated words He promised He would keep. It behooves Christians, including pastors, believers, and scholars, to emulate Christ's teaching in their Bibliology. . ." (Strouse in *Thou Shalt Keep Them*, 39)

- At this point it is instructive to note that no modern version differs with the KJB in terms of how Matthew 4:4 should read.

KJB	NIV	NASB	ESV
But he answered and said, It is written, Man shall not live by bread alone, but by every word that proceedeth out of the mouth of God.	Jesus answered, "It is written: 'Man shall not live on bread alone, but on every word that comes from the mouth of God.'	But He answered and said, "It is written, 'MAN SHALL NOT LIVE ON BREAD ALONE, BUT ON EVERY WORD THAT PROCEEDS OUT OF THE MOUTH OF GOD.'"	But he answered, "It is written, "'Man shall not live by bread alone, but by every word that comes from the mouth of God.'"

- The King James as well as the popular modern versions cited above all agree that man should live by "every word" that came from the mouth of God.

- Consequently, only the preservationist position is internally consistent with the totality of the Biblical data. How can the Lord Jesus Christ possess such confidence in the Old Testament scriptures if God Almighty had not promised to preserve them? Furthermore, how can any Christian scholar maintain that the reading before them in Matthew 4:4, in any version, is correct ("every word") without at the same time acknowledging the reality of Biblical preservation? How did the words get from the pen of Moses (Deuteronomy 8) to the time of Christ unless God preserved them?

- Only the King James reading of Psalm 12:6-7 is internally consistent with the totality of the Biblical data. Were the poor and the needy of David's day preserved until the time of Christ? No, certainly not. Were the words of David's day (Psalm 91) as well as the words of Moses (Deuteronomy 8:3) preserved until the time of Christ? Yes, absolutely or else how were both Christ and the Adversary able to quote them in Matthew 4?

- When one seeks to deny the clear teaching of one passage in order to support their theology, they create problems for themselves elsewhere. While the Bible is a book of books it should always be remembered that it is a unified document that was settled in heaven (Psalm 119:89) before God moved upon a single human author to reveal (revelation) and record his words (inspiration).

- *Matthew 4:4 and the Challenge of "Verbatim Identicality"*

- There is one final point from Strouse's essay that is important to our purposes in this class. Covering this point will set us up for the second part of our discussion regarding Matthew 4:4 next week. Strouse offers three reasons why Christ utilized the Hebrew Old Testament during his earthly ministry and not the Septuagint (LXX) Greek translation of the Old Testament.

    o "There are at least three Biblical arguments that defend the position that the Lord always used the Hebrew text and not the Greek LXX.

    The Lord referred to jots and tittles that make up the Hebrew language, not the Greek language (Mt. 5:17-18).

    The Lord referred to the three-fold division of the *Tanak*, not the LXX, which included the *Torah* (law), the *Nabi'im* (prophets), and *Kethubim* (writings), on several occasions (cf. Lk. 24:44)

    The Lord referred to the first and last books of the *Tanak* (Luke 11:50-52), describing the brutal deaths of the prophets Abel (Genesis 4:8) to Zacharias (II Chronicles 24:20-22). Although the Lord cited precisely the Hebrew of Matthew 4:4, it is clear upon close examination of Deuteronomy 8:3 that Christ did not quote the LXX, since at least two words are different." (Strouse in *Thou Shalt Keep Them*, 38)

- Luke 4:16-21 — I have long questioned the notion that Jesus and his Jewish apostles were using the Greek LXX at the time of Christ. It seems unlikely to me that a Jewish synagogue in Nazareth would not have been using the Hebrew Old Testament.

- Consequently, I think that Strouse's first two arguments are sound regarding why the Lord Jesus Christ would have used the Hebrew Old Testament during his earthly ministry over the Greek LXX. I believe that Jesus and the Apostles were using the Hebrew Old Testament not a Greek translation.

- That being said, Strouse's third argument hinges upon the standard of *"verbatim identicality."* According to his third point, Strouse reasons that Christ could not have used the LXX because it has two words that are different from the Hebrew text. In the footnote attached to point three quoted above Strouse states,

    o "The *LXX* adds ὁ (*ho*) and τo (*to*)." (Strouse in *Thou Shalt Keep Them*, 39)

- Strouse offers no explanation of whether these two Greek words alter the doctrinal content of the verses in question (Deuteronomy 8:3 and Matthew 4:4). The bottom line for Strouse is that the wording is not exactly the same. Therefore, one must be right and the other wrong.

- What happens, though, when one seeks to apply this standard to the KJB?

Deuteronomy 8:3	Matthew 4:4
. . . that he might make thee know that	But he answered and said, It is written,
man **doth** not live by bread **only**,	Man **shall** not live by bread **alone**,
but by every *word* that proceedeth out of the mouth of the **LORD doth man live**.	but by every word that proceedeth out of the mouth of God.

- Is Matthew 4:4 in your KJB an exact word for word quotation of Deuteronomy 8:3? No! Does that mean one of these is in error? No! They are both teaching the exact same doctrinal content without using the exact same words.

Matthew 4:4	Luke 4:4
But he answered and said, It is written, Man shall not live by bread alone, but by every word **that proceedeth out of the mouth** of God.	And Jesus answered him, saying, It is written, **That** man shall not live by bread alone, but by every word of God.

- So not only does Matthew's quotation of Deuteronomy 8:3 not match exactly, but the citations of Deuteronomy by both Matthew and Luke in the same context, they also do not match each other exactly and yet no one views these verses as differing substantively in terms of their doctrinal content.

- Going a step further, one should compare the Adversary's quotation of Psalm 91:11-12 with Matthew 4:6.

Psalm 91:11-12	Matthew 4:6
For he shall give his angels charge over thee, to keep thee in all thy ways. They shall bear thee up in *their* hands, lest thou dash thy foot against a stone.	He shall give his angels charge concerning thee: and in *their* hands they shall bear thee up, lest at any time thou dash thy foot against a stone.

- The Adversary did not quote Psalm 91 exactly as the Psalmist penned it. Yet, the Lord Jesus Christ did not correct Satan or quibble with him for not quoting God's word exactly as it was written.

- The same phenome is observable for the other "it is written" quotations of the Lord Jesus Christ during his temptation.

Deuteronomy 6:16	Matthew 4:7
Ye shall not tempt the LORD **your** God, . . .	Jesus said unto him, It is written again, **Thou** shalt not tempt the Lord **thy** God.

Deuteronomy 6:13	Matthew 4:10
Thou shalt **fear** the LORD thy God, and serve him, and shalt swear by his name.	Then saith Jesus unto him, Get thee hence, Satan: for it is written, Thou shalt **worship** the Lord thy God, and him **only** shalt thou serve.

- While I agree with Waite and Strouse that Matthew 4:4, and other verses like it are vital to the establishment of the doctrine of preservation, I maintain that they go too far in demanding *verbatim identicality* or identical wording as their standard of preservation.

- In the next Lesson we will consider the importance of the perfect tense and the passive voice upon this discussion.

WORKS CITED

Strouse, Thomas. "Every Word: Matthew 4:4" in *Thou Shalt Keep Them: A Biblical Theology of the Perfect Preservation of Scripture*. El Sobrante, CA: Pillar & Ground Publishing, 2003.

Waite, D.A. *Defending the King James Bible*. Collingswood, NJ: The Bible For Today Press, 2006.

Sunday, November 27, 2016—Grace Life School of Theology—*From This Generation For Ever*

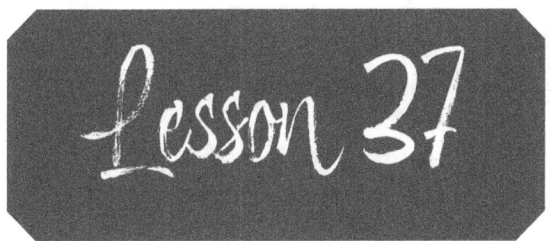

PRESERVATION: EXAMINING THE RELEVANT PASSAGES, MATTHEW 4:4 (PART 2)

INTRODUCTION

- Recall from Lesson 30 that we laid out the following three views of preservation.
    - View 1 — Denial of a Doctrine of Preservation
    - View 2 — Preservation in the KJV/TR/MT Tradition
    - View 3 — Preservation in the Totality of Manuscripts

- Please remember that we are in the process of studying the relevant passages that establish the fundamental promise of preservation. This is an important first step before we consider the extant and location of preservation.

- As part of this first step we have considered the following relevant passages regarding preservation:

    o Psalm 12:6-7 (Lessons 31 & 32)

    o Psalm 119:111, 152, 160 (Lesson 33)

    o Isaiah 30:8 (Lesson 34)

    o Isaiah 40:8 & I Peter 1:23-25 (Lesson 35)

    o Matthew 4:4 (Lesson 36 & 37)

- Last week in Lesson 36 we began discussing the impact of Matthew 4:4 upon the doctrine of preservation. At the outset, I acknowledged that Matthew 4:4 is often included in lists of verses used by preservationists to establish the doctrine of preservation but that little if any exposition has ever been offered on the verse. Two exceptions to this are found in the writings of Dr. D.A. Waite and Dr. Thomas M. Strouse.

- In Lesson 36, I laid out the following four points that we would be considering with respect to Matthew 4:4 and the doctrine of preservation:

    o D.A. Waite on Matthew 4:4

    o Thomas M. Strouse on Matthew 4:4

    o Matthew 4:4 and the Challenge of "Exact Sameness"

    o Impact on the Perfect Passive Tense

- The first three of these points were covered last week in Lesson 36. Our objective this morning is to consider the remaining point i.e., the Impact on the Perfect Passive Tense.

MATTHEW 4:4

- Last week, during our survey of the commentary on Matthew 4:4 offered by Waite and Strouse, I purposely left out any of their comments on the Perfect Passive Tense. This was a conscious decision on my part because the material on this point merited its own separate point.

Impact on the Perfect Passive Tense

- Twice in his essay "Every Word: Matthew 4:4," Strouse briefly mentions the importance of the passive tense upon the doctrine of preservation.
  - "The perfect tense, which He utilized, expresses a completed action with a resulting state of being. The result of the action continues from the past through the present and into the future." (Strouse in *Thou Shalt Keep Them*, 35)
  - "The Greek word Γεραπται (*Gegraptia*) is the 3ms perfect indicative passive of γράφω (*grapho*) meaning "it was, still is and will continue to remain written. Christ declared that the Hebrew text Dt. 8:3, ("not by bread alone shall man live, but by all [words] proceeding out of the mouth of Jehovah") was still intact, including the consonants and vowels, up to his day." (Strouse in *Thou Shalt Keep Them*, 38)

- Strouse offers no further exposition regarding the significance of the perfect passive tense but rather directs his readers to consider Chapter 8 of *Thou Shalt Keep Them* which contains an entire essay devoted to the matter titled "It Is Written" by David Sutton. We will consider the Sutton essay in a few moments.

- It is a textual fact that the verb *gegraptai* is in the perfect tense and passive voice.

- To see an interlinear view of KJB and the *Textus Receptus* please enter the following link into your internet browser: *https://www.blueletterbible.org/kjv/mat/4/4/t_conc_933004.*

- D.A. Waite offers a fuller explanation of why the perfect tense in Matthew 4:4 is significant when considering the doctrine of preservation. Regarding the matter Waite writes,

  o "The second thing I want to show you from that verse is that the word "written," which is recorded scores of times in the New Testament, is in the perfect tense in the Greek. Our English word "graphite," comes from this word, as well as the word, "mimeograph." *GraphO* is the Greek word for "write" and *gegraptai* is the perfect tense of that verb. There are three main past tenses in Greek. (1) There is the imperfect past tense, which is the progressive past, "was writing." (2) There is the aorist past, which is a spot or point action, "wrote." (3) Then you have another past tense, the perfect tense which is used here.

  According to *The Intermediate Grammar of the Greek New Testament* by Dana and Mantely, pages 200-205, the perfect tense indicates that an action has begun in the past and the results of that act continue right on down to the very present.

  This is the tense that the Lord Jesus Christ used when He said, "It is written." It means that the verse He quoted to Satan had been written down in the past in the Hebrew language by Moses and those very Hebrew words were preserved to the very day and hour when the Lord was quoting them to the Devil. Every time *gegraptai* is used or some other form of the perfect tense of that verb (and we have it scores of times in the New Testament) that is proof of the Bible's preservation. God's Words stand just as they were written down." (Waite, 9)

- By far, the fullest treatment of the impact of the perfect passive tense in Matthew 4:4 upon the doctrine of preservation can be found in David Sutton's essay "The Passive Perfect: "It is Written".

Sutton's work comprises Chapter Eight of *Thou Shalt Keep Them: A Biblical Theology of the Perfect Preservation of Scripture* edited by Kent Brandenburg. In the Introduction Sutton states:

- o "The New Testament declares the doctrine of preservation when it employs the phrase "it is written." When quoting passages in the Old Testament, this phrase translates the perfect passive verb *gegraptai* and succinctly states that the verse at hand was written in the past and the result continues to be written down. Believers, unbelievers, the Lord Jesus Christ, and even Satan evidence the reality of preservation by using *gegraptai*. If the nature of this perfect passive *gegraptai* means that particular verses from the Old Testament are preserved just as they were written, then one should conclude that *gegraptai* implies that all the Old Testament and all the New Testament are preserved just as they were written." (Sutton in *Thou Shalt Keep Them*, 75)

- Regarding the meaning of the perfect tense Sutton writes:

    - o "When God authored a perfect tense verb, He employed it over other tenses because the perfect tense expresses the unique idea that an event was accomplished in the past and the results continue in the present. . . the perfect tense shows completed past action with the results of that action continuing to the present. The perfect tense is different from the present tense, which, generally, is present, ongoing action. The perfect tense also must not be confused with the pluperfect (past perfect) tense, for the pluperfect tense views the action, along with its results, as terminating in the past." (Sutton in *Thou Shalt Keep Them*, 75-76)

- Meanwhile, the passive voice indicates the relationship between the verb and subject.

    - o "The passive voice shows that the action of the verb is being done to the subject by someone. In the passive, the subject is not doing the action to something (active voice) or to itself (middle voice); something or someone acts upon the subject." (Sutton in *Thou Shalt Keep Them*, 76)

- When the passive voice is combined with the perfect tense the following meaning is conveyed, according to Sutton.

    - "Combining the perfect tense with the passive voice shows that the action of the verb completed in the past by an agent other than the subject of the verb with the results of the action continuing into the present. The perfect tense, and the perfect passive in particular, is often used in Scripture to teach doctrine and illustrate preservation of truth." (Sutton in *Thou Shalt Keep Them*, 76)

- Consider the theological implications of both the perfect tense and the perfect passive in the following examples.

    - John 1:3—"The first two verbs in the verse ("were made" and "was made") are the aorist tense of *genomai* (ἐγενετο, *egeneto*). Thus, Jesus Christ, in six literal days, created all things. The last "was made" is the perfect tense form of the same verb. In other words, the results of what Jesus Christ created have continued." (Sutton in *Thou Shalt Keep Them*, 76)

    - John 1:18—"The verb "hath seen" is in the perfect tense. No one in the past had ever seen God (cf. Ex. 33:20), and that reality continued to the time of the writing of the Fourth Gospel. To this day, no man has seen God at any time." (Sutton in *Thou Shalt Keep Them*, 77)

    - II Timothy 1:12—"When Paul wrote the verbs translated "have believed" and "am persuaded," he used the perfect tense. Paul professed that in the past he began believing on the Son and was convinced that Christ was able to keep that which he had committed to Him. Both his belief and his conviction continued to persist to the point of writing the epistle. Very clearly, the perfect tense establishes actions as being completed in the past with the results continuing to the present." (Sutton in *Thou Shalt Keep Them*, 77)

    - John 19:30—"Having hung on the cross for six hours and having suffered the brutality of crucifixion, the Lord Jesus Christ said, "It is finished." *Tetelestai* is a perfect passive and can also be understood as "It has been finished." God's plan of offering His only begotten Son a sacrifice for man's sins and Christ's offering for them was complete for all time, yet the results of Christ's offering would continue... The perfect passive *tetelestai* teaches the eternal sufficiency of Christ's bloody death on the cross." (Sutton in *Thou Shalt Keep Them*, 77)

- o I Corinthians 15:3-4—"The perfect passive verb that Paul used for the resurrection of Christ signifies that Christ was raised at a moment in the past and the results of His resurrection continue . . . The perfect passive teaches that the results of the bodily resurrection of Jesus Christ continue." (Sutton in *Thou Shalt Keep Them*, 77)

- o Ephesians 2:8-9—"This classic verse on salvation gleans its eternal security teaching from the construction of the linking verb "are" and the perfect passive participle "saved". God is teaching believers that they are always in the state of being saved by God. In the past salvation came to the lost soul, and from that time on, he is always saved. The perfect passive clearly teaches the present results of past salvation." (Sutton in *Thou Shalt Keep Them*, 77)

- After explaining the meaning and significance of both the perfect tense and passive voice and applying it to non-preservation related texts by way of explanation and illustration, Sutton explains the significance with respect to the doctrine of preservation.

  - o "Sixty-three times in the NT the exact phrase "it is written" occurs. The perfect passive verb *gegraptai* underlies fifty-nine of these references, while the other four occasions represent the perfect passive participle *gegramenon*." (Sutton in *Thou Shalt Keep Them*, 78)

- So every occurrence of "it is written" in the New Testament corresponds with a perfect passive verb in Greek, according to Sutton.

- Sutton discusses the difference between the aorist and perfect tenses in Greek.

- o "One must not confuse the aorist tense with the perfect passive, for the aorist verb *egrapsa* is used differently from the perfect passive *gegraptai*. In the NT the aorist is constantly used to describe the composition of a personal letter (cf. Acts 15:23; I Cor. 7:1), the OT Law (cf. Jn. 5:46), or a NT epistle (cf. Eph. 3:3; Philm. 21). Punctiliar action appropriately denotes the writing process, because the author at a point in time penned words on some medium. However, *gegraptai* does not encompass the process of writing the message alone, but affirms the continuation of the written message. God carefully distinguished among the form of *grapho*; consequently, the occurrences of the perfect passive inform the reader of a significant reference to Scripture that enables or bolsters some particular belief or practice.

  Particular Words made up of distinguishable letters were deliberately written. Therefore, one should conclude that when God gave man the text of the Bible, He gave specific Words and not general thoughts. One should also conclude that if Words are preserved, then the letters forming those Words are also preserved." (Sutton in *Thou Shalt Keep Them*, 78)

- The first appearance of the perfect passive in the New Testament occurs in Matthew 2:5 and stands out as an example of its usage.

  - o "Herod had asked the chief priests and scribes where Christ should be born. Without hesitation these religious scholars referenced the OT and gave a confident answer, which relied on the precise prophecy of Micah the prophet. Their ability to identify the Messiah was based on the preserved prophecy of Christ's birthplace, which Divinely narrowed the possible candidates for Messiah. Since Micah 5:2 was preserved, and testified by *gegraptai*, the pinpoint knowledge of Messiah was preserved." (Sutton in *Thou Shalt Keep Them*, 78)

- After pointing out other similar usages of *gegraptai* in the New Testament, Sutton concurs with Strouse about the Adversary's own recognition of the preservation process.

- o "It is interesting that Satan understands Scriptures' preservation, for he too recognized that the Words of God were written in the past and continue to abide (Mt. 4:6; Lk. 4:10)." (Sutton in *Thou Shalt Keep Them*, 78)

- Sutton views the doctrine of preservation (Bibliology) as a necessary prerequisite for one's doctrine of salvation (Soteriology).

  - o "The doctrine of salvation is dependent upon preservation: if there were not preserved Words, then there would be no preached Word, and man could not believe on Jesus Christ; for "faith cometh by hearing, and hearing by the Word of God." ... Since God preserved His Word, man has sure footing on prophecy and its fulfillment. Without preservation of Scripture, prophecies of Christ would be obscure and even lost, and salvation by grace through faith would be impossible." (Sutton in *Thou Shalt Keep Them*, 80)

- Sutton concludes his essay on the impact and significance of the perfect passive upon the doctrine of preservation as follows:

  - o "The grammar of the perfect passive teaches that someone caused an event in the past and the results of that action continue to the present. Much doctrine that the believer holds is established in the perfect passive. Consistency demands that the perfect passive *gegraptai* means that the Scriptures were written in the past and they continue to be written down in the present. Based on their inspired use of the perfect passive *gegraptai*, the writers of Scripture believed in perfect preservation. Likewise, believers today should believe in the perfect preservation of Scripture, because "It is written."" (Sutton in *Thou Shalt Keep Them*, 81)

CONCLUSION

- I believe that the perfect passive is significant and does play a role in the establishment of the doctrine of preservation. To argue otherwise, would place one's theological understanding of other passages in jeopardy.

- That being said, I think that Strouse, Waite, and Sutton go too far in demanding *verbatim identiality* of wording as the standard for preservation. The standard adopted by Sutton would demand not just identical wording but identical spelling. Given the historical and textual facts that no two manuscripts are exactly the same, this standard demands more than one can prove and therefore does more to harm the pro-King James position than help it.

- As we saw in Lesson 35, one could not even apply this standard to the KJB given the fact that the New Testament citations of Old Testament verses do not possess identical wording.

WORKS CITED

Strouse, Thomas. "Every Word: Matthew 4:4" in *Thou Shalt Keep Them: A Biblical Theology of the Perfect Preservation of Scripture.* El Sobrante, CA: Pillar & Ground Publishing, 2003.

Sutton, David. "The Perfect Passive: "It is Written" in *Thou Shalt Keep Them: A Biblical Theology of the Perfect Preservation of Scripture.* El Sobrante, CA: Pillar & Ground Publishing, 2003.

Waite, D.A. *Defending the King James Bible.* Collingswood, NJ: The Bible For Today Press, 2006.

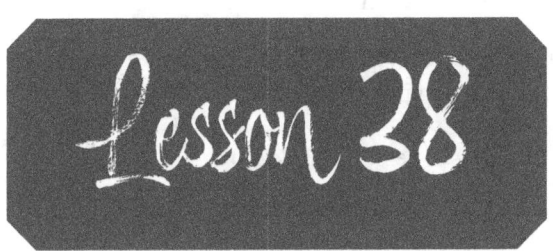

PRESERVATION: EXAMINING THE RELEVANT PASSAGES, MATTHEW 24:35

INTRODUCTION

Recall from Lesson 30 that we laid out the following three views of preservation:

- View 1 — Denial of a Doctrine of Preservation
- View 2 — Preservation in the KJV/TR/MT Tradition
- View 3 — Preservation in the Totality of Manuscripts

- Please remember that we are in the process of studying the relevant passages that establish the fundamental promise of preservation. This is an important first step before we consider the extant and location of preservation.

- As part of this first step, we have considered the following relevant passages regarding preservation.

    o Psalm 12:6-7 (Lessons 31 & 32)

    o Psalm 119:111, 152, 160 (Lesson 33)

    o Isaiah 30:8 (Lesson 34)

    o Isaiah 40:8 and I Peter 1:23-25 (Lesson 35)

    o Matthew 4:4 (Lesson 36 & 37)

- Today in Lesson 38 we want to look at one more passage that is often used to establish the fundamental promise of preservation – Matthew 24:35.

MATTHEW 24:35

- Non-preservationist Daniel B. Wallace argued in his 1992 essay "Inspiration, Preservation, and New Testament Textual Criticism" found in the *Grace Theological Journal,* that Matthew 24:35 does not teach the preservation of scripture. A note at the bottom of page 43 reads:

    o "Occasionally Matt 24:35 ("Heaven and earth will pass away. but my words will not pass away") is used in support of preservation. But once again, even though this text has the advantage of now referring to Jesus' words (as opposed to the OT), the context is clearly eschatological: thus the words of Jesus have certainty of fulfillment. That the text does not here mean that his words will all be preserved in written form is absolutely certain because

(1) this is not only foreign to the context, but implies that the written gospels were conceived at this stage in *Heilsgeschichte*—decades before a need for them was apparently felt; (2) we certainly do not have all of Jesus' words recorded-either in scripture or elsewhere (cf. John 20:30 and 21:25)." (Wallace in *Grace Theological Journal*, 43)

- Wallace sees Matthew 24:35 as dealing with the eschatological fulfillment of Christ's prophecy, not the preservation of the written text of scripture.

- Writing in 1997, W. Edward Glenny discusses Matthew 24:35 in a section titled *Eschatological Fulfillment* in his essay, "The Preservation of Scripture." As the section heading suggests, Glenny, like Wallace before him, sees the verse as pertaining to the fulfillment of prophecy as opposed to textual preservation. Glenny writes:

  o "That Matthew 24:35 also refers to fulfillment, not textual preservation, is evident from verse 34. These two verses read . . . (quotes the verse 34 & 35). Verse 35 itself cannot mean that all of Jesus' words will be perfectly preserved in the text of Scripture since all of His words were not recorded in the text of Scripture, or anywhere else for that matter (cf. John 20:30; 21:25). Also, Luke 16:17 states that no part of the Law will fail; in other words, it will all come to pass. Therefore, when read in their context, these passages do not guarantee that every word of the autographs of Scripture will be preserved intact in some text or text-type. Instead, they teach that the Word of God is true, and that the OT prophecies will all come to pass; none will fail." (Glenny in *The Bible Version Debate*, 87-88)

- Please note that Gleeny provides essentially the same argument as Wallace for why Matthew 24:35 is not talking about the preservation of scripture.

- Unwilling to state that Matthew 24:35 has anything to do with preservation, like Drs. Wallace and Glenny, Dr. William W. Combs of Detroit Baptist Seminary sees the verse as having an indirect application similar to Isaiah 40:8.

- o "Jesus' statement, "My words will not pass away," might first seem to be a direct promise of preservation . . . (quotes Waite) . . . However, this verse would seem to promise too much. It is simply not true that *all* of Jesus' words have been preserved. The apostle John reminds us that "there are also many other things which Jesus did, which if they were written in detail, I suppose that even the world itself would not contain the books that would be written" (John 21:25). Certainly, Jesus must have said some things that were not recorded in the NT, and some of those words have passed away. Though it is true that God (or Jesus) is the ultimate author of Scripture, this verse is not directly referring to any written revelation.

  Matthew 24:35 uses the same hyperbolic language as Matthew 5:18. "Not the smallest letter or stroke shall pass from the Law" is saying much the same thing as "My words will not pass away." Both the words of the Law and the words of Jesus are immutable; they cannot be set aside; they are unalterable. As the words of God, they "stand forever" (Isa. 40:8). And just as "not the smallest letter or stroke shall pass from the Law" speaks of the authority and validity of the Law, so the fact that Jesus' "words will not pass away" give them equal authority to the OT. Carson notes "The authority and eternal validity of God's words (Ps 119:89-90; Isa 40:6-8). But unlike Matthew 5:18, which clearly refers to the Scripture, 24:35 has reference to the authority of Jesus' oral words. And though it is true that some of Jesus' words were recorded in Scripture, written revelation is not the primary emphasis here. Any application to preservation would be indirect, much like Isaiah 40:8." (Combs, 24-25)

- In summation, Combs argues that Matthew 24:35 is referring to the authority of Jesus' spoken words all of which were not necessarily written down. Consequently, the passage only applies to the preservation of the scriptures indirectly. Please note that this is different from what Drs. Wallace and Glenny argued (see above).

- Dr. Kent Brandenburg is the general editor of *Thou Shalt Keep Them:*

A Biblical Theology of the Perfect Preservation of Scripture as well as being the author of Chapter Five titled, "My Words Shall Not Pass Away: Matthew 24:35." In his comments on the context of Matthew 24, Dr. Brandenburg points out that God puts his own credibility on the line when it comes to the issue of predictive prophecy. Given the fact that Matthew 24 and 25 constitute one of the great prophetic passages of the New Testament, its speaker; the Lord Jesus Christ, is likewise, putting His credibility as Israel's Messiah on the line.

- o "The Lord Jesus Christ is God, so He can speak prophetically, and He does in this text. Since He says that the events prophesied in these two chapters are going to occur, one can count on them occurring. . .The generation that witnesses the previously described signs will live to see the coming of the Lord Jesus Christ. This is the answer to the disciples' question concerning the "when" of his coming in v. 3. The generation of people that will see these things is the generation that will enter the tribulation period. . ." (Brandenburg in *Thou Shalt Keep Them*, 59-61)

- Dispensationally, we know that Matthew 24 and 25 await a yet future fulfillment. Moreover, we know that the revelation of the mystery and the formation of the body of Christ interrupted the prophetic timetable outlined by Christ in Matthew 24 and 25. Therefore, the generation that will see the fulfillment of Matthew 24 is still in the future. Yet, the words Christ uttered that day on the Mount of Olives have been recorded in the book of Matthew, a book we have access to during the dispensation of grace. Those to whom these words will directly apply during the Ages to Come will need access to what Christ said that day upon the Mount of Olives. They will have it the same way we have it, via the book of Matthew.

- In that context, there is no reason to assume that Christ's words that "shall not pass away," are anything other than the words recorded in Matthew 24. There is no reason to assume that this somehow violates that statement found in John 20:30 and 21:25. If words and deeds referred to in these Johannine verses were necessary for us to know they would have been added to the eternal written record.

- Contextually, Matthew 24:35 is referring to the words uttered by Christ during the Olivet Discourse. These words must be preserved in written form so that the people living in the ages to come, to whom these verses will directly apply, will know what God said. This is consistent with Isaiah 30:8 and why God wrote anything in a book. The same could be said for any prophetic statement whether spoken by Christ in His earthly ministry and later recorded by the gospel writers or the Old Testament prophets. In that context, Matthew 24:35 is stating that Christ's words in the Olivet Discourse "shall not pass away," by extension we could also conclude that none of the other words of Christ that the Holy Spirit elected to record for us via inspiration will pass away either.

- Dr. D.A. Waite presents the following Biblical argument for why Matthew 24:35 extends the fundamental promise of preservation to the totality of the New Testament in addition to the Old. Please note that all the text formatting exhibited in the following quotation below belongs to Waite.

    o "The Lord is talking of His Words, the New Testament. Not the Masoretic Hebrew Old Testament only, but His Words will not pass away. That means the promise extends to the New Testament. I believe, personally that the Lord Jesus was the Source and Author of every word of the Hebrew Old Testament text. He was the Revelator. He is the Word of God. In a very real sense, therefore, His *Words* include the entire Old Testament. He is also the Source and Author of all the New Testament books. Though we had human writers, the Lord Jesus Christ is the Divine Author and SOURCE of it all.

    a. Christ's Authorship of the Gospels. In John 14:26 Jesus said that the Holy Spirit would "*bring all things to your remembrance*," whatsoever I have said unto you." This includes the four Gospels: Matthew, Mark, Luke and John. John 14:26 says: (quotes the verse). He is talking to His disciples in the Upper Room. This includes everything He said in the four Gospels. His Words shall not pass away. The Holy Spirit of God will bring to these Apostles the exact words so that nothing is forgotten. The Holy Spirit is the MEANS.

b. Christ's Authorship of the Acts of the Apostles. Let us look at John 15:26-27 (quotes the verse). The Apostle bearing *"witness"* is written about in the Acts of the Apostles. The Holy Spirit of God bore witness through the Apostles, and the book of Acts is the record of their *witness*. When the Lord Jesus said that the Holy Spirit would *bring all things* to their remembrance, His statement included the book of Acts.

c. Christ's Authorship of the Epistles. Let us turn to John 16:12-13. The Lord Jesus said:

> *I have yet many things to say unto you [He's talking to His disciples], but ye cannot bear them now. [They couldn't understand them] (13) Howbeit when he, the Spirit of truth, is come, he will guide you into all truth: for he shall not speak of himself [from Himself, Himself being the source]; but whatsoever he shall hear, that shall he speak: and he will shew you things to come.*
>
> *The guiding into all truth includes the Epistles. Notice also that it is clear that the Holy Spirit is not the Source and Author of the Words of God, but it is the Lord Jesus Christ Who is the Source and Author.*

d. Christ's Authorship of Revelation. In John 16:13b, the Lord Jesus continued,

> *". . . and He will shew you things to come."*
>
> *Although it refers to the other New Testament prophetic books, the phrase "things to come" certainly refers also to the book of Revelation. So you have the book of Revelation, the Epistles, the Acts of the Apostles, all the Gospels written by the Lord Jesus, working through the Holy Spirit, using human writers.*
>
> *When He says, "My Words shall not pass away," the Lord Jesus is including the Gospels, Acts, Epistles, and Revelation. All of them are His Words. The whole New Testament is tied up in a bundle and can be held in your hand. He has promised to preserve the Words of the New Testament as well as the Old Testament. I want you to notice also in John 16:14, Jesus says:*
>
> *"He [the Holy Spirit] shall glorify me: for he shall receive of mine, and shall shew it unto you."*

> *That certainly is an answer to the Charismatic Movement which glorifies the Holy Spirit instead of glorifying Christ.*
>
> *In Matthew 24:35 the Lord Jesus Christ said: "Heaven and earth shall pass away. . ." What could be more stable than the heavens and earth? Now, we do have earthquakes, but we think of the earth as being solid. We call it terra firma. That means "firm earth." But the Lord Jesus said that heaven and earth shall pass away. Look at unbelievers and Christians who do not believe in God's preservation of His Words. They take the earth for granted. We walk on it. We assume it won't give way when we walk on it. It is a solid thing. But Jesus said, "Heaven and earth SHALL pass away, but My Words shall not pass away." There will be a new heaven and a new earth, but the Words of God will continue. They are forever settled in Heaven; they are preserved words. They are even more preserved and more settled than either the heaven or the earth!" (Waite, 11-13)*

- In Lesson 19 The Living Word's Attitude Toward the Written Word we studied how the Lord Jesus Christ gave "Advanced Authentication of the New Testament" before it was written. In doing so we utilized the exact same verses from John 14 and 16 that Waite just used in the above argument.

- Moreover, in Lesson 20 The New Testament Writer's Attitude Toward the Written Word we discussed how Paul and the other New Testament writers were penning the words of Christ.

  o Acts 22:14-15 — "And he said, The God of our fathers hath chosen thee, that thou shouldest know his will, and see that Just One, and shouldest hear the voice of his mouth. For thou shalt be his witness unto all men of what thou hast seen and heard."

  o Galatians 1:1-12 — "But I certify you, brethren, that the gospel which was preached of me is not after man. For I neither received it of man, neither was I taught *it*, but by the revelation of Jesus Christ."

    - Read the verse closely, it was not *by* the revelation from Christ, not just something sent to him, but it was the revelation *of* Jesus Christ. In other words, the Lord revealed himself to Paul and spoke with Paul face-to-face just like he did with Moses. He put his words in Paul's mouth, and Paul went out to preach and write those things down.

- o I Corinthians 14:37 — "If any man think himself to be a prophet, or spiritual, let him acknowledge that the things that I write unto you are the commandments of the Lord."
- o I Timothy 6:2-3 — ". . . These things teach and exhort. If any man teach otherwise, and consent not to wholesome words, *even* the words of our Lord Jesus Christ, and to the doctrine which is according to godliness;"
  - The words that Paul wrote down in I Timothy were the very words of the Lord Jesus Christ. Paul's words were the words of the glorified Christ. Not only are these passages from the pen of the Apostle Paul strong regarding Pauline authority, but they are also strong in regard to the doctrine of inspiration. The words of Christ to us today are found in Paul's epistles. Paul's epistles are not made up of Paul's interpretation of the things that Christ gave him. It is not just Paul's interpretation of the ministry of Christ, but you have the very words of the Lord Jesus Christ given to Paul and written down for you and for me.
- o II Corinthians 13:3 — "Since ye seek a proof of Christ speaking in me, which to you-ward is not weak, but is mighty in you."
  - Who is speaking in Paul? Christ is speaking in Paul. The words that Paul speaks came from Christ.

- If this line of argumentation was valid in establishing the inspired nature of the entire New Testament, it is not suddenly falsified when speaking about preservation. One cannot just sweep away the doctrine of preservation just because they do not like the implications. Dr. David Sorenson points out that the mere fact that the Bible exists today serves as *prima facie* (accepted as correct until proven otherwise) evidence that God preserved it.
  - o ". . . the fact that the Bible exists today is *prima facie* evidence that God has preserved it. History is replete with examples of attacks against the Bible down through the ages, yet it has

stood the test of time. Roman emperors ordered Scripture to be burned and large quantities of Bibles were. Yet, it continued. The Roman Catholic hierarchy hid it away in its cloisters, yet it continued. Catholic authorities burned at the stake men who translated the Scripture into vernacular tongues, yet it continued. Most are aware of the anecdote told of Voltaire who sneered that the day was coming when the only place one could find a Bible would be in a museum. Yet, his home today houses a Bible Society. The Communists banned and burned untold numbers of Bibles. Yet, even in places such as the former Soviet Union, the Word of God abounds. There is no question that whether it is the Old Testament or the New Testament, God has preserved His Word." (Sorenson, 55)

- Sorenson tackles the assertions of Wallace and Glenny regarding Matthew 24:35 head on:

  o "Some allege that Jesus was simply foretelling that His words would be fulfilled [reference in the footnote is to Glenny's essay quoted above]. That is to be sure. However, Jesus clearly said that His words would not pass away. First, the context of the verse lends itself to this view. The heavens and earth indeed someday will pass away. See 2 Peter 3:12-13. The earth in its present form will not last in perpetuity. However, in distinction to that, Jesus said that His words would. Second, the etymology of the word translated as "pass away" is instructive. Thayer's *Greek-English Lexicon of the New Testament* lists a number of possible ways in which the word might be translated. One sense is perish. Another is to go away. Jesus in effect said that though the heavens and earth will perish, His words will not. Or to put it another way, though the heavens and earth will go away, His words will not. Common sense dictates that if the plain sense makes sense to seek no other sense. In the eschatological context of Matthew 24, verse 35 clearly bespeaks the preservation of the words of Christ.

  The same critics object that these are His *spoken* words and not His *written* Word (again the reference in the footnotes is to Glenny). Thus implied is that though His spoken words may last forever, His written Word will not (Glenny's notion is contrary to what we saw in Isaiah 30:8. The whole reason God had Isaiah "note it in a book" is so that it would stand forever.)! However, what these selfsame critics seem to miss is that the Holy Spirit inspired the very words of Jesus which he saw fit to record as Scripture. To infer that the written Word of God is anything less than eternal is inconceivable. The Psalmist wrote, "Concerning thy testimonies, I have known of old that thou has founded them for ever" (Ps. 119:152). The word translated founded also has the sense of established. David clearly implied that God's Word is established forever. . . Likewise, Ps. 119:160 says, "Thy word is true from the beginning; and every one of thy righteous judgements endureth for ever" (Please recall from Lesson 33 that Dr. Combs views both Ps. 119:152 and 160 as clear promises of preservation.) . . . The Bible clearly teaches that God has promised to preserve His Word." (Sorenson, 52-55)

CONCLUSION

- The totality of the Biblical evidence is overwhelming, Matthew 24:35 is teaching the eternal preservation of the words of Christ. To claim otherwise creates more problems than it solves. As Dr. Sorenson stated, common sense dictates that we seek no other sense.

WORKS CITED

Brandenburg, Kent. "My Words Shall Not Pass Away: Matthew 24:35" in *Thou Shalt Keep Them: A Biblical Theology of the Perfect Preservation of Scripture*. El Sobrante, CA: Pillar & Ground Publishing, 2003.

Combs, William W. "The Preservation of Scripture?" in *Detroit Baptist Seminary Journal*. Fall 2000.

Glenny, W. Edward. "The Preservation of Scripture" in *The Bible Version Debate: The Perspective of Central Baptist Theological Seminary*. Minneapolis, MN: Central Baptist Theological Seminary, 1997.

Sorenson, David H. *Touch Not the Unclean Thing: The Text Issue and Separation*. Duluth, MN: Northstar Baptist Ministries, 2001.

Waite, D.A. *Defending the King James Bible*. Collingswood, NJ: The Bible For Today Press, 2006.

Wallace, Daniel B. "Inspiration, Preservation, and New Testament Textual Criticism" in *Grace Theological Journal*. 1992.

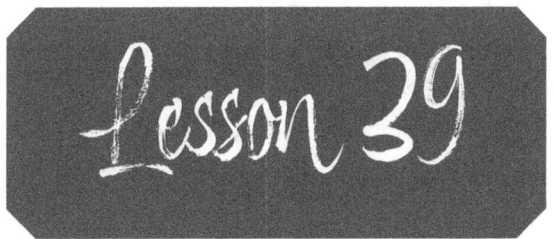

PRESERVATION: FAITH IN THE PROMISE OF GOD

REVIEW: WHAT HAVE WE SEEN SO FAR?

In Lesson 28 & 29 we began the second term of the class with an Introduction to Preservation. After reviewing some key points regarding inspiration from the first term we took stock of the following facts.

- Fact 1 — the original autographs are not extant i.e., they no longer exist.
- Fact 2 — no two Greek manuscripts are exactly the same.
  - Alexandrian manuscripts ℵ (Codex Sinaiticus) and B (Codex Vaticanus), the two so-called oldest and best, differ with each other in over 3,000 places in the gospels alone.

- The manuscripts comprising the Alexandrian Text Type differ from those comprising the Byzantine Text Type.
- No two Byzantine manuscripts read exactly the same.

○ Fact 3 — no two printed editions of the Greek New Testament are exactly the same.
- Editions of the TR are not exactly the same.
- The TR differs from the Critical Text.
- Critical Text editions are not exactly the same.
- United Bible Society
- Nestle-Aland

○ Fact 4 — no two editions of the King James Bible are exactly the same.
○ Fact 5 — the King James differs from modern versions.
○ Fact 6 — no two modern versions read exactly the same.

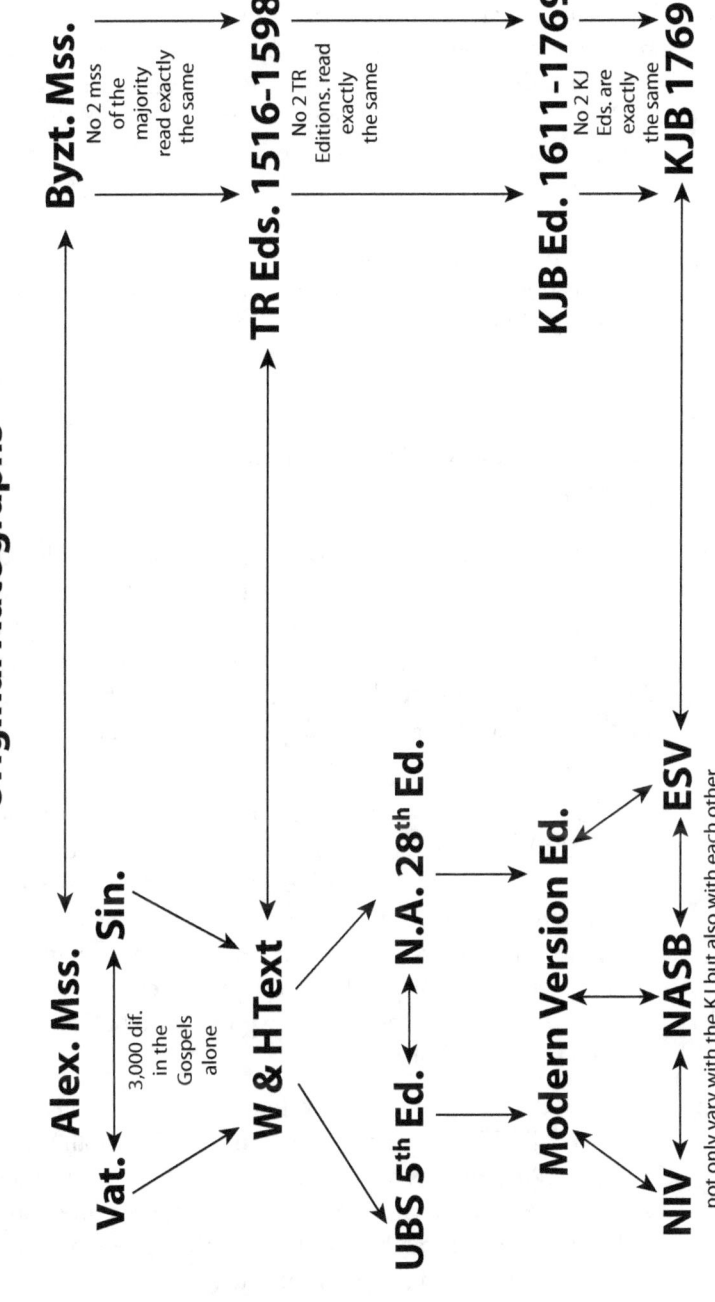

- Summary Statement:

  - "If the preservation of the Word of God depends upon exact preservation of the words of the original documents, then the situation is dire. No two manuscripts contain exactly the same words. No two editions of the Masoretic Text contain exactly the same words. No two editions of the *Textus Receptus* contain exactly the same words. No two modifications of the King James Version contain exactly the same words and the Bible nowhere tells us which edition, if any, does contain the exact words of the originals. These are not speculations, these are plain facts." (Bauder, 155)

- In Lesson 29 we used the Book of Jeremiah as a case study to prove that God could preserve his word without preserving the original autographs.

  - Jeremiah 51:61-63—Jeremiah writing at the bidding of God the Holy Spirit tells Seraiah to destroy Original #2 by tying a stone to it and throwing it into the Euphrates River after it is read in Babylon. God almighty orders the destruction of Original #2. Why would God do this? Didn't God know that a bunch of Fundamentalists in the 20th and 21st century would be looking for the originals?

  - Daniel 9:2 — over 70 years later Daniel comes to understand, by reading the book of Jeremiah, that the captivity was supposed to last 70 years. How is that possible if Original #2 was destroyed? Copies were made prior to the captivity. Once the copies were made, God did not care what happened to the original. The original contents of Original #2 were preserved via the copying process. Daniel had access to the inspired word of God through the copy he had in front of him.

  - Matthew 2:17-18 — contains a quotation from Jeremiah 31:15. First, how did Matthew have access to what Jeremiah said over 470 years (70-year captivity + 400 years of silence) later if God had not preserved His word? So, God secured the contents of the book of Jeremiah despite directing Jeremiah to have Original #2 thrown in the Euphrates River.

In Lesson 30 after discussing the Core Issue of Preservation versus Restoration we studied how the textual facts presented in Lesson 28 & 29 have given birth to the following three views on the doctrine of preservation:

- View 1 — Denial of a Doctrine of Preservation
- View 2 — Preservation in the KJV/TR/MT Tradition
- View 3 — Preservation in the Totality of Manuscripts

- With these three views in mind, Lesson 31 through 38 were devoted to determining whether the scriptures teach their own preservation.
  - Psalm 12:6-7 (Lessons 31 & 32)
  - Psalm 119: 111, 152, 160 (Lesson 33)
  - Isaiah 30:8; 40:8; I Peter 1:23-25 (Lessons 34 & 35)
  - Matthew 4:4 (Lessons 36 & 37)
  - Matthew 24:35 (Lesson 38)

INTRODUCTION

- In this Lesson we want to conclude our consideration of the fundamental promise of preservation. To accomplish this task, we will consider the following four points:
  - Preservation: The Bible's Claim for Itself
  - Preservation: God Keeps His Promises
  - Preservation: The Superiority of the Fideistic Approach
  - Preservation: The Historic Position of the Reformers

PRESERVATION: THE BIBLE'S CLAIM FOR ITSELF

- After studying the relevant passages as well as the scholarly comments made thereupon, I unequivocally maintain that preservation is the Bible's claim for itself. In other words, the Bible does assert and establish a doctrine of preservation.

- Even Dr. William W. Combs, a supporter of View 3 concludes that the Bible does establish a doctrine of preservation. Combs also concludes that the position advanced by Wallace and Glenny (View 1) to "discount the force of these passages on preservation is unconvincing."

    o "It has been demonstrated that many of the verses commonly claimed by those in the KJV/TR camp to directly prove a doctrine of preservation have been misinterpreted and misapplied. On the other hand, at least two verses Psalms 119:152 and 160, would seem to suggest a more direct promise of preservation, with Isaiah 40:8 and Matthew 24:35 supplying more indirect support. In addition, Matthew 5:18 and John 10:35 also strongly imply a doctrine of preservation with their emphasis on the continuing authority of Scripture — an argument that will be explored shortly. The attempt by Wallace and Glenny to discount the force of these passages for preservation is unconvincing." (Combs, 26)

- That being said, Combs does not agree with View 2 either, he disagrees with the KJV/TR camp regarding the *method* and *extent* of preservation.

    o "Thus we conclude that some of the verses discussed above do teach a doctrine of preservation, some more directly and other more indirectly. However, they do not support the view of preservation that is put forth by the KJV/TR camp — that God has perfectly preserved the Bible to our day. Instead, they only suggest a general promise of preservation without specifying how (what method) or to what extent (how pure) God has chosen to preserve his Word." (Combs, 26)

- Questions regarding the *method* and *extent* of preservation will be addressed in further Lessons.

- Given the scope of our discussion so far, the following points are inescapable:

    o God did promise to preserve His word.

    - Psalms 12:6-7; 105:5; 119:111, 152, 160; Isaiah 30:8; 40:8; Matthew 4:4, 24:35; I Peter 1:23-25

    o God did not see fit to preserve His word by preserving the originals.

    - This is self-evident because the originals no longer exist.

    o God did not supernaturally over-take the pen of every scribe, copyist, or typesetter who ever handled the text to ensure that no differences of any kind entered the text.

    - Differences exist at every level of this discussion.

    o If the standard for preservation is "plenary" or "pristine" identicality, i.e., "*verbatim identicality*" why did God not just preserve the originals and thereby remove all doubt?

PRESERVATION: GOD KEEPS HIS PROMISES

- Given the fact that God has indeed promised to preserve his word, the belief in preservation is really a question of faith in the promises of God. The following scriptures demonstrate that God keeps his word and is incapable of lying.

- I Kings 8:24 — "God promised and fulfilled with His hand. He promised the temple. It was built by Solomon who praised God for His faithfulness in keeping His promises." (Waite, 15)
- Romans 4:20-21 — "Here, the capability of God is exalted, as well as the fact that God keeps His promises. Though both Abraham and Sarah had passed the age of being parents, God told Abraham that he would have a son by Sarah. He was *"fully persuaded"* to believe *"the promise of God."*" (Waite, 15)
- Titus 1:2 — "Here is a promise-keeping God, One who has not lied, One who *cannot lie*, and One Who keeps His promises." (Waite, 15)
- Hebrews 10:23 — "Yes, God is *faithful* and He keeps His promises." (Waite, 15)

PRESERVATION:
THE SUPERIORITY OF THE FIDEISTIC APPROACH

- God's fundamental promise of preservation coupled with His inability to lie as well as His faithfulness to accomplish His promises, serve as the basis for the Fideistic (Faith) Approach to Textual Criticism. Either God kept his promise regarding preservation, or he did not.

- If God did so act it would be inappropriate and high minded for humans to think they can reconstruct what God promised to preserve.

- o "The hypothesis that God did not preserve His Words, so man needs to restore them, lies at the root of textual criticism. This line of thinking rejects what Scripture states about preservation, depending instead on the uninspired words of men, both contemporary and historical... Any application of the pertinent passages on preservation that does not leave one with the assurance the he has a Bible will all the Words of God cannot be accepted from a position of faith. The position that all the Words exist somewhere, but are still yet to be found, does not fit into the teaching of Scripture, and, therefore must be rejected." (Brandenburg in *Thou Shalt Keep Them*, 262)

- Man's wisdom works contrary to God's wisdom as many scriptures attest.

  - o Proverbs 3:5
  - o Isaiah 55:8-9
  - o I Corinthians 1:27-31; 2:5 — what is your faith about God's word standing in? The wisdom of men or the power of God?

- Kent Brandenburg summarizes the situation as follows:

  - o "The basis for perfect preservation is faith; other views are built on human rationalism, "the doctrine of human reason, unaided by Divine revelation, is an adequate or the sole to attainable religious truth." People who take a view that is "unaided by Divine revelation" are not normally known as Bible-believers, therefore, most people that profess to be Bible-believers do not usually want to consider their positions rationalistic.

    Those who espouse the "majority" text view claim to simply determine what words are found in the majority of the manuscripts, and the words that survive that test are essentially deemed to be the text of Scripture. Counting is the sole criterion. This is rationalistic. The proponents of the minority text view use the humanely devised laws of textual criticism, which treat the Bible like uninspired books, in an attempt to ascertain the readings most likely found in the original manuscripts. This view also applies human reason as the sole guide. Neither of these could be considering that God of the Bible, for neither of them provides perfection, and God is perfect. He is perfect, and He is powerful enough to keep something perfect, from the soul of a man to every Word of Scripture. In contrast, the received text position receives what God has supernaturally preserved by faith. Some advocates of the received text do not believe in perfect preservation, basing their position upon Divine providence alone. However, received text people at least depend on Scriptural principles to defend their position. In many cases, the other points of view do their best to argue away as many texts on preservation as possible (cites Combs in the footnote), and contend that faith is an invalid criterion for receiving the perfect text of Scripture (cites Larry D. Pettegrew's essay in *The Bible Version Debate: The Position of Central Baptist Theological Seminary* in the footnote)." (Brandenburg in *Thou Shalt Keep Them*, 263-264)

- Later Brandenburg points out that the position of the "rationalist-preservationist" is nothing more than "conceptual preservation."

    o "Instead of just believing God, men speculate on the percentage of error assumed to exist. The wobbly foundation upon which the rationalist preservationist stands is the assertion that "all of the doctrines alone have been preserved," which effectually leaves the believer with a conceptual preservation." (Brandenburg in *Thou Shalt Keep Them*, 265)

- Since God set forth his doctrine via words written in a book, what sense does it make to argue that God could preserve the book but not the words? Yet, as we will see in a future lesson, this is precisely the position of Dr. W. Edward Glenny; God preserved the *documents* but not the words that comprise those documents.

Wallace on the Fideistic Approach

Dr. Dan Wallace excoriates the fideistic approach arguing that the theological *a priori* belief in preservation has "no place in textual criticism."

- "The fideistic formula violates all known historical data. Such a dogmatic affirmation results in a procrusteanizing of the data on a massive scale in the name of orthodoxy. For example, the Byzantine text did not become the majority until the ninth century—and even then "majority" must be qualified: There are almost twice as many Latin MSS as there are Greek and, to my knowledge, none of them belongs to the Byzantine text." (Wallace in *JETS*, 202)

- "In sum, a theological *a priori* has no place in textual criticism. Since this is the case it is necessary to lay aside fideism in dealing with the evidence. The question, since we are dealing fundamentally with historical inquiry, is not what is possible but what is probable. With the stance of faith of the traditionalists in place, textual criticism become so intertwined with orthodoxy that the evidence cannot objectively be interpreted. But once dogma is evacuated from the discussion, no position can be comfortable merely with what is possible." (Wallace in *JETS*, 204)

Notice plainly what Wallace is asserting: 1) the doctrine of preservation has no place in the discipline of textual criticism, 2) the faith approach is a hindrance to dealing with the historical evidence, and 3) only when the doctrine of preservation (*dogma*) is abandoned can one objectively evaluate the historical data.

Explaining away the doctrine of preservation is just as central to Wallace's position as faith is to the preservationist. Therefore Wallace must declare that passages such as Isaiah 40:8 and I Peter 1:23-25 do not assert a doctrine of preservation. He must first explain away the verses before he can advance his so-called objective argument.

- o "Traditionalists make the rather facile assumption that when God's word is mentioned the reference must be to the written text—specifically, the text of the NT. Yet neither the written text nor the NT per se is in view in these passages. The most satisfactory exegesis of all such passages is that they are statements concerning either divine ethical principles (i.e., more laws that cannot be violated without some kind of consequence) or the promise of fulfilled prophecy." (Wallace in *JETS*, 202-203)

Wallace is arguing for a naturalistic approach to textual criticism using rationalistic means. This approach is rooted in the notion that the Bible is the same as any other book and should be approached by the same principles.

PRESERVATION: THE HISTORIC POSITION OF THE REFORMERS

- The following doctrinal Confessions of the Reformation Era all allude to the doctrine of preservation:

    - o 1646 — The Westminster Confession of Faith (Reformed)
    - o 1658 — The Savoy Declaration of Faith and Order (Reformed)
    - o 1689 — The London Baptist Confession (Baptistic)
    - o 1742 — The Philadelphia Baptist Confession (Baptistic)

- Given that the wording is virtually identical in all four Confessions, we will limit our quotes to Chapter I Of the Holy Scriptures, Article VIII from *The Westminster Confession of Faith*:

-○ "The Old Testament in Hebrew (which was the native language of the people of God of old), and the New Testament in Greek (which, at the time of the writing of it, was most generally known to the nations), being immediately inspired by God, and, by His singular care and providence, kept pure in all ages, are therefore authentical; so as, in all controversies of religion, the Church is finally to appeal unto them. But, because these original tongues are not known to all the people of God, who have right unto, and interest in the Scriptures, and are commanded, in the fear of God, to read and search them, therefore they are to be translated in to the vulgar language of every nation unto which they come, that, the Word of God dwelling plentifully in all, they may worship Him in an acceptable manner; and, through patience and comfort of the Scriptures, may have hope."

- All four *Confessions* hold that the Hebrew Old Testament, and the Greek New Testament were "inspired by God" and "kept pure in all ages." If this is not a belief in preservation, I don't know what is. Moreover, the saints responsible for these *Confessions* assert the need for these pure Hebrew and Greek words to be translated in the "vulgar language of every nation unto which they come." This is a strong appeal for the accurate and proper translation of the pure Hebrew and Greek words into the vernacular languages of all peoples.

- These *Confessions* demonstrate the historic Protestant belief in the notion of preservation or the idea that God kept his word pure in all ages. This belief was held across denominational traditions (Reformed & Baptistic) as well as geographical boundaries (Old & New World).

- It is also important to note that the drafters of these *Confessions* were ascribing these statements to the Masoretic Hebrew Text and the Greek *Textus Recptus*, the only Greek text they had available to them. It was the act of translating the *Textus Receptus* into the vernacular languages of Europe that drove the Reformation and touched off the greatest era of Christian mission work the world has ever seen. These are historical facts that cannot be disputed.

CONCLUSION

- Before we go further let me ask you the following question: how many of you believe the following statements?

    - God created the world in six days.
    - God destroyed the earth through a flood saving only Noah and his family.
    - God confounded the languages of men and scattered them across the face of the earth.
    - God through Moses delivered Israel out of Egyptian slavery through the Red Sea.
    - David killed Goliath.
    - Jonah was swallowed by a whale.
    - Jesus Christ was the incarnated, Virgin Born Son of God who died on the cross for our sins and rose again the third day.
    - The resurrected and ascended Lord Jesus Christ appeared to Saul of Tarsus on the Damascus Road.

- Why do you believe these things? Because you believe the Bible.

- So then why, when it comes to the issue of textual criticism and the identification of the Biblical text and its translation into English do so many believers leave the viewpoint of faith in favor of naturalistic textual theories?

- We need to believe what the Bible teaches about itself. We need to remember that the Bible is God's book. Remember from our studies of inspiration in term one, when we interact with the Bible, we are interacting with God himself. We need to adopt the viewpoint of faith.

- If God promised to preserve his word, and God cannot lie, and God always fulfills his promises then it would make more sense to believe in preservation than to deny it. To adopt a contrary position, one would have to subscribe to one of the following suppositions regarding God's foundational nature and character:

- God didn't mean what He said (Never issued such a promise.).
- God's word cannot be trusted (Because he has lied about his intention to preserve his word.).
- God is unwilling or unable to fulfill his promises.

- From this we conclude that of the following three views, View 1 is false and is to be rejected outright. There is a Doctrine of Preservation; this is the Bible's claim for itself.
  - View 1 — Denial of a Doctrine of Preservation
  - View 2 — Preservation in the KJV/TR/MT Tradition
  - View 3 — Preservation in the Totality of Manuscripts

- In the coming weeks we will begin studying the *nature* and *extent* of preservation by beginning an investigation into whether preservation is the corollary of inspiration.
- From this we will endeavor to determine the accuracy of Views 2 and 3.

WORKS CITED

Bauder, Kevin T. "An Appeal to Scripture" in *One Bible Only? Examining the Exclusive Claims for the King James Bible*. Grand Rapids, MI: Kregel Publications, 2001.

Combs, William W. "The Preservation of Scripture?" in *Detroit Baptist Seminary Journal*. Fall 2000.

Waite, D.A. *Defending the King James Bible*. Collingswood, NJ: The Bible For Today Press, 2006.

Wallace, Daniel B. "The Majority-Text Theory: History, Methods, and Critique" in *Journal of the Evangelical Theological Society*. June 1994.

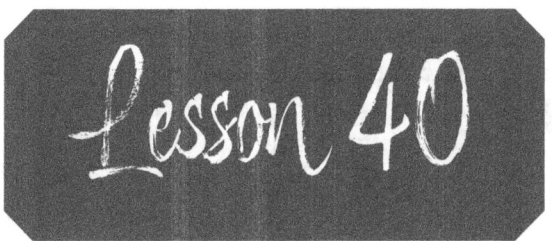

WHY PRESERVATION MATTERS

INTRODUCTION

- Since Lesson 30, we have been discussing the following three views of preservation identified by Dr. William Combs in his essay "The Preservation of Scripture."

  o View 1 — Denial of a Doctrine of Preservation

  o View 2 — Preservation in the KJV/TR/MT Tradition

  o View 3 — Preservation in the Totality of Manuscripts

- Last week in Lesson 39 we concluded that View 1 is false and that the scriptures do teach/promise their own preservation. This is the Bible's claim/promise for itself.

- In this Lesson, before beginning a secondary consideration regarding the *nature* of preservation, I would like to consider why preservation matters.

THE PERSPECTIVE OF HISTORICAL THEOLOGY

- Lesson 39 demonstrated that a belief in the promise of preservation was maintained by the Reformers and written into their Creeds and Catechisms. This belief in preservation was exemplified by Reformed and Baptistic Statements of Faith in both the Old and New Worlds. Setting the standard was *The Westminster Confession of Faith* from 1646 which states the following in Chapter 1 Article VIII:

    - "The Old Testament in Hebrew (which was the native language of the people of God of old), and the New Testament in Greek (which, at the time of the writing of it, was most generally known to the nations), being immediately inspired by God, and, by His singular care and providence, kept pure in all ages, are therefore authentical; so as, in all controversies of religion, the Church is finally to appeal unto them."

- Louis Gaussen captured the Reformation Era belief in preservation in his seminal 1840 work *Theopneustia* (*The Divine Inspiration of the Bible*). Gaussen articulated the prevailing notion that inspiration without preservation is meaningless. Gaussen clearly depicts God as being an active agent in the preservation of scripture. According to Gaussen, preservation was providential, not merely circumstantial, or historical.

    - "The Lord has watched miraculously over his Word. This the facts of the case have demonstrated.

        In constituting as its depositaries, first, the Churches of the Jewish people, and then those of the Christian people, his providence had by this means to see to the faithful transmission of the oracle of God to us. . . all these vast labors have so convincingly established the atoning preservation of that text, copied nevertheless so many thousands of times (in Hebrew during thirty-three centuries, and in Greek during eighteen hundred years), that the hopes of the enemies of religion, in this quarter, have been subverted." (Gaussen, 167-168)

- "When one thinks that the Bible has been copied during thirty centuries, as no book of man has ever been, or ever will be; that it was subject to all the catastrophes and all the captives of Israel; that it was transported seventy years to Babylon; that it has seen itself so often persecuted, or forgotten, or interdicted, or burnt, from the days of the Philistines to those of the Seleucid; -- when one thinks that, since the time of Jesus Christ, it had to traverse the first three centuries of the imperial persecutions, when persons found in possession of the holy books were thrown to the wild beasts; next the 7th, 8th, and 9th centuries, when false books, false legends, and false decretals, were everywhere multiplied; the 10th century, when so few could read, even among princes; the 12th, 13th, and 14th centuries, when the use of the Scriptures in the vulgar tongue was punished with death, and when the books of the ancient fathers were mutilated, when so many ancient traditions were garbled and falsified, even the very acts of the emperor, and those of the councils; – then we can perceive how necessary it was that the providence of God should have always put forth its mighty power, in order that, on the one hand, the Church of the Jews should give us, in its integrity, that Word which records its revolts, which predicts its ruin, which describes Jesus Christ; and, on the other, that the Christian Churches (the most powerful of which, and the Roman sect in particular, interdicted the people from reading the sacred books, and substituted in so many ways the traditions of the middle ages from the Word of God) should nevertheless transmit to us, in all their purity, those Scriptures, which condemn all their traditions, their images, their dead languages, their absolutions, their celibacy; which say, that Rome would be the seat of a terrible apostasy, where "the Man of Sin would be sitting as God in the temple of God, waging war against the saints, forbidding to marry, and to use meats which God created; . . ." (Gaussen, 169-170)

- "This intervention of God's providence in the preservation of the Old Testament becomes still more striking in our eyes if we compare the astonishing integrity of the original Hebrew (at the close of so many centuries) with the rapid and profound alteration which the Greek version of the Septuagint has undergone in the days of Jesus Christ (after the lapse of only two hundred years)." (Gaussen, 172-173)

- "We repeat, these facts, placed in contrast with the astonishing preservation of the Hebrew text (older than that of the LXX by more than twelve hundred years), proclaim loudly enough how necessary it was that the mighty hand of God should intervene in the destinies of the sacred book." (Gaussen, 174)

- "We desire, however, to give such of our readers as are strangers to sacred criticism, two or three other and still more intelligible means of estimating that providence which has for thirty centuries watched over our sacred text." (Gaussen, 175)

- "Here, then, the thing is evident: such is the real insignificance of the various readings about which so much noise was made at first. Such has been the astonishing preservation of the Greek manuscripts of the New Testament that have been transmitted to us." (Gaussen, 186)

- Yet, now in our day, Protestant Theologians have spilt much ink arguing that the Bible never promises its own preservation and that no such doctrine exists. Standard Systematic Theology books are completely silent and devoid of any discussion of preservation in their chapters/discussions of Bibliology (See Lesson 4.). Evangelical scholars have asserted that *a priori* belief in the Biblical promise of preservation has no seat at the table of textual criticism. In fact, it is only when the *dogma* of preservation is jettisoned that true objectivity can be obtained and progress made in evaluating the historical/textual data, according to leading Evangelical scholarship (See comments by Wallace in Lesson 39.).

- How did we get to this place? How did we go from having a belief in the promise of preservation written into the major Creedal statements of the Protestant Reformation to the outright denial of a clear Biblical promise?

- The answer is the crucible of the late 19th century. During the period between 1859 with the publication of *On the Origin of the Species* by Charles Darwin till the end of the century, Biblical Christianity was turned inside out by a torrent of destructive forces including: 1) Evolution, 2) Liberalism, 3) Modernism, and 4) German Higher Criticism. The net effect of these forces was the reshaping of Protestant Bibliology.

- Important doctrines such as inspiration and inerrancy experienced complete overhauls during the years between 1860 and 1900. Moreover, the entire field of textual criticism was transformed by naturalists who asserted that the Bible was like any other book and should be treated accordingly.

Inspiration

- Throughout church history prior to 1860, Christian theologians conceived of verbal inspiration as having been accomplished through a process of dictation (see Lessons 14 & 15).

- During the thirty years between the publication of Gaussen's *Divine Inspiration* in 1840 and Charles Hodges' *Systematic Theology* in 1871 the theological landscape had changed drastically. The intervening thirty years saw the publication of *On the Origin of the Species* by Charles Darwin, the growth and influence of German Higher Criticism, and the resulting theological liberalism of the Modernists. In response to the controversy, these men and their contemporaries altered many Protestant doctrines in an attempt to answer their critics. The doctrine of inspiration is one such example.

- It has only been in the last 150 years or so that the notion of Divine Dictation has fallen out of favor among professional theologians. For the majority of the history of the dispensation of grace, Christian thinkers, theologians, and philosophers had no problem with viewing dictation as the means by which inspiration was accomplished.

- It was also during this time period (1860-1900) that the phrase "in the original autographs" was added to doctrinal statements on inspiration (See Lesson 4 for a discussion of the "Originals Only" position.). This language is completely foreign to the doctrinal statements of the Reformation Era. In fact, creedal statements of the Reformation Era clearly extend inspiration beyond the original languages themselves. There was no notion that translations were incapable of extending the inspired text beyond the original documents or languages. Consider the rest of Chapter I Article VIII from *The Westminster Confession of Faith* as a case in point:

  - "But, because these original tongues are not known to all the people of God, who have right unto, and interest in the Scriptures, and are commanded, in the fear of God, to read and search them, therefore they are to be translated in to the vulgar language of every nation unto which they come, that, the Word of God dwelling plentifully in all, they may worship Him in an acceptable manner; and, through patience and comfort of the Scriptures, may have hope."

- In 1840, Louis Gaussen comments on the relationship between inspiration and translation in his seminal work *Theopneustia* (*The Divine Inspiration of the Bible*). Gaussen outlines the four forms God's word passed through via inspiration so that it could be intelligible to human beings:

  - "First, it was from all eternity in the mind of God. Next it was passed by Him into the mind of man. In the third place, under the operation of the Holy Ghost and by a mysterious process, it passed from the prophets' thoughts, into the types and symbols of an articulate language it took shape in words. Finally, after having undergone this first translation, alike important and inexplicable, men have reproduced and counter-chalked it, by a new translation, in passing from one human language into another human language." (Gaussen, 154-155)

- Regarding the fourth form of translating from one human language (Hebrew or Greek) into another human language such as French or

English, Gaussen writes:

- o "The operation by which the sacred writers express with words the mind of the Holy Ghost, is, we have said, itself a rendering not of words by words, but of divine thoughts by sensible symbols. Now this first translation is an infinitely nice matter, more mysterious and more liable to error (if God puts not his hand to it) than the operation can be afterwards, by which we should render a Greek word of that primitive text, by its equivalent in another language. . . The divine thought being already incarnated, as it were, in the language of the sacred text, what remains to be done in translation is no longer the giving of it a body, but only the changing of its dress, making it say in French what it had already said in Greek, and modestly substituting for each of its words an equivalent word. Such an operation is comparatively very inferior, very immaterial, without mystery, and infinitely less subject to error than the preceding. It even requires so little spirituality, that it may be performed *to perfection* by a trustworthy pagan who should possess *in perfection* a knowledge of both languages... The more, then, one reflects on this first consideration, the more immeasurable ought the difference to appear between these two orders of operations; to wit, between the translation of the divine thoughts into the words of human language, and the translation of the same thoughts into the equivalent terms of another language. No longer, therefore, be it said, "What avails it to me, if the one be human, that the other is divine?" (Gaussen, 155-157)

- This is a high view of inspiration that extends the results of inspiration beyond the original autographs alone. It was a rationalistic response to German Higher Criticism that caused Christian theologians of the late 19th century to limit inspiration to the autographs only.

Inerrancy

- During the Grace History Project, I taught two Lessons (63 & 64) on the history of the doctrine of inerrancy. Lesson 63 laid out the pre-modern history of the topic by looking at the writings of Irenaeus, Augustine, Luther, and Calvin. *The Westminster Confession of Faith Chapter I Article V* states the following regarding infallibility and inerrancy:

    o "We may be moved and induced by the testimony of the Church to a high and reverent esteem of the Holy Scripture. And the heavenliness of the matter, the efficacy of the doctrine, the majesty of the style, the consent of all the parts, the scope of the whole (which is, to give all glory to God), the full discovery it makes of the only way of man's salvation, the many other incomparable excellencies, and the entire perfection thereof, are arguments whereby it does abundantly evidence itself to be the Word of God: yet notwithstanding, our full persuasion and assurance of the infallible truth and divine authority thereof, is from the inward work of the Holy Spirit bearing witness by and with the Word in our hearts."

- Our investigation of these writings revealed that these men believed the scriptures were inerrant simply because they were the word of God. The belief that the scriptures were infallible was based upon "the inward work of the Holy Spirit bearing witness by and with the Word in our hearts." There was no formal theological doctrine of inerrancy, and it was certainly not limited to the original autographs only.

- The Civil War in the United States in the 1860s and changes in science after Charles Darwin published *On the Origin of the Species* in 1859 led many to challenge the idea that the Bible was literally the word of God and factually true in every respect. Arguments about evolution and biblical authority for slavery divided churches and led to a revised view of inerrancy among some factions that claimed only the original manuscripts of the Bible to be without error.

- A.A. Hodge and B.B. Warfield expressed a new view on inerrancy in the April 1881 edition of the *Presbyterian Review*. The expression "original autograph(s)(ic)" is found six times in the 1881 "Inerrancy" article by A.A. Hodge and B.B. Warfield. Consider the following from the pen of Ernest R. Sandeen:

    o "Verbal and inerrant inspiration was claimed not for the Bible as we now find it, but for the books of the Bible as they came from the hands of the authors—the original autographs. This emphasis upon the original manuscripts is another example of the way in which the Princeton doctrine of the Scriptures was refined and tightened in the face of growing critical opposition. A.A. Hodge said nothing of the original autographs in the first (1860) edition of his Outlines of Theology but saw fit to introduce it into the 1879 edition. The collaborative article of A.A. Hodge and B.B. Warfield in the Princeton Review (1881) elevated the concept to an especially prominent place in the Princeton doctrine of inspiration. That this concept of the original autographs had been recently added to their apologetic was never mentioned by Warfield and Hodge." (Sandeen, 127- 128)

    o "This new emphasis was introduced just at the time that the number of biblical errors or discrepancies turned up by the critics was growing too large to be ignored. One could no longer dismiss them as had Charles Hodge—as flecks of sandstone in the Parthenon marble. A.A. Hodge and B.B. Warfield retreated. In the first place, they stated that their theory of inspiration did not cover the preservation of the accuracy of the biblical manuscripts; inerrancy was claimed for the manuscripts only as they came from the hands of their authors. Copyists' errors could not invalidate the inerrancy of the Bible. Even this much hedging on the part of the Princeton professors has been widely criticized. As we have seen, the Princeton theology of inspiration served to define and describe the way in which God had provided an inerrant source of knowledge concerning Christianity. But what possible good can a nineteenth-century Christian derive from a Bible which, although once inerrant, is now riddled with mistakes through the carelessness of copyists? The Princeton claim to an inerrant Bible was maintained only by resource to lost and completely useless original autographs. Once again, the completely scholastic, theoretical nature of the Princeton mind is illustrated. And once again Princeton is caught propagating a dogma which is flatly contradicted by the Westminster Confession. In that creed, the Scriptures are declared to be authentic not only at the moment of their description but now: "being immediately inspired by God, and, by His singular care and providence, kept pure in all ages, are therefore authentical."" (Sandeen, 128)

- Defenders of an inerrant Bible assumed that the Bible was true as a starting point; however, their defense took shape as a logical syllogism that worked backward toward the rationalists. Since the Bible is true as an assumption, and since only verifiable historical events can be true (thus accepting the premise of the rationalists), then the Bible must contain only actual and verifiable historical events and can contain no error. Thus, inerrancy as a very rationalistic response to the rationalists, was born. (Bratcher)

- The rationalistic doctrine of inerrancy forged at Princeton during the crucible of controversy was picked up by fundamentalists during the later 19th and early 20th centuries and codified into their revised doctrinal statements where it has become the new orthodoxy. Mark well that it was a new understanding of inerrancy that was impacted by the era of controversy between 1860 and 1900.

Textual Criticism

- It was also during the time period in question (1860-1900) that naturalistic textual criticism gained a foothold within Protestant scholarship thereby replacing the traditional Greek text of the Protestant Reformation with a completely new text developed using rationalists' precepts and critical methodology.

- As we saw in Lesson 28, Drs. Westcott and Hort were the chief architects of the critical methodology and authors of the so-called new and improved Greek text. They began their work with the presupposition that the Bible was like any other book and should be treated using the same rules of textual criticism as the writings of Plato, Aristotle, or any other work of antiquity. Moreover, they infer that textual corruption could have entered the text via the hands of the original authors or their amanuensis.

    o "The principles of criticism explained in the foregoing section hold good for all ancient texts preserved in a plurality of documents. In dealing with the text of the New Testament no new principle whatever is needed or legitimate. (Westcott and Hort, 73)

    o "Little is gained by speculating as to the precise point at which such corruptions came in. They may be due to the original writer, or his amanuensis if wrote from dictation, or they may be due to one of the earliest transcribers." (Westcott and Hort, 280-281)

- On this point Hort stands in opposition to modern Evangelical scholarship in that he allows for "corruption" to have entered the text via the "original writer." Such a position explains why Hort is reluctant to ascribe infallibility to the text in any form. In a letter addressed to J.B. Lightfoot dated May 1, 1860, Hort stated in part:

    o "I am convinced that any view of the Gospels, which distinctly and consistently recognizes for them a natural and historical origin (whether under a special Divine superintendence or not) and assumes that they did not drop down ready-made from heaven, must and will be 'startling' to an immense portion of educated English people. But so far, at least, Westcott and I are perfectly agreed, and I confess I had hoped that you (Lightfoot) would assent. . . If you make a decided conviction of the absolute infallibility of the N.T. practically a *sine qua non* for co-operation, I fear I could not join you, even if you were willing to forget your fears about the origin of the Gospels. I am most anxious to find the N.T. infallible, and have a strong sense of

> the Divine purpose guiding all its parts; but I cannot see how the exact limits of such guidance can be ascertained except by unbiased a posterior criticism. . . (Regarding the question of "Providence" in Biblical Hort writes) Most strongly I recognize it; but I am not prepared to say that it necessarily involves absolute infallibility." (Hort, 419-421)

- This is the type of textual criticism that Dr. Edward F. Hills is referring to when he talks about the "naturalistic method" in the *King James Version Defended*. He is speaking about an approach to the scriptures that doubts their supernatural origin, doubts their infallibility even in the original autographs, and treats the Bible as though it were any other book. Such was the approach of Drs. Westcott and Hort.

- Later in this class we will study the textual theories of Westcott and Hort in detail. For the time being, understand that their approach to the text was completely different from the approach adopted by the Reformers. Moreover, their methodology is the seedbed for all modern textual criticism. In other words, their work has given rise to the modern eclectic method. Put another way, modern eclecticism is built over the top of the foundation laid by Westcott and Hort. Modern textual critics who follow the eclectic method are the intellectual great grandchildren of Westcott and Hort.

CONCLUSION

- Thus, was Protestant Bibliology completely reshaped by the forces of science, liberalism, and German Higher Criticism during the latter half of the 19th century. Preservation was abandoned altogether, inspiration and inerrancy were confined to nonexistent original autographs, and textual criticism was reinvented under rationalistic and naturalistic principals. Consider the following table summarizing these findings:

Before	1860	After
Preservation—"... being immediately inspired by God, and, **by His singular care and providence, kept pure in all ages,** are therefore authentical..." (Westminster Confession of Faith)		Preservation—the promise of preservation was dropped from doctrinal statements; Systematic Theology books completely overlook the topic; modern theologians argue that the scriptures do not promise their own preservation.
Inspiration—Divine Dictation accepted descriptor for how inspiration was accomplished; not limited to the original autographs and extended to vernacular languages via translation. (WCF)		Inspiration—Divine Dictation falls out of favor as a descriptor for how inspiration was accomplished. Inspiration is limited to the nonexistent original autographs.
Inerrancy—no formal doctrine of inerrancy; the scriptures were believed to be inerrant because they are the word of God; the Holy Spirit bears witness with the believer's spirit that the scriptures are infallible. (WCF)		Inerrancy—formal doctrine was developed that limited infallibility and inerrancy to the original autographs only. Took shape in a logical syllogism that meet the German Higher Critics on their own terms. Rewrote Protestant Bibliology.
Textual Criticism—began with the notion the scriptures were the Inspired word of God and of Divine origin; what God gave by inspiration was preserved and "kept pure in all ages" and was available to be translated into the vernacular languages of the nations.		Textual Criticism—was completely reworked staring with the rationalistic/naturalistic notion that the Bible is like any other book and should be treated like any other book of antiquity. Replaced the text of the Reformation (TR) with a "new and improved" Greek text. Modern Textual Criticism is built on top of the Rationalistic suppositions of Westcott & Hort.

Pastor Bryan Ross—Grace Life Bible Church—Grand Rapids, MI

- These core changes to the Protestant view of the Bible have shaped Fundamentalism and later Evangelicalism throughout the 20th and 21st centuries.

THE AGNOSTICISM OF BART EHRMAN: THE LOGICAL CONCLUSION OF THE PREVAILING VIEW

- Dr. Bart Ehrman is a New York Times Bestselling author and professor of Religious Studies at The University of North Carolina at Chapel Hill. He is one of North America's leading scholars in his field, having written and edited thirty books, including three college textbooks. He has also achieved acclaim at the popular level, authoring five *New York Times* bestsellers. Ehrman's work focuses on textual criticism of the New Testament, the historical Jesus, and the development of early Christianity. (Wikipedia Entry)

- In the introduction to his bestselling book *Misquoting Jesus: The Story Behind Who Changed the Bible and Why* from 2005, Dr. Ehrman recounts his personal history. After recounting his early years in a conservative household in Lawrence, Kansas, Ehrman was "born-again" as a sophomore in high school. In 1973, Ehrman entered Moody Bible Institute where he decided to major in Bible and Theology. Naturally this required taking a lot of Bible study and Systematic Theology courses. It was while at Moody that he first encountered the prevailing Evangelical orthodoxy with respect to the scriptures:

    o "Only one perspective was taught in these courses, subscribed to by all the professors (they had to sign a statement) and by all the students (we did as well): The Bible is the inerrant word of God. It contains no mistakes. It is inspired completely and in its very words — "verbal, plenary inspiration." All the courses I took presupposed and taught this perspective; any other was taken to be misguided or even heretical. . .

There was an obvious problem, however, with the claim that the Bible was verbally inspired — down to the very words. As we learned at Moody in one of the first courses in the curriculum, we don't actually have the original writings of the New Testament. What we have are copies of these writings, made years later — in most cases, many years later. Moreover, none of these copies is completely accurate, since the scribes who produced them inadvertently and/or intentionally changed them in places. All scribes did this. So rather than actually having the inspired words of the autographs (i.e., the originals) of the Bible, what we have are the error-ridden copies of the autographs. One of the most pressing of all tasks, therefore, was to ascertain what the originals of the Bible said, given the circumstances that 1) they were inspired and 2) we don't have them." (Ehrman, 4-5

- The position described by Ehrman above is the same one I was taught in Bible College. Ehrman has summarized the "Originals Only" position in a nutshell. Ehrman describes an experience very similar to my own; many of his friends at Moody were content to rest on the claim that the autographs were inspired despite the obvious problem that they no longer exist. It was this problem that first interested Ehrman in the field of textual criticism.

    o "For me, though, this was a compelling problem. It was the words of scripture themselves that God had inspired. Surely we have to know what those words were if we want to know how he had communicated to us, since the very words were his words, and having some other words (those inadvertently or intentionally created by scribes) didn't help us much if we wanted to know His words.

    This is what got me interested in the manuscripts of the New Testament, already as an eighteen-year-old." (Ehrman, 5)

- After completing his studies at Moody in 1976, Ehrman enrolled in Wheaton College, one of the most prestigious Evangelical institutions of higher learning in the country and the *alma mater* of Billy Graham. It was at Wheaton that Ehrman began his study of the Greek language thereby increasing his misgiving regarding inspiration.

- o "At the same time, this started making me question my understanding of scripture as the verbally inspired word of God. If the full meaning of the words of scripture can be grasped only by studying them in Greek (and Hebrew), does this mean that most Christians, who don't read ancient languages, will never have complete access to what God wants them to know (this was not the position of Gaussen in 1840)? And doesn't this make the doctrine of inspiration a doctrine only for the scholarly elite, who have the intellectual skills and leisure to learn the languages and study the text by reading them in the original? What does it do to say that the words are inspired by God if most people have absolutely no access to these words, but only to more or less clumsy renderings of these words into a language, such as English, that has nothing to do with the original words?

    My questions were complicated even more as I began to think increasingly about the manuscripts that conveyed the words. The more I studied Greek, the more I became interested in the manuscripts that preserve the New Testament for us, and in the science of textual criticism, which can supposedly help us reconstruct what the original words of the New Testament were. I kept reverting to my basic question: how does it help us to say that the Bible is the inerrant word of God if in fact we don't have the words God inerrantly inspired, but only the words copied by scribes—sometimes correctly but sometimes (many times!) incorrectly? What good does it to say that the autographs (i.e., the originals) were inspired? We don't have the originals! We have only error-ridden copies, and the vast majority of these are centuries removed from the originals and different from them, evidently, in thousands of ways." (Ehrman, 6-7)

- These lingering doubts drove Ehrman deeper into his studies of textual criticism in hopes of understanding "what the Bible really was." As a result, he decided to attend Princeton Theological Seminary and study textual criticism from the world's leading expert, Bruce M. Metzger. Doubts raised via Ehrman's continued study of textual criticism coincided with a difficulty in expounding upon the text of Mark 2:26 regarding the identification of the high priest in opening the floodgates of agnosticism. Ehrman's professor (not Metzger) wrote at the end of his term paper regarding his exposition of Mark 2:26, "Maybe Mark just made a mistake." This coupled with his lingering doubts, over a long period of time, were the catalysts that led to Ehrman's complete reevaluation of the doctrine of inspiration and the Bible itself. (Ehrman, 8-10)

- Ultimately, it was a lack of understanding regarding the promise of preservation that caused Ehrman to doubt inspiration. Nowhere in his formal education in Christian Academia did he ever encounter instruction in the doctrine of preservation. Why? Because preservation was discarded in the late 19th century response to German Higher Criticism.

  o "If one wants to insist that God inspired the very words of scripture, what would be the point if we don't have the very words of scripture? In some places, as we will see, we simply cannot be sure that we have reconstructed the original text accurately. It's a bit hard to know what the words of the Bible mean if we don't even know what the words are!

  This became a problem for my view of inspiration, for I came to realize that it would have been no more difficult for God to preserve the words of scripture than it would have been for him to inspire them in the first place. If he wanted his people to have his words, surely he would have given them to them (and possibly even given them the words in a language they could understand, rather than Greek and Hebrew). The fact that we don't have the words surely must show, I reasoned, that he did not preserve them for us. And if he didn't perform that miracle, there seemed to be no reason to think that he performed the earlier miracle of inspiring those words." (Ehrman, 11)

- Ehrman is simply following the contents of his theological training to its logical conclusion. While I do not agree with Ehrman, I at least can applaud him for being intellectually honest. Without preservation inspiration is in jeopardy. Notice also that Ehrman is working off the perceived standard of *verbatim identicality* of wording.

- The following paragraph captures the net effect of all this upon Ehrman's views on inspiration and the Bible. In the end, Ehrman takes the naturalistic/rationalistic starting point of the current Evangelical Orthodoxy to its logical conclusion; the Bible was not inspired and is a human work that is no different from any other book.

    o "In short, my study of the Greek New Testament, and my investigation into the manuscripts that contain it, led to a radical rethinking of my understanding of what the Bible is. This was a seismic change for me. Before this—starting with my born-again experience in high school, through my fundamentalist days at Moody, and on through my evangelical days at Wheaton—my faith had been based completely on a certain view of the Bible as the fully inspired, inerrant word of God. Now I no longer saw the Bible that way. The Bible began to appear to me as a very human book. Just as many scribes had copied, and changed, the texts of scripture, so too had human authors originally written the texts of scripture. This was a human book from beginning to end. It was written by different human authors at different times and in different places to address different needs. Many of these authors no doubt felt they were inspired by God to say what they did, but they had their own perspectives, their own beliefs, their own views, their own needs, their own desires, their own understandings, their own theologies; and these perspectives, beliefs, views, needs, desires, understandings, and theologies informed everything they said. In all these ways they differed from one another. Among other things, that meant that Mark did not say the same thing that Luke said because he didn't mean the same thing as Luke. John is different from Matthew—not the same. Paul is different from Acts. And James is different from Paul. Each author is a human author and needs to be read for what he (assuming they were all men) has to say, not assuming that what he says is the same, or conformable to, or consistent with what every other author has to say. The Bible, at the end of the day, is a very human book." (Ehrman, 11-12)

- In Ehrman we see the next effect the naturalistic/rationalistic approach to scripture first advanced in the late 19th century. It is only by ignoring the obvious questions and inconsistencies that the prevailing Evangelical Orthodoxy is held together. Without the promise of preservation, the system comes crashing down upon the one honest enough to take things to their logical conclusion.

CONCLUSION

- As the title of this Lesson suggests (Why Preservation Matters) our goal herein has been to demonstrate the high cost associated with denying the promise of preservation by providing a practical real-life example in Bart Ehrman.

- In his book *On Guard: Defending Your Faith with Reason and Precision*, William Lane Craig offers the following advice for dealing with a determined skeptic:

    o "Now the determined skeptic can deny any conclusion if he is willing to pay the price of rejecting one of its premises. But what you can do is raise the price of rejecting the conclusion by giving good evidence for the truth of the premises. . . we want to raise the price of denying the conclusion as high as we can. We want to help the unbeliever see what it will cost him intellectually to resist the conclusion. Even if he is willing to pay that price, he may at least come to see why we are not obligated to pay it. . ." (Craig, 25)

- Following Professor Craig's advice, notice how Ehrman's denial of inspiration is identical with the position on the Bible enunciated by atheist Richard Dawkins:

    o "To be fair, much of the Bible is not systematically evil but just plain weird, as you expect of a chaotically cobbled-together anthology of disjointed documents, composed, revised, translated, distorted and 'improved' by hundreds of anonymous authors, editors and copyists, unknown to us and mostly unknown to each other, spanning nine centuries." (Dawkins, 268)

- Therefore, the promise of preservation matters. Theologically, the promise of preservation protects what God gave by inspiration. Next time we will begin to study the extent of this linkage by considering whether preservation is the corollary of inspiration.

Why Preservation Matters: Flow Chart of Ehrman's Error

Between 1860 & 1900 Protestant Bibliology was rewritten in response to the following forces: 1) Evolution, 2) Liberalism/Modernism, 3) German Higher Criticism, and 4) Rationalism.
- *Inspiration*—was limited to the nonexistent original autographs, Divine Dictation was dropped as a descriptor for how inspiration was accomplished.
- *Preservation*—the promise of preservation was dropped from doctrinal statements.
- *Inerrancy*—formal doctrine developed that limited inerrancy and infallibly to the nonexistent original autographs; took shape in a logical syllogism that meet the German Higher Critics on their own terms.
- *Textual Criticism*—was completely reworked starting with the rationalistic/naturalistic notion that the Bible is like any other book and should be treated in like manner to any work of antiquity. Replaced the text of the Reformation (*TR*) with a "new and improved" Greek text. Modern Textual Criticism is built on top of the Rationalistic suppositions of Westcott & Hort.

Became the new Protestant Orthodoxy on the Bible that was carried forward into the 20th century by Fundamentalists in their doctrinal statements.

In the 1970s Bart Ehrman attended Moody Bible Institute and Wheaton College where he was taught the new Protestant Orthodoxy on the Bible that had been forged in the crucible of controversy between 1860 & 1900 (See previous box.). This Orthodoxy is devoid of the promise of preservation. Having been removed from Protestant doctrinal statements for the better part of a century, modern Systematic Theology books as well as Christian higher education do not teach the doctrine of preservation. Ehrman questioned the feasibility of his formal education along the following lines: 1) only the original autographs were inspired, 2) the original autographs are not extant, 3) all we possess are copies which are subject to error, 4) therefore, the doctrine of inspiration was a doctrine of the scholarly elite since it required knowledge of Hebrew and Greek in order to really know what God said, 5) knowledge of the original languages is of no practical consequence given the nonexistent nature of the inspired original autographs.

In the 1980s Bart Ehrman enrolled in Princeton Theology Seminary to study textual criticism from Bruce M. Metzger, the world's leading expert in the field. While at Princeton, Ehrman came to believe that Mark made a mistake in Mark 2:26 in identifying the high priest. This along with his previous misgivings led Ehrman to completely rethink what the Bible is. Ehrman explains this process in his 2005 book *Misquoting Jesus* in which he states that if God could not preserve His words there was no reason to think He inspired them perfectly in the first place. Recall that Ehrman was not taught to believe in the promise of preservation because it had been dropped from Protestant Bibliology in the late 19th century. In this way Ehrman followed his education to its logical conclusion and reasoned that without preservation, inspiration is meaningless.

Ehrman's denial of inspiration led to the logical conclusion that the Bible "was a human book from beginning to end." Recall from above that Westcott & Hort began their textual work with the premise that the Bible was the same as any other book and should be treated accordingly. In this way, we see in Ehrman, the logical outcome of the train of thought initiated by Westcott & Hort. When dealt with honestly, in the absence of the promise of preservation, the Protestant Bibliology forged in the late 19th century logically leads to the conclusion enunciated by Ehrman. In his argumentation there are no formal or informal fallacies that I am aware of, and his conclusion naturally follows from his premises. To follow the same line of reasoning and arrive at a different conclusion is questionable to say the least. More recently, theologians such as Daniel B. Wallace and W. Edward Glenny have spilt much ink denying the Biblical promise of preservation. The *a priori* belief in the *dogma* of preservation is excoriated by Wallace as a hindrance to objectivity. Yet Wallace insists upon "faith" in the scholar's ability to reconstruct the text in order to avoid Ehrman's conclusion. Ehrman essentially says, "you Christians don't actually have the word of God." Meanwhile, Wallace who is supposed to be opposing him says, "you are right Bart but some day we will and when we do you will be sorry." In the end, it seems that Ehrman the Agnostic, has been more honest about where the prevailing Orthodoxy leads.

Pastor Bryan Ross--Grace Life Bible Church--Grand Rapids, MI

WORKS CITED

Bratcher, Dennis. *The Modern Inerrancy Debate.* www.cresourcei.org/inerrant.htm.

Craig, William Lane. *On Guard: Defending Your Faith with Reason and Precision.* Colorado Springs, CO: David C. Cook, 2010.

Dawkins, Richard. *The God Delusion.* Bantam Press, 2006.

Ehrman, Bart D. *Misquoting Jesus: The Story Behind Who Changed the Bible and Why.* New York, NY: HarperCollins, 2005.

Gaussen, Louis. *The Divine Inspiration of the Bible.* Grand Rapids, MI: Kregel Publications, 1971.

Hort, Fenton John Anthony. *Life and Letters of Fenton John Anthony Hort, Vol. I.* London: Macmillian and Company LTD, 1896.

Sandeen, Ernest R. *The Roots of Fundamentalism: British & American Millenarianism, 1800-1930.* Chicago, IL: The University of Chicago Press, 1970.

Westcott, Brooke Foss & Fenton John Anthony Hort. *The New Testament in The Original Greek.* London: Macmillian and Company LTD, 1896.

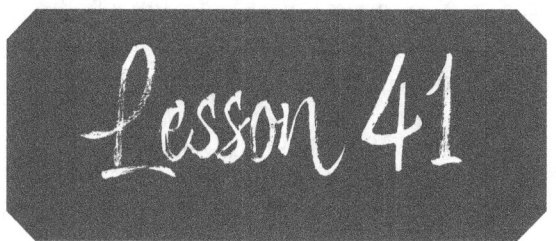

PRESERVATION THE COROLLARY OF INSPIRATION

INTRODUCTION

In Lesson 30 after discussing the Core Issue of Preservation versus Restoration, we studied how the textual facts presented in Lesson 28 and 29 have given birth to the following three views on the doctrine of preservation:

- o View 1 — Denial of a Doctrine of Preservation
- o View 2 — Preservation in the KJV/TR/MT Tradition
- o View 3 — Preservation in the Totality of Manuscripts

- In Lesson 39 we concluded that View 1 is false, and the Bible does promise preservation as a theological reality. In other words, preservation is the Bible's doctrinal/theological claim for itself.

- Last week in Lesson 40 we considered "Why Preservation Matters" by using Bart Ehrman as a case study to demonstrate the high cost associated with denying preservation.

- Now, having duly established that preservation is a Bible doctrine, we want to begin a secondary consideration that will help distinguish between the truthfulness of Views 2 and 3. That consideration is the *extent* or *nature* of preservation.

- After giving much thought to where/how to begin this discussion I have elected to commence with a consideration of whether preservation is the corollary of inspiration. Much has been said in the scholarly literature regarding this question.

- For organizational purposes, we will study this topic by tackling the following points:

    o What is a Corollary?

    o Preservation is the Corollary of Inspiration

    o Problems Created by a Denial of a Corollary

- Lastly, an Appendix at the end has been provided outlining the position of Dr. Daniel B. Wallace on the Corollary.

WHAT IS A COROLLARY?

- Noah Webster's *American Dictionary of the English Language* defines the English word corollary as follows:

    o "A conclusion or consequence drawn from premises, or from what is advanced or demonstrated. If it is demonstrated that a triangle which has equal sides, has also equal angles, it follows as a *corollary* that a triangle which has three equal sides, has its three angles equal."

- Google defines a corollary as:

  o *Noun* — a proposition that follows from (and is often appended to) one already proved.

    - direct or natural consequence or result.

  o *Adjective* — forming a proposition that follows from one already proved.

    - associated; supplementary.

- Dr. William W. Combs explains how the term "corollary" is used in the conversation regarding inspiration and preservation.

  o "Webster defines *corollary* as 1) a proposition inferred immediately from a proved proposition with little or no additional proof, (2a) something that naturally follows: result, and (2b) something that incidentally or naturally accompanies or parallels. Thus to say that preservation is the corollary of inspiration means that preservation is a doctrine that can be "inferred immediately" from the "proved position" of inspiration; preservation "naturally follows" or "parallels" inspiration. To say that there is a correlation or parallel between inspiration and preservation does not reveal anything about the exact nature of preservation." (Combs, 27)

- Edward F. Hills asserts that preservation is the corollary of inspiration in the *King James Version Defended* when he writes:

  o "If the doctrine of divine inspiration of the Old and New Testament Scripture is a true doctrine, the doctrine of the providential preservation of the Scriptures must also be a true doctrine. It must be that down through the centuries God has exercised a special providential control over the copying of the Scriptures and the preservation and use of the copies, so that trustworthy representatives of the original text have been available to God's people in every age. God must have done this, for if He gave the Scriptures to His Church by inspiration as the perfect and final revelation of His will, then it is obvious that He would not allow this revelation to disappear or undergo any alteration of its fundamental character." (Hills, 2)

PRESERVATION IS THE COROLLARY OF INSPIRATION

- While Combs would not agree with Edward F. Hills as to the *extent* of the corollary, he does nonetheless assert that a corollary exists.

    o "It is perfectly reasonable to assert a corollary between inspiration and preservation without asserting that preservation be in every way equal to inspiration . . ." (Combs, 27)

- Combs quotes John H. Skilton's essay on "The Transmission of the Scriptures" to support the notion that, "A right understanding of the corollary suggests that there is no real purpose or value in inspiring a document that is not preserved." (Combs, 27) Skilton observes:

    o "But we must maintain that the God who gave the Scriptures, who works all things after the counsel of his will, has exercised a remarkable care over his 'Word, has preserved it in all ages in a state of essential purity, and has enabled it to accomplish the purpose for which he gave it. It is inconceivable that the sovereign God who was pleased to give his Word as a vital and necessary instrument in the salvation of his people would permit his Word to become completely marred in its transmission and unable to accomplish its ordained end. Rather, as surely as that he is God, we would expect to find him exercising a singular care in the preservation of his written revelation." (Skilton in *TIW*, 143)

- After quoting Skilton, Combs offers the following strong evidence in favor of a corollary between inspiration and preservation:

    o "To illustrate, we might ask, what would be the purpose of producing an authoritative record (inspiration) and letting it perish? Why, for instance, let Paul write an inspired letter to the Romans and then have it perish on the way to Rome? Of course, that did not happen, but could it have happened? If one denies a corollary between inspiration and preservation, Paul's letter could have perished before it got to Rome.

    The purpose of inspiration was to produce γραφή (2 Tim 3:16), a written record, a deposit of divine truth for the readers, not the writer. Without preservation the purpose of inspiration would be invalidated. Since it was clearly God's intention that Paul's inspired letter to the Romans be read by the Romans — it could not have perished — there must have been a divine work of preservation at work for at least a few weeks or months until the letter was received by the Romans. This suggests that there is some degree of correlation between inspiration and preservation. And the letter to the Romans was not meant just for the Romans. No Scripture was intended for just the original recipients — "For whatever was written in earlier times was written for our instruction, that through perseverance and the encouragement of the Scriptures we might have hope" (Rom 15:4). Similarly, Paul warns the Corinthians using the example of Israel's failure: "Now these things happened to them as an example, and they were written for our instruction, upon whom the ends of the ages have come" (1 Cor 10:11). If the Old Testament Scriptures ("these things") were "written," that is, inspired for the purpose of instructing future believers ("our instruction") that purpose for the inspired writings demands their preservation." (Combs, 27-28)

PROBLEMS CREATED BY A DENIAL OF A COROLLARY

- In the main body of his essay "The Preservation of Scripture", Dr. W. Edward Glenny of Central Baptist Theological Seminary denies the notion that preservation is the corollary of inspiration.

    - "The first historical problem mentioned above is the assumption that preservation is a necessary corollary of inspiration and that for inspiration to be true God must have preserved the NT text inerrantly. The difficulty with this assumption becomes obvious when it is carried to its logical conclusion." (Glenney, 77)

- Glenny, like Bart Ehrman, Harry A. Sturz, and Daniel B. Wallace (see Appendix A) before him, denies any corollary between preservation and inspiration on the grounds that there is not "*verbatim identicality*" or exact same wording in the extant manuscript witnesses.

- Glenny's main concern in denying the corollary in the main body of his essay on preservation is to disprove the notion of "perfect preservation" or the idea that all the words were preserved exactly/identically as they were given under inspiration. As we have seen in previous lessons, this is the standard of preservation advocated for by preservationists Thomas M. Strouse, David Sutton, and Kent Brandenburg.

- By denying any corollary between preservation and inspiration to answer the TR/King James position of "perfect preservation," even Professor Combs believes that Glenny has overstated his case. To prove this, Combs cites footnote thirty-six from Glenny's essay on "The Preservation of Scripture" in which Glenny recants his denial of the corollary found in the main body of the essay. (Combs, 28) Combs writes the following regarding Glenny's denial of the corollary, "since this denial creates an untenable problem for his doctrine of the canon, Glenny permits the corollary to enter through the back door." (Combs, 28)

- After denying a corollary in the body of the essay, Glenny states the following in footnote thirty-six:

    - "The criteria for determining whether God's word has been preserved are self-evident, i.e., does it still exist? Our belief in the preservation of God's Word is different from our belief in the canon in that preservation does not follow directly from inspiration nor are given criteria in Scripture by which we are to determine or prove the preservation of scripture. But there is a similarity between preservation of Scripture and the doctrine of the canon in that, the recognition of the exact books which are to be included in the canon does not follow directly from the biblical teaching on inspiration from the criteria given in Scripture to identify them. These criteria must be applied to the historical evidence ... Based on the historical evidence we believe certain books are included in the canon just as we believe on the basis of historical evidence that God has preserved His word. My point is that just as we use historical evidence to recognize which books meet the criteria necessary to be included in the canon, in the same way we use historical evidence to recognize the fact that God has preserved His Word.

        An obvious truth is that a document which is to be included in the canon must be preserved. Therefore, since inspiration implies canonicity, in an indirect way inspiration is related to the preservation of the *documents* which are included in the canon. However, the preservation I have addressed and evaluated in this chapter is not the preservation of the *documents* which are in the canon, but rather the perfect preservation of the words of *the text of all of the documents*." (Glenny, 104-105)

- Please note that Glenny, based upon his doctrine of the Canon is forced to admit at least an *indirect* corollary between inspiration and preservation. Combs points this out in his essay when he states:

    - "Why is it that "a document that is to be included in the canon *must* be preserved"? (emphasis added) Obviously, it is because God wanted the documents he *inspired* to be in the canon, and if he wanted his *inspired* documents to be in the canon, he "must" have preserved them. This line of reasoning ultimately is based on a corollary between inspiration and preservation." (Combs, 28-29)

- In other words, without the preservation of what was inspired, how is one to know historically what books should be included in the Canon? Furthermore, by so arguing, Glenny is admitting that preservation must be a historical reality while at the same time not believing it to be a theological necessity. Recall that Glenny does not believe that the Bible teaches its own preservation.

- Moreover, Glenny has God preserving the *documents* or the material objects themselves upon which God's words were written; without at the same time preserving the *words* found on/in those documents. Does this even make any sense at all? How is it that preservation can be a historical reality necessary for determining canonicity yet at the same time not be a theological necessity?

WORKS CITED

Combs, William W. "The Preservation of Scripture?" in *Detroit Baptist Seminary Journal*. Fall 2000.

Glenny, W. Edward. "The Preservation of Scripture" in *The Bible Version Debate: The Perspective of Central Baptist Theological Seminary*. Minneapolis, MN: Central Baptist Theological Seminary, 1997.

Hills, Edward F. *The King James Version Defended*. Des Moines, IA: Christian Research Press, 1956.

Skilton, John H. "The Transmission of the Scriptures" in *The Infallible Word*. https://www.the-highway.com/transmission1_Skilton.html.

THE POSITION OF DANIEL B. WALLACE ON THE COROLLARY

INTRODUCTION

- As we saw in the main body of Lesson 41, Dr. W. Edward Glenny denies a corollary between preservation and inspiration in the main body of his essay "The Preservation of Scripture." Yet, in footnote thirty-six, Glenny allows a corollary in through the back door due to historical considerations and his position on canonicity. Glenny argues for the preservation of the *documents* but not the words written on those documents.

- Dr. Glenny was preceded by Dr. Daniel B. Wallace in denying that the scriptures teach a doctrine of preservation as well as a corollary between preservation and inspiration.

- - "Both Wallace and Glenny put forth two major arguments against preservation. First, preservation is not a necessary corollary of inspiration; that is, while inspiration is a true doctrine, there is nothing in the doctrine itself that demands that what God inspired he was bound to preserve. Second, the biblical texts that are used to support a doctrine of preservation have been misinterpreted and, in fact, do not teach such a doctrine." (Combs, 8)

- So, we have seen Drs. Wallace and Glenny deny the doctrine of preservation on two grounds: 1) while inspiration is true it does not demand preservation and 2) the Biblical texts used to assert preservation have been misinterpreted and do not assert said doctrine (see Lessons 31-38).

DANIEL B. WALLACE ON THE COROLLARY

- In 1992, Dr. Daniel B. Wallace authored an essay in the *Grace Theological Journal* called "Inspiration, Preservation, and New Testament Textual Criticism." In a section titled "The Critique," Wallace offers his critique of preservationists such as Jasper James Ray, David Otis Fuller, John William Burgon, Wilbur Pickering, Edward F. Hills, and Theodore Letis.

- Wallace's critique of the doctrine of preservation as enunciated by these men is made along the following three lines of argumentation: 1) a question-begging approach, 2) faulty assumptions, and 3) a non-biblical doctrinal basis. The third point coincides with what we have seen so far in Lessons 31 through 38, that no Biblical text supports the doctrine of preservation, according to Wallace.

- Wallace deals with the question of the corollary between inspiration and preservation under point two, "faulty assumptions." After quoting the passage above from Edward F. Hills (see main part of the Lesson), Wallace states the following:

- "In other words, preservation proceeds from and is a necessary consequence of inspiration. Or, in the words of Jasper James Ray, "the writing of the Word of God by inspiration is no greater miracle than the miracle of preservation. . ." (Wallace in *GTJ*, 31)

- Wallace then quotes Bart Ehrman to buttress his point. It is important to note that Dr. Glenny, writing in 1997, quotes the same passage from Ehrman as well as providing virtually identical argumentation to what Wallace presented in 1992. Parties doubting this fact are encouraged to compare Wallace's essay from 1992 (pages 31-33) with Glenny's piece from 1997 (see pages 77-78). The Ehrman quote reads as follows:

  - "Any claim that God preserved the New Testament text intact, giving His church actual, not theoretical, possession of it, must mean one of three things—either 1) God preserved it in all the extant manuscripts so that none of them contain any textual corruptions, or 2) He preserved it in groups of manuscripts, none of which contain any corruptions, or 3) He preserved it in a solitary manuscript which alone contains no corruptions." (quoted by Wallace in *GTJ*, 32)

- As follow-up to Ehrman, Wallace writes (also see Glenny page 77):

  - "The problem with these first and second possibilities is that neither one of them is true: no two NT manuscripts agree completely—in fact, there are between six and ten variations per chapter for the closest two manuscripts.

    Is it possible that the NT text was preserved intact in a single manuscript? No one argues this particular point, because it is easily demonstrable that every manuscript has scribal errors in it." (Wallace in *GTJ*, 32)

- Notice once again what the standard is for this discussion. It is none other than "exact sameness." For Wallace, the lack of "exact sameness" or identical wording across the manuscript witnesses is enough to negate preservation as the corollary of inspiration. Moreover, Wallace is pleased to allow TR advocates to take on "exact sameness" as their standard for preservation because he can then point out historically that identical wording does not exist. In this sense pro-TR preservationists have played into the hands of their critics by overstating the case with respect to preservation.

- Two years later, in June of 1994, Wallace authored an even more aggressive diatribe against TR preservationists in the *Journal of the Evangelical Theological Society*. In an article titled "The Majority-Text Theory: History, Methods, and Critique" Wallace addresses the "doctrinal underpinning of the traditional-text theory," by denouncing those who believe in the "dogma of preservation" as a starting point for discussing the matter.

    o "First, and most importantly, I must speak to the theological a priori. MT advocates need the dogma of preservation at all points where the evidence will not easily yield to their interpretation." (Wallace in *JETS*, 201)

- Wallace quotes Theodore P. Leits' essay, "In Reply to D.A. Carson's "The King James Version Debate"" to illustrate his point.

    o "When reviewing the defense of the Majority Text, one dominating consideration emerges: a prior commitment to what the Bible has to say concerning itself with regard to inspiration and preservation. For the Majority Text apologists, this is an all-consuming consideration to which everything else must be subordinated. Their arguments, therefore, are not directed to some neutral bar of determination (as if such a thing existed) but are consciously directed to those who also have the same priority." (Letis, 192)

- After quoting Letis, Wallace states the following regarding the corollary between inspiration and preservation:

- o "To them, verbal inspiration necessitates preservation. Pickering tells us that "the doctrine of Divine Preservation of the New Testament depends upon the interpretation of the evidence which recognizes the Traditional Text to be the continuation of the autographa.
- o In order to make preservation support the MT it must infer accessibility: "God has preserved the text of the New Testament in a very pure form and it has been readily available to His followers in every age throughout 1900 years." Hence the MT position is based on a corollary (accessibility) of a corollary (preservation) of a particular dogmatic stance (verbal inspiration)." (Wallace in *JETS*, 201)

PRESERVATION: HISTORICAL NOT THEOLOGICAL

- Wallace denies the scriptures a doctrine of preservation while at the same time arguing that preservation is a historical reality, not a theological necessity. In other words, Wallace denies that preservation is the corollary of inspiration because the relevant verses do not teach preservation. Yet, at the same time, in the face of agnostic objections against the word of God leveled by Bart Ehrman, Wallace argues for the historical reality of preservation.
- While Wallace denies a doctrine of preservation, he cannot deny the historical reality of the surviving manuscript copies. For Wallace, these copies exist not because of God's promise of preservation but are the product of a mere circumstantial historical reality. In other words, the historical reality is not the result of God's fundamental promise of preservation but circumstantial happenings in the same manner that would affect any other ancient documents.
- Wallace's view maintains that any book of antiquity for which we still possess manuscript copies is preserved is because God exercises sovereign control over the universe. This standard would

apply equally to secular writings such as Caesar's *Commentaries on the Gallic War* or the Bible. On this view, any ancient document that is extant today owes its present existence to God's preservation. Moreover, on this view there is no difference between the Bible and Caesar's *Commentaries*. God is under no obligation to preserve the one over the other. Rather, it just so happens that copies have survived.

- In his book *Myths about the Modern Bible Versions* David W. Cloud states the following about "circumstantial preservation:"

    o "Another popular myth surrounding the modern Bible versions is the idea that while God inspired the Scriptures infallibly, He has preserved the Scriptures only in a more general sense. To put this another way, while inspiration was miraculous, preservation has been merely circumstantial. . . The doctrine of preservation lies at the very heart of the Bible text debate. The Bible cannot be treated as any other book. It is God's Word. God gave it and God has promised to preserve it. The underlying thesis, though, of modern textual criticism is that the Bible became corrupted through the centuries and it is the task of textual criticism to restore it in original purity. . . The bottom line is that the same Bible that claims to be infallibly inspired also claims to be infallibly preserved. My faith in this is not based on common sense (though it is sensible to believe that if God gave a perfect Bible He would preserve that very Bible). My faith in this matter is based on the promises of a God that cannot lie." (Cloud, 98-102)

CONCLUSION

- In summation, Wallace rejects any corollary between inspiration and preservation because he does not believe the scriptures teach their own preservation. That being said, he argues rationally that preservation must be a historical reality or else we would not have any extant copies. The reason Wallace's position on preservation is so confusing to some is because Wallace is trying to have his cake and eat it too. God did not promise to preserve his word, yet He did, circumstantially, in a historical sense.

WORKS CITED FOR APPENDIX A

Cloud, David W. *Myths About the Modern Bible Versions*. Oak Harbor, WA: Way of Life Literature, 1999.

Combs, William W. "The Preservation of Scripture?" in *Detroit Baptist Seminary Journal*. Fall 2000.

Hills, Edward F. *The King James Version Defended*. Des Moines, IA: Christian Research Press, 1956.

Letis, Theodore P. *The Majority Text: Essays and Reviews in the Continuing Debate*. Institute for Biblical and Textual Studies, 1987.

Wallace, Daniel B. "Inspiration, Preservation, And New Testament Textual Criticism" in *Grace Theological Journal*. 1992.

Wallace, Daniel B. "The Majority-Text Theory: History, Methods, and Critique" in *Journal of the Evangelical Theological Society*. June 1994.

Westcott, Brooke Foss & Fenton John Anthony Hort. *The New Testament in The Original Greek*. London: Macmillan and Company LTD, 1896.

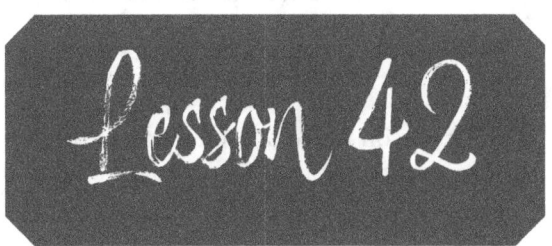

PRESERVATION THE COROLLARY OF INSPIRATION, PART 2

INTRODUCTION

- Last week in Lesson 41 we began our consideration of the *extent* or *nature* of preservation by looking at whether preservation is the corollary of inspiration. We accomplished this through a consideration of the following points:

    o What is a Corollary?
    o Preservation is the Corollary of Inspiration
    o Problems Created by a Denial of a Corollary

- Today we want to conclude our discussion of the corollary by considering the following points:

    o Harry A. Sturz: Preservation but No Corollary

    o The Solution: Dropping the Standard of "Verbatim Identicality"

From here we will move on into a consideration of passages that prove that the standard of "exact sameness" for preservation was overreaching.

HARRY A. STURZ: PRESERVATION BUT NO COROLLARY

- Harry A. Sturz is the author of the 1984 work *The Byzantine Text-Type and New Testament Textual Criticism*. Sturz was a Professor of Greek, and Chairman of the Theology Department at Biola University for many years.

- In footnote number 21 of his essay "The Preservation of Scripture," Dr. William W. Combs informs his readers that Harry Sturz was the former teacher of Daniel B. Wallace. Combs reports that while Sturz denies any corollary between inspiration and preservation, he does argue contrary to Wallace that preservation is promised in scripture. (Combs, 7)

- First, we need to establish that Professor Sturz maintains a belief in the promise of preservation. Regarding the matter he states:

    o "Preservation of the Word of God is promised in Scripture... It may very well be that the Scriptures used to attest the promise to preserve God's Word do involve preservation... But while God promised that his Word would be preserved, "Heaven and earth shall pass away, but my words will not pass away... (Matt. 24:35)" (Sturz, 38)

- Despite maintaining a belief in the promise of preservation (doctrine of preservation), Sturz cautions his readers regarding preservation as the necessary corollary of inspiration. Regarding this matter, he states,

    o "The chief weakness in the Burgon-Hills theory seems to be the foundation upon which the entire structure is built. To present preservation as the necessary corollary of inspiration, then to imply that preservation of the Scripture must be as faithful and precise as the inspiration of the Scripture, appears to be taking a position that is both unscriptural and impossible to demonstrate. Hills insists that;

    > . . . if the doctrine of divine inspiration of the Old and New Testament Scriptures is a true doctrine, the doctrine of providential preservation of these Scriptures must also be a true doctrine. It must be that down through the centuries God has exercised a special providential control. . . God must have done this. . .

    It should be pointed out that providential preservation is not a necessary consequence of inspiration. Preservation of the Word of God is promised in Scripture, and inspiration and preservation are related doctrines, but they are distinct from each other, and there is danger in making one the necessary corollary of the other. . . It may very well be that the Scriptures used to attest the promise to preserve God's Word do involve preservation. The point is that this is a different matter than insisting that God, because He inspired the Scriptures, is ipso facto obligated to preserve them; or further, that He is obligated to preserve them in a particular way." (Sturz, 38-39)

- It is because of the lack of "*verbatim identicality*" in the manuscript copies that Sturz advises caution in confounding preservation with inspiration.

    o "One danger of such a positon is that the faith of some has been weakened when they have become aware of variant readings in the manuscripts precisely because they have confounded preservation with inspiration. Though both are biblical doctrines, the Scripture does not link them inexorably." (Sturz, 38)

- This is a point I have been driving at now for weeks. When one believes in the promise of preservation it is natural to assume that preservation occurred with the same precision as inspiration. Given enough time, one will eventually run into the facts that there are variant readings even in the manuscript tradition supporting the KJB. When one encounters these facts, they are faced with some hard choices: 1) ignore them and pretend like variant readings do not exist and persist it their position unaltered; 2) leave a pro-TR King James stance in favor of the prevailing orthodoxy; or 3) let the Scriptures teach them how to think about textual variants and amend their pro-TR/King James stance accordingly.

- Even though Sturz does not use my terminology ("*verbatim identicality*"), he is arguing for caution with respect to the corollary because he knows that even within the Byzantine text-type (the preferred text of TR/King James advocates) there is not "*verbatim identicality*" of wording.

    o "If providential preservation of the Scriptures is tied to inspiration, is placed on a level with inspiration, and is understood to mean that not one jot or tittle shall pass out of the Byzantine text-type, the theory is on shaky ground due to the fact that even the Byzantine text with its high degree of homogeneity is composite (i.e., there are strands within its homogeneity). Through the research of von Soden at least five principal strands have been identified, some of them with an array of subordinates, within the Byzantine text-type. Even if it were agreed for the sake of argument that the Byzantine text were the best text—the text of God's special providential care—one who holds an orthodox view of inspiration would still be unable to say that the preserved Byzantine text paralleled exactly and in every detail the verbally inspired original... It is a mistake to put preservation on the same level of precision of operation as inspiration..." (Sturz, 39)

- Sturz goes on to make some additional arguments that we will cover in future lessons. The point for now is this, Sturz believes in the promise of preservation but does not view it as the corollary of inspiration because of the lack of *verbatim identicality* of wording in the manuscript copies. Despite his honesty on this matter, he offers no way of overcoming the problem. He only points out that the defense of the TR/King James offered by Edward F. Hills possesses certain inaccuracies that need to be overcome.

THE SOLUTION: DROPPING THE STANDARD OF *"VERBATIM IDENTICALITY"*

- After studying the matter, I have come to believe that dropping the standard of *"verbatim identicality"* for preservation is the solution to the entire problem on both ends of the spectrum.

- I believe in the doctrine of preservation for the same reason I believe in inspiration; it is the Bible's claim for itself (See Lesson 31-38). My position begins with faith in the promise of God and confidence that He did what He said He would do.

- Given the fact that conservatives believe in plenary verbal inspiration or the inspiration of every word, it is reasonable to assume and perhaps expect that preservation would also be both verbal and plenary. It is, therefore, easy to see why many preservationists have demanded *identical* wording (or Xeroxed identicality) as their standard for preservation. They view this conclusion as following logically from the doctrine of plenary verbal inspiration.

- However, when one looks at the historical data, they encounter the fact that no two Greek manuscripts (even Byzantine); editions of the TR, or printings of the KJB, are exactly the same. This is a source of concern for many given their prior belief in and demand for *"verbatim identicality"* as the standard for preservation. Recall the following comment from Sturz above:

- o "One danger of such a positon is that the faith of some has been weakened when they have become aware of variant readings in the manuscripts precisely because they have confounded preservation with inspiration." (Sturz, 38)

- Running headfirst into the facts, one is forced to decide. Are they going to turn away from the doctrine of preservation in favor of a rationalistic/naturalistic explanation of the facts, or, look to the scriptures to inform their understanding of the *nature* of preservation? Please recall the following statements from <u>Lesson 5 Overcoming the Problem of Exact Sameness</u>:

  - o "The "Originals Only" and "King James Inspired" positions are seeking to address the problem of "Exact Sameness." It is a known fact that there are textual variations in the Hebrew and Greek manuscripts supporting the English Bible. One side seeks to deal with the problem by appealing to the nonexistent "Originals" while the other side sees the KJB as a divine act on par with the inspiration of the originals in the first place.

  - o The "Originals Only" position (see <u>Lesson 4</u>), largely ignores the doctrine of preservation. Meanwhile, many King James defenders want to argue that preservation assures the "exact sameness" of every word as originally written under inspiration. Unfortunately, this type of "exact sameness" or "verbatim" wording understanding of preservation cannot be sustained by a consideration of the historical and textual facts. Even among the manuscripts comprising the Byzantine Text Type and utilized by both the Majority Text and the *TR* positions, there is not "exact sameness" or "verbatim" wording across all the manuscripts witnesses.

  - o The manuscripts in the Byzantine Text-Type, while not possessing "exact sameness" or "verbatim" wording across the board, demonstrate an "agreeance" as to doctrinal content of how passages should read." (Amended from Lesson 5.)

- These facts do not overthrow my belief in God's promise to preserve His word. These facts do not lead me to deny or to doubt the clear promise of God.

- Rather, I look back to the scriptures to inform my thinking on the topic. When I do, I realize that my prior insistence upon the standard of *"verbatim identicality"* was excessive and an overstating of the case for preservation to begin with. A careful study of the KJB will confirm this conclusion for anyone who is skeptical of its veracity.

- I can adopt this modified position on preservation based upon faith in God's written word. After studying the issue, I have come to believe that the challenge of *"verbatim identicality"* is the central problem in the textual/Bible version debate.

- Most King James advocates maintain that it is perfect in every detail. If that is truly the case, they need to let the KJB inform their thinking on the issues of textual variations. Even within the KJB the New Testament does not quote the Old with exact identicality.

- Please consider the following table comparing Isaiah 61:1-2 and Luke 4:18-19 as a case in point. In Luke 4 Jesus is in the synagogue in Nazareth where He stands up to read and is handed a copy of the book of Isaiah. In other words, Christ is not just making a free quotation of the Old Testament, rather he is reading from a manuscript copy of the book of Isaiah. Jesus then proceeds to read Isaiah 61 out of the manuscript copy that was handed to him. A side-by-side comparison reveals that even within the KJB there is not exact identicality in wording between the two passages.

Isaiah 61:1-2	Luke 4:18-19
"The Spirit of the Lord **GOD** is upon me; because the **LORD** hath anointed me to preach **good tidings** unto the **meek**; he hath sent me **to bind up** the brokenhearted, to **proclaim liberty** to the captives, and the **opening of the prison** to them that are **bound**; To **proclaim** the acceptable year of the LORD,	"The Spirit of the Lord is upon me, because **he** hath anointed me to preach **the gospel** to the **poor;** he hath sent me **to heal** the brokenhearted, to **preach deliverance** to the captives, **(and recovering of sight to the blind)**, to **set at liberty** them that are **bruised**, To **preach** the acceptable year of the Lord.

- These passages from within the KJB do not exhibit "*verbatim identicality*" yet the Lord Jesus Christ called the copy He was reading from in Nazareth "scripture." What this illustrates is that different words can have the same meaning. The words we possess convey the exact same doctrinal content expressed in the originals without necessitating we possess the exact same words. If the Lord Jesus Christ could call what he read in Luke 4 "scripture" yet it does not match Isaiah 61 exactly in my KJB, then that tells me that demanding more from the doctrine of preservation than Christ did is not wise. We need to be careful not to demand more from our doctrine than the Bible claims for itself.

- The preceding comparison between Isaiah 61 and Luke 4 highlights the fact that there is a difference between 1) a different way of saying the same thing and 2) a substantive difference in meaning. At the end of the day, the reason King James advocates reject modern versions and their underlying texts is because their wording has been changed so much so as to substantively alter the doctrinal content of the Bible (See examples provided in <u>Lesson 10</u>). Some, in their zeal, have overstated the case and adopted a standard for preservation that cannot be sustained in light of the historical/textual facts.

- Psalms 12:6-7—what the doctrine of preservation assures is exactly what verse 6 states, namely the preservation of a Pure Text i.e., a text that does not report information about God, His nature or character, His doctrine, His dispensational dealings with mankind, history, archeology, or science that is false. In short, God's promise to preserve His word assures the existence of a text that has not been altered in its "fundamental character" or "doctrinal content" despite not being preserved in a state of "*verbatim identicality.*"

- Once one has adjusted their view of preservation to accord with the textual facts, by dropping "*verbatim identicality*" as their standard for preservation; there is nothing wrong with viewing the doctrine as a corollary of inspiration. As we saw last week in Lesson 41, an attempt to deny any corollary creates just as many problems as overstating the case.

- In the next Lesson we will consider further examples of why "*verbatim identicality*" of wording is demanding too much for the doctrine of preservation.

WORKS CITED

Sturz, Harry A. *The Byzantine Text-Type & New Testament Textual Criticism.* Nashville, TN: Thomas Nelson Publishers, 1984.

EXAMPLES OF ALTERED DOCTRINAL CONTENT BETWEEN THE KJB AND MODERN VERSIONS

- **Note:** this appendix was created using excerpts from Lesson 10.

SUBSTANTIVE DIFFERENCES AFFECTING THE ACCURACY OF THE TEXT

- There is no doubt in my mind that there are substantive differences in meaning that affect the accuracy of the text between the *TR* and the Critical Text and their representative translations into English. Please consider the following examples. For the sake of clarity and consistency we will compare the King James with other literal translations, namely, the New American Standard Bible (NASB) and the English Standard Version (ESV).

Mark 1:2-3

KJB	NASB	ESV
2) As it is written **in the prophets**, Behold, I send my messenger before thy face, which shall prepare thy way before thee. 3) The voice of one crying in the wilderness, Prepare ye the way of the Lord, make his paths straight.	2) As it is **written in Isaiah the prophet**: "BEHOLD, I SEND MY MESSENGER AHEAD OF YOU, WHO WILL PREPARE YOUR WAY; 3) THE VOICE OF ONE CRYING IN THE WILDERNESS, 'MAKE READY THE WAY OF THE LORD, MAKE HIS PATHS STRAIGHT.'"	2) As it **is written in Isaiah the prophet**, "Behold, I send my messenger before your face, who will prepare your way, 3) the voice of one crying in the wilderness: 'Prepare the way of the Lord, make his paths straight,'"

- Mark 1:2-3 contains quotations from Malachi 3:1 (Mark 1:2) and Isaiah 40:3 (Mark 1:3) as the KJB accurately reports with the use of "prophets" plural. Meanwhile the modern versions quoted above both read "As it is written in Isaiah the prophet" singular. This is a flat-out mistake in the NASB and ESV; one can read Isaiah from now till the rapture and not find the contents of Mark 1:2 in the book of Isaiah.

- This is not a translation issue. It is a textual issue. The issue here is not how to properly translate individual Greek words into English. The reason the English texts differ is because their underlying Greek texts differ. This is an example of a substantive difference in meaning. They cannot both be correct.

- This is a clear-cut case where modern versions and their underlying Greek text are wrong. They present information that is false. The Old Testament quotation found in Mark 1:2 cannot be found in the book of Isaiah.

Matthew 5:22

KJB	NASB	ESV
But I say unto you, That whosoever is angry with his brother **without a cause** shall be in danger of the judgment: and whosoever shall say to his brother, Raca, shall be in danger of the council: but whosoever shall say, Thou fool, shall be in danger of hell fire.	"But I say to you that everyone who is angry with his brother shall be guilty before the court; and whoever says to his brother, 'You good-for-nothing,' shall be guilty before the supreme court; and whoever says, 'You fool,' shall be guilty *enough to go* into the fiery hell.	But I say to you that everyone who is angry with his brother will be liable to judgment; whoever insults his brother will be liable to the council; and whoever says, 'You fool!' will be liable to the hell of fire.

- The phrase "without a cause" is missing from both the NASB and ESV. The reason the phrase is missing from both modern versions is because the underlying Greek text from which they are translated does not contain the phrase.

- The omission of the phrase "without a cause" seems to be a minor oversight in Matthew 5 but, when cross referenced with Mark 3:5, a theological problem is encountered. In Mark 3:5 Jesus gets angry due to the hardness of the heart exhibited by those in the synagogue. Does Jesus have cause to be angry? Yes. The omission of the phrase, "without a cause" in the Critical Text and its corresponding modern translations in Matthew 5 creates a doctrinal problem in Mark 3 when Jesus gets angry. Practically, the omission of the phrase "without a cause" results in Jesus condemning Himself out of His own mouth.

Luke 2:33

KJB	NASB	ESV
And **Joseph** and his mother marveled at those things which were spoken of him.	And **His father** and mother were amazed at the things which were being said about Him.	And **his father** and his mother marveled at what was said about him.

- Once again why do these versions read differently in English? Because their underlying Greek texts are not the same. The *TR* and its subsequent translation into English via the KJB maintain the doctrinal integrity of the virgin birth. Joseph was not the father of Jesus as the modern translations of the Critical Text imply.

Colossians 2:18

KJB	NASB	ESV
Let no man beguile you of your reward in a voluntary humility and worshipping of angels, intruding into those things which he **hath not seen**, vainly puffed up by his fleshly mind,	Let no one keep defrauding you of your prize by delighting in self-abasement and the worship of the angels, taking his stand on *visions* he **has seen**, inflated without cause by his fleshly mind,	Let no one disqualify you, insisting on asceticism and worship of angels, going on in detail about visions, puffed up without reason by his sensuous mind,

- Here we have a situation where the *TR* and the Critical Text are directly contradictory. This is not just a situation where one text leaves something out that the other one includes. One text, the Critical Text, says that people "*have seen*" angels and visions while the other one (the *TR*) says that you *have not*. The reason they contradict in English is because they contradict in Greek.

- Here the principles of *Noncontradiction* and *Excluded Middle* absolutely apply because the two readings are directly contradictory and teach opposites. One reading says you have seen a thing while the other one says that you have not.

- Both readings cannot be correct because they possess substantive differences in meaning. One of them must be right and one of them has to be wrong or they are both wrong. We cannot even entertain the notion that they are both wrong on account of the doctrine of preservation.

- This passage is dealing with the doctrine of *Angelology* during the dispensation of grace. How many believers in our day claim to have guardian angels, seen angels, or heard messages from angels or received visions and revelations based upon their personal experience? Colossians 2:18 is the clearest verse in the Pauline epistles informing us that anyone making such claims does not know what they are talking about and is not to be trusted. More importantly, anyone entertaining this type of spiritual mysticism is not holding Christ as the head in the next verse (Colossians 2:19).

- Furthermore, the readings found in the NASB and ESV for Colossians 2:18, create an internal contradiction within the book of Colossians. Colossians 1:16 teaches that the principalities and powers in heavenly places and those beings occupying them are "invisible" i.e., you cannot see them. Now, one chapter later in chapter 2, modern versions have people seeing things that chapter 1 said were invisible.

- I fail to see how this difference does not affect doctrine as it relates to the body of Christ. I have dealt with many Pentecostals who have claimed to have had angelic visitations and have seen into the spirit world based upon the authority of Colossians 2:18 in their modern version.

John 1:18

KJB	NASB
No man hath seen God at any time; **the only begotten Son**, which is in the bosom of the Father, he hath declared him.	No one has seen God at any time; **the only begotten God** who is in the bosom of the Father, He has explained *Him*.

- Is Jesus Christ the "only begotten Son" or the "only begotten God" as the NASB states? The wording of the NASB asserts that Jesus Christ is a lesser God created by God Almighty and is not coequal with the Father. Theologically this is very close to what the Jehovah's Witnesses believe about Christ i.e., that he was not co-equal with God the Father but is a lesser created being. Once again it seems to me that this reading affects doctrine.

BASIC FACTUAL IRREGULARITIES

- The examples cited above do not even consider the scores of omitted verses in the Critical Text or the fundamental lack of agreeance amongst Critical Text translations on even basic textual or historical details. As we studied in Lesson 3, this is not simply a King James versus modern versions problem. Even among modern versions, which subscribe to the same theories of textual criticism, there are substantive differences in meaning and lack of agreement about even basic facts. See the following examples:

II Samuel 15:7

KJB	NASB	ESV
And it came to pass after **forty years**, that Absalom said unto the king, I pray thee, let me go and pay my vow, which I have vowed unto the LORD, in Hebron.	Now it came about at the end of **forty years** that Absalom said to the king, "Please let me go and pay my vow which I have vowed to the LORD, in Hebron.	And at the end of **four years** Absalom said to the king, "Please let me go and pay my vow, which I have vowed to the LORD, in Hebron.

Ecclesiastes 8:10

KJB	NASB	ESV
And so I saw the wicked buried, who had come and gone from the place of the holy, and they **were forgotten in the city** where they had so done: this *is* also vanity.	So then, I have seen the wicked buried, those who used to go in and out from the holy place, and they **are *soon*** forgotten in the city where they did thus. This too is futility.	Then I saw the wicked buried. They used to go in and out of the holy place and **were praised in the city** where they had done such things. This also is vanity.

Luke 10:1

KJB	NASB	ESV
After these things the Lord **appointed other seventy** also, and sent them two and two before his face into every city and place, whither he himself would come.	Now after this the Lord **appointed seventy others**, and sent them in pairs ahead of Him to every city and place where He Himself was going to come.	After this the Lord **appointed seventy-two others** and sent them on ahead of him, two by two, into every town and place where he himself was about to go.

Matthew 12:47

KJB	NASB	ESV
Then one said unto him, Behold, thy mother and thy brethren stand without, desiring to speak with thee.	Someone said to Him, "Behold, Your mother and Your brothers are standing outside seeking to speak to You."	Omitted

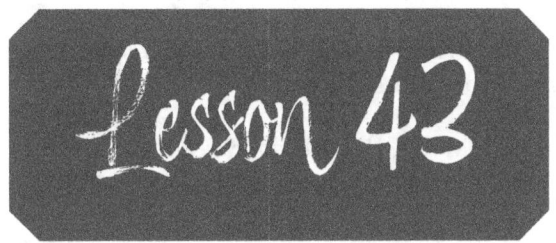

PASSAGES PROVING PLENARY PRESERVATION IS PRESUMPTUOUS

INTRODUCTION

- Last week in Lesson 42 we concluded that dropping the standard of *"verbatim identicality"* was the solution for solving the corollary problem.

- To help illustrate this point we compared Isaiah 61 and Luke 4 and noted that Luke's account of what Christ read in the synagogue in Nazareth does not match exactly with the passage He is reading from in Isaiah 61, even in a KJB.

- I would like to use this Lesson to offer further proof from scripture that demanding *"verbatim identicality"* as the standard for preservation is excessive and out of step with how the Bible itself would teach you to think about the matter.

- Noah Webster's *American Dictionary of the English Language* defines the word "verbatim" as follows:

    o   VERBA'TIM adv. [L.] Word for word; in the same words; as, to tell a story verbatim as another has related it.

- The goal of this lesson is to show that the testimony of the scriptures does not require verbatim phraseology but simply equivalent meaning. It is possible to say the exact same thing using different words.

    o   "At 3:30, I drove to the store."
    o   "I drove to the store at half past three."

- Consider the following example from II Timothy 2:15:

    o   Geneva — ". . . dividing the word of truth aright."
    o   King James — "…rightly dividing the word of truth."

- In both examples, the order of words and the words themselves are different but the substance is equivalent. This highlights a point that I have been making since Lesson 5, there is a difference between 1) a different way of saying the same things, and, 2) a substantive difference in meaning.

- There are four proofs that scripture approves of substantive doctrinal equivalence (*content equivalence* not dynamic equivalence) and does not require *verbatim identicality*:

    o   The fact that New Testament quotes of the Old Testament do not match verbatim.

- o The fact that Old Testament quotations of the Old Testament do not match verbatim.
- o The fact that New Testament quotations of the New Testament do not match verbatim.
- o II Kings 19 and Isaiah 37 do not match verbatim.

NEW TESTAMENT QUOTES OF THE OLD TESTAMENT

- In this category I would like to consider the following two categories of passages:

  - o "Scripture" Passages
  - o "It is written" Passages

"Scripture" Passages

- This category explores instances where a New Testament figure is reading from a manuscript copy of the Old Testament, yet the manuscript copies that are read from in the New Testament do not match exactly with the Old Testament texts that are being read in the KJB.

Isaiah 61:1-2 & Luke 4:18-19

Isaiah 61:1-2	Luke 4:18-19
The Spirit of the Lord **GOD** is upon me;	The Spirit of the Lord is upon me,
because the **LORD** hath anointed me to preach **good tidings** unto the **meek**;	because **he** hath anointed me to preach **the gospel** to the **poor**;
he hath sent me **to bind up** the brokenhearted,	he hath sent me **to heal** the brokenhearted,
to **proclaim liberty** to the captives,	to **preach deliverance** to the captives,
and the **opening of the prison** to them that are **bound**;	**(and recovering of sight to the blind)**,
	to **set at liberty** them that are **bruised**,
To **proclaim** the acceptable year of the LORD,	To **preach** the acceptable year of the Lord.

- We have already seen this example in Lessons 5 and 42. The manuscript copy that Christ is reading from in Luke 4 is not an exact match with the King James text of Isaiah 61, the passage the Lord is reading from. Yet, the Lord Jesus Christ calls the manuscript copy He is reading from scripture. The passages are substantively equivalent in their doctrine despite not possessing verbatim wording.

Isaiah 53:7-8 & Acts 8:32-33

Isaiah 53:7-8	Acts 8:32-33
He was oppressed, and he was afflicted, yet he opened not his mouth: he is **brought as a lamb** to the slaughter, and **as a <u>sheep</u> before <u>her</u> shearers is** dumb, so **he openeth** not his mouth. **He was taken from prison and from judgment**: and who shall declare his generation? For **he was cut off out of the land of the living**: for the transgression of my people was he stricken.	He was **led as a sheep** to the slaughter; and **like a <u>lamb</u> dumb before <u>his</u> shearer,** so **opened he** not his mouth: **In his humiliation his judgment was taken away**: and who shall declare his generation? for **his life is taken from the earth**.

- Acts 8:26-30—the Ethiopian Eunuch is on his way home to Ethiopia from Jerusalem in his chariot reading a manuscript copy of the book of Isaiah. When Philip is prompted by the angel of Lord to join himself unto the Eunuch's chariot, Philip finds him reading the passage above from Isaiah 53.

- When one compares the text of Acts 8:32-33 with Isaiah 53:7-8 the wording is far from identical, yet the doctrinal substance is unaltered despite not possessing verbatim wording.

- Acts 8:32-35—twice in this passage the Holy Spirit calls the text of verses 32 and 33 scripture despite the lack of verbatim wording with Isaiah 53:7-8 in the KJB. Once again, this proves that demanding *verbatim identicality* in wording as the standard for preservation is overreaching. God the Holy Spirit does not even demand that in his word.

"It is written" Passages

- In Lessons 36 and 37 we devoted two lessons to a study of how the phrase "it is written" impacts the doctrine/promise of preservation. In Lesson 37 we considered the impact of the Perfect Tense and Passive Voice upon the doctrine of preservation.

    - "The perfect tense, which He utilized, expresses a completed action with a resulting state of being. The result of the action continues from the past through the present and into the future." (Strouse in *Thou Shalt Keep Them*, 35)

    - "Combining the perfect tense with the passive voice shows that the action of the verb was completed in the past by an agent other than the subject of the verb with the results of the action continuing into the present. The perfect tense, and the perfect passive in particular, is often used in Scripture to teach doctrine and illustrate preservation of truth." (Sutton in *Thou Shalt Keep Them*, 76)

- After explaining the meaning and significance of both the perfect tense and passive voice and applying it to non-preservation related texts by way of explanation and illustration, Sutton explains the significance with respect to the doctrine of preservation. Every occurrence of "it is written" in the New Testament corresponds with a perfect passive verb in Greek, according to Sutton:

    - "Sixty-three times in the NT the exact phrase "it is written" occurs. The perfect passive verb *gegraptai* underlies fifty-nine of these references, while the other four occasions represent the perfect passive participle *gegramenon*." (Sutton in *Thou Shalt Keep Them*, 78)

- In Lesson 36 we noted places where the phrase "it is written" occurred yet there was not verbatim identicality in how the New Testament quoted the Old Testament.

Deuteronomy 8:3 & Matthew 4:4

Deuteronomy 8:3	Matthew 4:4
. . . that he might make thee know that man **doth** not live by bread **only**, but by every *word* that proceedeth out of the mouth of the **LORD doth man live**.	But he answered and said, **It is written**, Man **shall** not live by bread **alone**, but by every word that proceedeth out of the mouth of God.

- Is Matthew 4:4 in your KJB an exact word for word quotation of Deuteronomy 8:3? No! Does that mean one of these is in error? No! They are both teaching the exact same doctrinal content without using the exact same words.

Matthew 4:4 & Luke 4:4

Matthew 4:4	Luke 4:4
But he answered and said, **It is written**, Man shall not live by bread alone, but by every word **that proceedeth out of the mouth** of God.	And Jesus answered him, saying, **It is written**, **That** man shall not live by bread alone, but by every word of God.

- So not only does Matthew's quotation of Deuteronomy 8:3 not match exactly but the citations of Deuteronomy by both Matthew and Luke, in the same context, do not match each other exactly. Yet no one views these verses as differing substantively in terms of their doctrinal content.

- The same phenomena are observable for the other "it is written" quotations of the Lord Jesus Christ during his temptation.

Deuteronomy 6:16 & Matthew 4:7

Deuteronomy 6:16	Matthew 4:7
Ye shall not tempt the LORD **your** God, ...	Jesus said unto him, **It is written** again, **Thou** shalt not tempt the Lord **thy** God.

Deuteronomy 6:13 & Mathew 4:10

Deuteronomy 6:13	Matthew 4:10
Thou shalt **fear** the LORD thy God, and serve him, **and shalt swear by his name**.	Then saith Jesus unto him, Get thee hence, Satan: for **it is written**, Thou shalt **worship** the Lord thy God, and him **only** shalt thou serve.

There are literally scores of these types of examples that we could cite. Please consider these few in addition to what we saw in Lesson 36.

Micah 5:2 & Matthew 2:5-6

Micah 5:2	Matthew 2:5-6
But thou, Bethlehem **Ephratah**, *though* thou be little among the thousands of Judah, *yet* out of thee shall he come forth **unto me** *that is* to be **ruler** in Israel; **whose goings forth** *have been* from of old, from everlasting. NIV—"... from ancient times." ESV—"... from ancient days."	And they said unto him, In Bethlehem of Judaea: for thus **it is written** by the prophet, And thou Bethlehem, *in* the land of Juda, art not the least among the princes of Juda: for out of thee shall come a **Governor**, that shall rule **my people** Israel.

Zechariah 13:7 & Matthew 26:13

Zechariah 13:7	Matthew 26:13
Awake, O sword, against my shepherd, and against the man *that is* my fellow, saith the LORD of hosts:	Then saith Jesus unto them, All ye shall be offended because of me this night: for **it is written,**
smite the shepherd,	**I will** smite the shepherd,
and the sheep shall be scattered:	and the sheep **of the flock** shall be scattered **abroad**.
and I will turn mine hand upon the little ones.	

Psalms 69:25 & Acts 1:20

Psalms 69:25	Acts 1:20
Let their habitation be desolate; *and* let none dwell in their tents.	For **it is written** in the book of Psalms, Let **his** habitation be desolate, **and let no man dwell therein: and his bishoprick let another take**.

Isaiah 59:20 & Romans 11:26

Isaiah 59:20	Romans 11:26
And **the Redeemer** shall come to Zion, and **unto them** that **turn from transgression in Jacob,** saith the LORD.	And so all Israel shall be saved: as **it is written,** There shall come out of Sion **the Deliverer,** and **shall turn away ungodliness from Jacob:**

Isaiah 29:14 & I Corinthians 1:19

Isaiah 29:14	I Corinthians 1:19
Therefore, behold, I will proceed to do a marvellous work among this people, *even* a marvellous work and a wonder:	For **it is written,**
for the wisdom of their wise *men* shall perish, and the understanding of their prudent *men* shall be hid.	**I will destroy the wisdom of the wise, and will bring to nothing the understanding of the prudent.**

- Many more examples like these could be presented for consideration. In fact, I challenge readers to look at each occurrence of the phrase "it is written" in the New Testament and compare the associated quotation with its Old Testament counterpart. I have not been able to find one that is completely *verbatim*, the closest one I could locate is II Corinthians 8:15's quotation of Exodus 16:18.

- So, in the above examples, which verse is right-the NT or the OT passage? The answer is that they are both right. From this we can make the following observations:

    o The NT quotations of the OT are not *verbatim* and are sometimes considerably different.

    o The NT quotations specifically say, "it is written," when in fact those exact words are not written.

    o This proves that scripture considers the NT phrasing to be the *equivalent* of the OT verse even though the words are not *verbatim*.

    o It is thus possible for different phrasings to be *equivalent*, and be both be the word of God even though they are not *verbatim*.

Old Testament Quotes of the Old Testament & New Testament Quotes of the New Testament

- In case one is tempted to argue that the examples cited in this section are illegitimate because the Old Testament was written in Hebrew and the New Testament in Greek, they need to mark well that the same phenomena occur within each Testament. The Old Testament does not quote the Old Testament with "verbatim identicality." Likewise, for the New Testament.

Deuteronomy 24:16 & II Chronicles 25:4

Deuteronomy 24:16	II Chronicles 25:4
The fathers shall not **be put to death** for the children, neither shall the children **be put to death for** the fathers: every man shall **be put to death** for his own sin.	But he slew not their children, but *did as it is* written in the law in the book of Moses, where the LORD commanded, **saying,** The fathers shall not **die for the children,** neither shall the children **die for** the fathers, but every man shall **die** for his own sin.

I Timothy 5:18 & Luke 10:7

Luke 10:7	I Timothy 5:18
And in the same house remain, eating and drinking such things as they give: For the labourer is worthy of his **hire**. Go not from house to house.	For the scripture saith, Thou shalt not muzzle the ox that treadeth out the corn. And, The labourer *is* worthy of his **reward**.

- I Timothy 5:18 clearly states "the scripture saith" yet when it quotes Luke 10:7 it does not do so with *verbatim identicality*.

- In this way the word of God instructs us that demanding *verbatim identicality* in wording as the standard for preservation was an excessive and unbiblical assumption. This false assumption has caused many to err to one of the following extremes:

    o **Option 1: Originals Only Position**—this position confines inspiration, infallibility, and inerrancy to the non-existent original autographs as a means of dealing with the variant readings. Advocates argue that it is their job to reconstruct the Biblical text. This position is nonscientific and non-falsifiable. In the absence of the originals how does one know whether they have accurately reconstructed the text? This position is of no practical consequence and cannot be maintained by faith in God's word.

    o **Option 2: Faith for Faith's Sake**—pretends like the variant readings do not exist and insist upon Plenary Verbal Preservation. Some incorrectly insist that God re-inspired His Word in English between 1604 and 1611 as a means of providing the verbatim identicality of wording that this view of Preservation demands. This view has the correct starting point, and is consistent with the fedeistic (believing) approach to Scripture; but it carries the corollary between Preservation and Inspiration too far.

- Please consider the following chart titled, A Scriptural Model for Dealing with Textual Variants. Begin reading in the upper left corner and follow the arrows as you work your way through the flow-chart.

Scriptural Model for Dealing with Textual Variants

Plenary Verbal Inspiration—Bible's assertion for itself (II Tim. 3:16; II Pet. 1:21).

⬇

Promise of Preservation—Bible's claim for itself (Ps. 12:6-7; 119:111, 152, 160; Is. 30:8, 40:8; Matt. 4:4; 24:35; I Pet. 1:23-25).

⬇

Preservation is the Corollary of Inspiration—it is reasonable to conclude that Preservation occurred with the same precision as Inspiration (i.e. Plenary Verbal), but many mistakenly assume that this requires *verbatim identicality* of wording. This false assumption underlies the entire textual variant discussion and leads to unscriptural conclusions.

{ Belief in the Scriptures leads one to maintain a belief in both Inspiration & Preservation }

⚠ **CAUTION**

Variant Readings are a Historical Fact—no two Greek manuscripts (even Byzantine); editions of the *TR*, or printings of the KJB are identical. Leads to the realization that Preservation did not occur with *verbatim identicality* of wording.

⬇

Option 1: Originals Only Position—this position confines inspiration, infallibility, and inerrancy to the non-existent original autographs as a means of dealing with the variant readings. Advocates argue that it is their job to reconstruct the Biblical text. This position is nonscientific and non-falsifiable. In the absence of the originals how does one know whether they have accurately reconstructed the text. This position is of no practical consequence and cannot be maintained by faith in God's word.

Option 2: Faith for Faith's Sake—pretends like variant readings do not exist and insists upon Plenary Verbal Preservation. Some incorrectly assert that God re-inspired his Word in English between 1604 and 1611 as a means of providing the verbatim identicality of wording this view of Preservation demands. Has the correct starting point, is consist with the believing approach to Scripture; but carries the corollary between Preservation and Inspiration too far.

Option 3: Biblically Amend One's Position on Preservation—the facts need not overthrow one's belief in the Promise of Preservation. Rather one should look back to the Scriptures which taught them to believe in Preservation in the first place to learn how to think about variant readings. When one does this, they will conclude that the insistence upon the standard of *"verbatim identicality"* was excessive and an overstatement of what the Scriptures teach about Preservation.

⬇

Result: A Biblically Amended Position on Preservation—drop *verbatim identicality* as the standard for Preservation. If one allows the KJB to teach them about the *nature* of Preservation, they will conclude that demanding *verbatim identicality* as the standard for Preservation was overreaching to begin with. There are at least four Scriptural proofs found within the KJB that support this conclusion:

1) How the OT quotes OT
2) How the NT quotes the OT
3) How the NT quotes the NT
4) Comparison between II Kings 19 & Isaiah 37

Observing these realities allows one to maintain their belief in the Promise of Preservation without overstating the facts. This Biblically revised position can still be maintained by faith in God's word without abandoning the believing approach to Scripture.

Pastor Bryan Ross–Grace Life Bible Church–Grand Rapids, MI

II KINGS 19 AND ISAIAH 37

- II Kings 19 and Isaiah 37 represent a different case than we observed in the previous point. In this case both passages are found in the Old Testament and were originally written in Hebrew. Moreover, they portray the exact same event, and yet, they are not identical.

- These chapters are not like the gospels where they are different accounts that provide different perspectives and contain different information. These are nearly identical in content but have different wording. Matthew, Mark, Luke, and John are different accounts that are written for different purposes. Therefore, when they record the same events, they include different details.

    o   Differ in length

    o   Some have a genealogy, some do not

    o   Those that do have a genealogy do not match

    o   They record different events

II Kings 19	Isaiah 37
1) And it came to pass, when king Hezekiah heard *it*, that he rent his clothes, and covered himself with sackcloth, and went into the house of the LORD.	1) And it came to pass, when king Hezekiah heard *it*, that he rent his clothes, and covered himself with sackcloth, and went into the house of the LORD.
2) And he sent Eliakim, **which** *was* over the household, and Shebna the scribe, and the elders of the priests, covered with sackcloth, **to** Isaiah the prophet the son of Amoz.	2) And he sent Eliakim, **who** *was* over the household, and Shebna the scribe, and the elders of the priests covered with sackcloth, **unto** Isaiah the prophet the son of Amoz.
3) And they said unto him, Thus saith Hezekiah, This day *is* a day of trouble, and of rebuke, and blasphemy: for the children are come to the birth, and *there is* not strength to bring forth.	3) And they said unto him, Thus saith Hezekiah, This day *is* a day of trouble, and of rebuke, and of blasphemy: for the children are come to the birth, and *there is* not strength to bring forth.

4) It may be the LORD thy God will hear **all** the words of Rabshakeh, whom the king of Assyria his master hath sent to reproach the living God; and will reprove the words which the LORD thy God hath heard: wherefore lift up *thy* prayer for the remnant that **are** left.	4) It may be the LORD thy God will hear the words of Rabshakeh, whom the king of Assyria his master hath sent to reproach the living God**,** and will reprove the words which the LORD thy God hath heard: wherefore lift up *thy* prayer for the remnant that **is** left.
5) So the servants of king Hezekiah came to Isaiah.	5) So the servants of king Hezekiah came to Isaiah.
6) And Isaiah said unto them, Thus shall ye say to your master, Thus saith the LORD, Be not afraid of the words **which** thou hast heard, **with which** the servants of the king of Assyria have blasphemed me.	6) And Isaiah said unto them, Thus shall ye say unto your master, Thus saith the LORD, Be not afraid of the words **that** thou hast heard, **wherewith** the servants of the king of Assyria have blasphemed me.
7) Behold, I will send a blast upon him, and he shall hear a rumour, and **shall** return to his own land; and I will cause him to fall by the sword in his own land.	7) Behold, I will send a blast upon him, and he shall hear a rumour, and return to his own land; and I will cause him to fall by the sword in his own land.
8) So Rabshakeh returned, and found the king of Assyria warring against Libnah: for he had heard that he was departed from Lachish.	8) So Rabshakeh returned, and found the king of Assyria warring against Libnah: for he had heard that he was departed from Lachish.
9) And when he heard say **of** Tirhakah king of Ethiopia, **Behold**, he is come **out to fight** against thee: he sent messengers again unto Hezekiah, saying,	9) And he heard say **concerning** Tirhakah king of Ethiopia, He is come **forth to make war** with thee. **And when he heard *it*,** he sent messengers to Hezekiah, saying,
10) Thus shall ye speak to Hezekiah king of Judah, saying, Let not thy God in whom thou trustest deceive thee, saying, Jerusalem shall not be **delivered** into the hand of the king of Assyria.	10) Thus shall ye speak to Hezekiah king of Judah, saying, Let not thy God, in whom thou trustest, deceive thee, saying, Jerusalem shall not be **given** into the hand of the king of Assyria.
11) Behold, thou hast heard what the kings of Assyria have done to all lands, by destroying them utterly and shalt thou be delivered?	11) Behold, thou hast heard what the kings of Assyria have done to all lands by destroying them utterly; and shalt thou be delivered?

12) Have the gods of the nations delivered them which my fathers have destroyed; *as* Gozan, and Haran, and Rezeph, and the children of Eden which *were* in **Thelasar**?	12) Have the gods of the nations delivered them which my fathers have destroyed, *as* Gozan, and Haran, and Rezeph, and the children of Eden which *were* in **Telassar**?
13) Where *is* the king of Hamath, and the king of Arpad, and the king of the city of Sepharvaim, of Hena, and Ivah?	13) Where *is* the king of Hamath, and the king of Arphad, and the king of the city of Sepharvaim, Hena, and Ivah?
14) And Hezekiah received the letter **of** the hand of the messengers, and read it: and Hezekiah went up **into** the house of the LORD, and spread it before the LORD.	14) And Hezekiah received the letter **from** the hand of the messengers, and read it: and Hezekiah went up **unto** the house of the LORD, and spread it before the LORD.
15) And Hezekiah prayed **before** the LORD, **and said**, O LORD God of Israel, **which** dwellest *between* the cherubims, thou art the God, *even* thou alone, of all the kingdoms of the earth; thou hast made heaven and earth.	15) And Hezekiah prayed **unto** the LORD, **saying,**
	16) O LORD **of hosts**, God of Israel, **that** dwellest *between* the cherubims, thou *art* the God, *even* thou alone, of all the kingdoms of the earth: thou hast made heaven and earth.
16) **LORD, bow down thine ear**, and hear: **open, LORD, thine eyes**, and see: and hear the words of Sennacherib, which hath sent **him** to reproach the living God.	17) **Incline thine ear, O LORD**, and hear; **open thine eyes, O LORD,** and see: and hear **all** the words of Sennacherib, which hath sent to reproach the living God.
17) Of a truth, LORD, the kings of Assyria have **destroyed** the nations and their **lands,**	18) Of a truth, LORD, the kings of Assyria have **laid waste all** the nations, and their **countries,**
18) And have cast their gods into the fire: for they *were* no gods, but the work of men's hands, wood and stone: therefore they have destroyed them.	19) And have cast their gods into the fire: for they *were* no gods, but the work of men's hands, wood and stone: therefore they have destroyed them.

19) Now therefore, O LORD our God, **I beseech thee**, save **thou** us **out of** his hand, that all the kingdoms of the earth may know that thou *art* the LORD **God**, *even* thou only.	20) Now therefore, O LORD our God, save us **from** his hand, that all the kingdoms of the earth may know that thou *art* the LORD, *even* thou only.
20) Then Isaiah the son of Amoz sent **to** Hezekiah, saying, Thus saith the LORD God of Israel, *That* **which** thou hast prayed to me against Sennacherib king of Assyria **I have heard**.	21) Then Isaiah the son of Amoz sent **unto** Hezekiah, saying, Thus saith the LORD God of Israel, **Whereas** thou hast prayed to me against Sennacherib king of Assyria:
21) This *is* the word **that** the LORD hath spoken concerning him; The virgin the daughter of Zion hath despised thee, *and* laughed thee to scorn; the daughter of Jerusalem hath shaken her head at thee.	22) This *is* the word **which** the LORD hath spoken concerning him; The virgin, the daughter of **Zion**, hath despised thee, *and* laughed thee to scorn; the daughter of Jerusalem hath shaken her head at thee.
22) Whom hast thou reproached and blasphemed? and against whom hast thou exalted *thy* voice, and lifted up thine eyes on high? *even* against the Holy *One* of Israel.	23) Whom hast thou reproached and blasphemed? and against whom hast thou exalted *thy* voice, and lifted up thine eyes on high? *even* against the Holy One of Israel.
23) By thy **messengers** thou hast reproached the Lord, and hast said, **With** the multitude of my chariots I am come up to the height of the mountains, to the sides of Lebanon, and will cut down the tall **cedar trees** thereof, *and* the choice fir trees thereof: and I will enter into the **lodgings** of his **borders**, *and* **into** the forest of his Carmel.	24) By thy **servants** hast thou reproached the Lord, and hast said, **By** the multitude of my chariots am I come up to the height of the mountains, to the sides of Lebanon; and **I** will cut down the tall **cedars** thereof, *and* the choice fir trees thereof: and I will enter into the **height** of his **border**, *and* the forest of his Carmel.
24) I have digged and drunk **strange waters**, and with the sole of my feet have I dried up all the rivers of besieged places.	25) I have digged, and drunk **water**; and with the sole of my feet have I dried up all the rivers of **the** besieged places.
25) Hast thou not heard long ago *how* I have done it, *and* of ancient times that I have formed it? now have I brought it to pass, that thou shouldest be to lay waste **fenced** cities *into* ruinous heaps.	26) Hast thou not heard long ago, *how* I have done it; *and* of ancient times, that I have formed it? now have I brought it to pass, that thou shouldest be to lay waste **defenced** cities *into* ruinous heaps.

26) Therefore their inhabitants **were** of small power, they were dismayed and confounded; they were *as* the grass of the field, and *as* the green herb, *as* the grass on the housetops, and *as corn* blasted before it be grown up.	27) Therefore their inhabitants **were** of small power, they were dismayed and confounded: they were *as* the grass of the field, and *as* the green herb, *as* the grass on the housetops, and *as corn* blasted before it be grown up.
27 But I know thy abode, and thy going out, and thy coming in, and thy rage against me.	28 But I know thy abode, and thy going out, and thy coming in, and thy rage against me.
28) Because thy rage against me and thy tumult is come up into mine ears, therefore I will put my hook in thy nose, and my bridle in thy lips, and I will turn thee back by the way by which thou camest.	29) Because thy rage against me**,** and thy tumult**,** is come up into mine ears, therefore will I put my hook in thy nose, and my bridle in thy lips, and I will turn thee back by the way by which thou camest.
29) And this *shall be* a sign unto thee, Ye shall eat this year **such things as grow of themselves**, and **in** the second year that which springeth of the same; and in the third year sow ye, and reap, and plant vineyards, and eat the **fruits** thereof.	30) And this *shall be* a sign unto thee, Ye shall eat *this* year **such as groweth of itself**; and the second year that which springeth of the same: and in the third year sow ye, and reap, and plant vineyards, and eat the **fruit** thereof.
30) And the remnant that is escaped of the house of Judah shall **yet** again take root downward, and bear fruit upward.	31) And the remnant that is escaped of the house of Judah shall again take root downward, and bear fruit upward:
31) For out of Jerusalem shall go forth a remnant, and they that escape out of mount Zion: the zeal of the LORD **of hosts** shall do this.	32) For out of Jerusalem shall go forth a remnant, and they that escape out of mount Zion: the zeal of the LORD **of hosts** shall do this.
32) Therefore thus saith the LORD concerning the king of Assyria, He shall not come into this city, nor shoot an arrow there, nor come before it with **shield**, nor cast a bank against it.	33) Therefore thus saith the LORD concerning the king of Assyria, He shall not come into this city, nor shoot an arrow there, nor come before it with **shields**, nor cast a bank against it.
33) By the way that he came, by the same shall he return, and shall not come into this city, saith the LORD.	34) By the way that he came, by the same shall he return, and shall not come into this city, saith the LORD.
34) For I will defend this city**,** to save it, for mine own sake, and for my servant David's sake.	35) For I will defend this city to save it for mine own sake, and for my servant David's sake.

35) **And it came to pass that night, that** the angel of the LORD went **out**, and smote in the camp of the Assyrians **an** hundred fourscore and five thousand: and when they arose early in the morning, behold, they *were* all dead corpses.	36) **Then** the angel of the LORD went **forth**, and smote in the camp of the Assyrians a hundred **and** fourscore and five thousand: and when they arose early in the morning, behold, they *were* all dead corpses.
36) So Sennacherib king of Assyria departed, and went and returned, and dwelt at Nineveh.	37) So Sennacherib king of Assyria departed, and went and returned, and dwelt at Nineveh.
37) And it came to pass, as he was worshipping in the house of Nisroch his god, that Adrammelech and Sharezer his sons smote him with the sword: and they escaped into the land of Armenia. And Esarhaddon his son reigned in his stead.	38) And it came to pass, as he was worshipping in the house of Nisroch his god, that Adrammelech and Sharezer his sons smote him with the sword; and they escaped into the land of Armenia: and Esarhaddon his son reigned in his stead.

- This comparison between II Kings 19 and Isaiah 37 within the KJB yields the following baseline data (Not claiming these statistics are infallible. It is very possible that I miscounted something.):
    o   2 completely identical verses
    o   2 different prepositions
    o   4 different punctuations
    o   4 cases where singular and plural can both be correct
    o   9 different words and phraseologies
    o   12 different spellings
    o   15 different verse divisions
    o   35 different phrasings

CONCLUSION

- Based upon the textual facts observed in this lesson, it would be wrong to require *verbatim identicality* as the standard for preservation. This standard cannot even be sustained within the King James text. Consequently, it is not helpful or productive for King James advocates to adopt a standard for preservation that cannot even be sustained in the very Bible they are asserting is "perfect."

- The example set forth in scripture is that God's word can be expressed in multiple different phrasings that are equivalent. Requiring "verbatim identicality" as the standard for preservation is demanding more than the Bible claims for itself.

- I believe in "perfect preservation" if by perfect one means the existence of a pure text that does not report information about God, His nature or character, His doctrine, His dispensational dealings with mankind, history, archeology, or science that is false. In short, God's promise to preserve His word assures the existence of a text that has not been altered in its "fundamental character" or "doctrinal content" despite not being preserved in a state of *verbatim identicality*.

WORKS CITED

Reid, David W. *Ridge Farm Bible Conference Notes (2012)*. Columbus, OH: Columbus Bible Church.

Strouse, Thomas. "Every Word: Matthew 4:4" in *Thou Shalt Keep Them: A Biblical Theology of the Perfect Preservation of Scripture*. El Sobrante, CA: Pillar & Ground Publishing, 2003.

Sutton, David. "The Perfect Passive: "It is Written" in *Thou Shalt Keep Them: A Biblical Theology of the Perfect Preservation of Scripture*. El Sobrante, CA: Pillar & Ground Publishing, 2003.

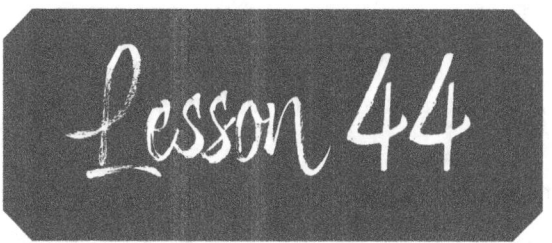

JOT AND TITTLE PRESERVATION, MATTHEW 5:17-18

INTRODUCTION

- In Lesson 42, I demonstrated using Scripture that demanding *verbatim identicality* as the standard for preservation was overreaching and not supported by the Biblical data. Based upon the textual facts observed in Lesson 42, we concluded that it would be wrong to require "verbatim identicality" as the standard for preservation. This standard cannot even be sustained within the King James text. Consequently, it is not helpful or productive for King James advocates to adopt a standard for preservation that cannot even be sustained in the very Bible they are asserting is "perfect."

- In addition, Lesson 43 demonstrated that the testimony of the scriptures does not require verbatim phraseology but simply equivalent meaning. It is possible to say the exact same thing using different words.
    - "At 3:30, I drove to the store."
    - "I drove to the store at half past three."

- Consider the following example from II Timothy 2:15.
    - Geneva — "... dividing the word of truth aright."
    - King James — "... rightly dividing the word of truth."

- The following four proofs that scripture approves of substantive doctrinal equivalence and does not require verbatim identicality were offered in Lesson 43:
    - The fact that New Testament quotes of the Old Testament do not match verbatim.
    - The fact that Old Testament quotations of the Old Testament do not match verbatim.
    - The fact that New Testament quotations of the New Testament do not match verbatim.
    - II Kings 19 and Isaiah 37 do not match verbatim.

- Our comparison between II Kings 19 and Isaiah 37 within the KJB produced the following baseline data (I am not claiming these statistics are infallible. It is very possible that I miscounted something.):
    - 2 completely identical verses
    - 2 different prepositions
    - 4 different punctuations
    - 4 cases where singular and plural can both be correct

- o 9 different words and phraseologies
- o 12 different spellings
- o 15 different verse divisions
- o 35 different phrasings

- The lack of identicality in both phraseology and punctuation exhibited by this comparison calls into question how King James advocates have traditionally understood Christ's statement in Matthew 5:17-18. The goal of this lesson is to consider the meaning of Matthew 5:17-18 considering the textual/historical facts.

- To accomplish this purpose, we will consider the following points:

  - o Use of Matthew 5:17-18 by King James Only Advocates
  - o Use of Matthew 5:17-18 by those critical of the King James Only position

USE OF MATTHEW 5:17-18 BY KING JAMES ONLY ADVOCATES

- Many King James Only advocates have used Matthew 5:17-18 as a proof text for their belief that preservation occurred with exact identicality. In the past, I have used these verses to make the argument for verbatim identicality; so, I know whereof I speak.

- Gary C. Webb's chapter titled "Not One Jot or One Tittle Matthew 5:17-18" in *Thou Shalt Keep Them: A Biblical Theology of the Perfect Preservation of Scripture* stands out as a case in point of this thinking.

- In the introduction, Webb argues that Matthew 5:17-18 establishes the doctrine of verbal plenary preservation or the preservation of "the precise wording of the text of Scripture." Webb states:

- - "The precise wording of the text of Scripture provides the authority of the inspired, inerrant Word of God. When one combines Jesus' promise that "one jot or one tittle shall in no wise pass from the law" with His assertion that spiritual greatness belongs to those who keep and teach the "least commandments," His statements demand a doctrine of verbal and plenary preservation of the text of Scripture." (Webb in *Thou Shalt Keep Them*, 41)

- In a section titled "The Apologetic Assertion of Matthew 5:17-20" Webb identifies the "jot" and "tittle" as follows:

  - "Jesus continued His defense with a solemn statement of the plenary infallibility of the law. He indicated the authority of the smallest portion of the teaching of the Old Testament by referring to the smallest portions of the Hebrew text itself. The "jot" refers to the smallest Hebrew consonant. Modern scholars normally define the "tittle" as only referring to a bend or point in the actual Hebrew letters themselves. Jesus asserted that no portion of the teaching of the Old Testament would pass out of existence, lose its authority, or be annulled until every bit of it had its fulfillment. Indeed, he declared that such an occurrence is an absolute impossibility." (Webb in *Thou Shalt Keep Them*, 43)

- If Webb would have stopped here, I would be inclined to agree with him. Jesus is saying that no detail of the law is going to go unfulfilled. Webb certainly does not stop there, he goes on to argue that Matthew 5:17-18 means that even the "jots" and "tittles" would be preserved with exact identity to what was given under inspiration.

- "The Application of the Passage to the Textual Debate: The Demand for the Verbal Preservation of the Text of Scripture" comprises one of the major sections of Webb's essay. In this section, Webb clearly equates "Verbal Preservation" with exact identicality of wording as the standard for preservation.

- o "Could the changing of one letter in the Hebrew or Greek text change a word and thereby affect the meaning of a command or doctrine? Certainly it could and usually does. What if a Christian, facing severe repercussions, struggles with the issue of complete honesty in a certain situation? The day of importance arrives, and he rises early to meet with his God. His soul agonizes as he opens his New American Standard Version of the Bible to the seventh chapter of John's Gospel, the place assigned by his daily reading schedule. In that passage, he reads that Jesus lied to his brothers, saying that he would not go to the feast in verse 8, when in fact verse 10 says He did go up later. Suppose to read this about Jesus, he nevertheless believes he has his answer from God. A "proper" interpretation of the text tells him he can lie in some circumstances. That "proper" interpretation would also nullify the sinlessness of Christ and render Him incapable of accomplishing our redemption." (Webb in *Thou Shalt Keep Them*, 45-46)

- In this example, Webb is referring to the fact that the NASV follows the Critical Text in John 7:8 in omitting the word "yet" as it reads in the TR and KJB.

John 7:8 (KJB)	John 7:8 (NASV)
Go ye up unto this feast: I go not up **yet** unto this feast; for my time is not yet full come.	"Go up to the feast yourselves; I do not go up to this feast because My time has not yet fully come."

- The problem in verse 8 resides in the fact that in verse 10 in both versions Jesus goes up to the feast.

John 7:10 (KJB)	John 7:10 (NASV)
But when his brethren were gone up, then went he also up unto the feast, not openly, but as it were in secret.	But when His brothers had gone up to the feast, then He Himself also went up, not publicly, but as if, in secret.

- Notice carefully what is going on here. Webb has correctly identified that the NASV's reading in John 7:8 creates a problem with verse 10 by its dropping of the word "yet." Why is the problem created? Because they are not identical in their wording or because they differ substantively? It is because they differ substantively i.e., the Critical Text's omission of the word "yet" creates a textual difficulty within John 7 for the NASB but, more than that, it asserts something that is *opposite* from the TR/KJB. In other words, both readings cannot be factually correct because they teach opposites. Therefore, Webb's example does not prove what he is arguing for, namely that every "jot" and "tittle" must be preserved with *verbatim identicality*. Rather it proves that preservation excludes substantive differences in meaning.

- According to Webb, a reading must have exact precision to be considered the word of God. One wonders what Webb would say about the following pre-King James English translations of the *TR*. The Geneva Bible and the Bishops Bible both contain the word "yet" in John 7:8 but are not identical in the totality of their wording. Yet, they do not differ from each other substantively in terms of their doctrinal content. In other words, they are substantively equivalent without possessing *verbatim identicality*.

Geneva Bible	Bishops Bible	King James
Go ye vp vnto this feast: I wil not go vp yet vnto this feast: for my time is not yet fulfilled.	Go ye vp vnto this feast: I wyll not go vp yet vnto this feast, for my tyme is not yet full come.	Go ye up unto this feast: I go not up yet unto this feast; for my time is not yet full come.

- Webb clearly argues for the preservation of the "exact wording" as his standard for preservation based upon Matthew 5:17-18.

  o "But, as the Lord indicated, the authority and validity of the least command or any command in Scripture depends upon the exact wording of that command in the Scriptural text. . . Jesus immediately states man's obligation to obey and teach all the commands, even the least of them, which demands that we must have the very jots and tittles that express those commands." (Webb in *Thou Shalt Keep Them*, 47)

- Later in this section, Webb provides an example of doubling down on verbal preservation for faith's sake.

  o "Some scholars and textual critics mock this clear, unbiased, derived doctrine of verbal preservation, claiming that the "evidence" of copies containing errors refutes the Bible doctrine (Wallace and Glenny would be a case in point.) . . . (Quotes Rom. 3:3-4) . . . The "evidence" claimed by evolutionists does not cause the believer to give up the Bible doctrine of creation. Why? Because he knows that the evolutionist's humanistic presuppositions have caused him to view and judge the "evidence" wrongly. Likewise, the scholar who follows the humanistic precepts of modern textual criticism makes the same type of error, judging the evidence with rationalistic presuppositions rather than by those in Scripture." (Webb in *Thou Shalt Keep Them*, 47)

- While I agree with Webb concerning the "rationalistic presuppositions" of modern textual criticism, his answer is simply to double down on faith for faith's sake in his understanding of verbal preservation. In doing so, he is demanding *verbatim identicality* of wording as his standard for preservation.

- On page 57 in footnote 59 Webb quotes from Samuel Schnaiter's "Textual Criticism and the Modern English Version Controversy" in Biblical Viewpoint Vol. XVI, No. 1 from 1982. In this quote, Schnaiter states the following regarding Wilbur N. Pickering's view of preservation:

- o "Pickering shows that he has fallen into the error of equating inspiration with preservation as described above. He also demonstrates that his view of the authority of God's Word depends on the recovery of the original wording of the New Testament text. And if it is true that his concept of authority is dependent on the preservation of precise wordings, then it is scarcely conceivable that even such a scholar as he has arrived at his conclusions from the evidence as much as from his predisposition. Knowledge that Pickerings' concept of authority depends upon preservation of precise wordings brings into question his entire procedure." (Webb in *Thou Shalt Keep Them*, 47)

- Just as modern textual criticism has been built upon a set of rationalistic presuppositions, Schnaiter is pointing out that the verbal plenary positon has as well. No one arguing for "the preservation of the precise wordings" can point to which manuscript, TR edition, or edition of the KJB got everything exactly correct. Therefore, this position suffers from the "predisposition" or presupposition that preservation demands *verbatim identicality* of wording. Ruckman knew this, but instead of looking back to the Bible to inform his beliefs as to the *nature* of preservation, he argued that the King James translators were inspired in the same sense as the Biblical writers as a means of providing the *identicality* of wording demanded by this position.

- Watch how Webb doubles down on his own presupposition in footnote 59 following the above quotation from Schnaiter. Webb states the following in response:

  - o "How could a Christian who professes to believe in verbal inspiration make such a statement? Verbal inspiration guarantees "precise wordings," which are the basis for every Christian doctrine. If we do not have "precise wordings," we do not have "the faith which was once delivered unto the saints" (Jude 3). For the Christians, the "predisposition" of a preserved text of Scripture which provides "precise wordings" should underlie our conclusion on the textual debate just as it does our conclusion on every other issue of faith and practice." (Webb in *Thou Shalt Keep Them*, 47)

- This is where Webb's fedeistic (believing) approach needs to be Biblically adjusted by allowing the Bible to teach him how to think about variant readings. If Webb were honest, he would admit that he cannot sustain this standard within the printed history of the KJB-the very Bible he is arguing reproduced the "precise wordings" of the originals.

- In the "Conclusion" to his essay on Matthew 5:17-18 Dr. Webb writes:

  o "In defending Himself against the possible criticism that He came to "destroy" the teaching of the Old Testament, Jesus gave Christians an absolute assurance in Matthew 5:18-19 of the verbal and plenary preservation of the text of Scripture. His Words demand that Christians concerned about textual criticism return to a position of faith, a position that builds its textual method on the teaching of the Bible. Modern textual criticism does not do this but ignores or discounts Jesus' exact assurance.

    Whom then should Christians believe? Did God leave the preservation of the texts of the Old and New Testaments to fallible copyists? Do Christians have only the evidence of history to support the doctrine of preservation? Or did Jesus mean what He taught when He said, "For verily I say unto you, Till heaven and earth pass, one jot or one tittle shall in no wise pass from the law, till all be fulfilled?" Jesus taught that the authority of God's Word rested upon the Divine preservation of the text. Belief in this doctrine leads men today to reject modern textual criticism with its invalid texts and to accept the texts (and the methods that produced them) behind the King James Version of the Bible." (Webb in *Thou Shalt Keep Them*, 50)

- Webb is clearly using Matthew 5:17-18 to advance the notion that preservation extends to the very "jots" and "tittles" and requires *verbatim identicality*. Webb's position is correct in principle regarding the faith approach, but he fails to fully apply his own principle and thereby fails to arrive at a sound and sustainable understanding of preservation. In the end, Webb's essay is an example of Option 2 Faith for Faith's Sake from our chart in Lesson 43.

- *Use of Matthew 5:17-18 in Other King James Only Literature*

- Webb is certainly not alone in using Matthew 5:17-18 as a proof text for the notion of verbal plenary preservation or the notion that preservation occurred with *verbatim identicality*. The following pro-King James authors include the passage in their lists of verses that teach preservation but offer little direct commentary upon the verse:

  o 1975 — *Counterfeit or Genuine: Mark 19? John 8?* Edited by David Otis Fuller

    - See the essay "The Preservation of the Scriptures" by Donald L. Brake on pages 182-183.

  o 1999 — *Forever Settled: A Survey of the Documents and History of the Bible* by Jack A. Moorman

  o 2000 — *Crowned with Glory: The Bible from Ancient Text to Authorized Version* by Dr. Thomas Holland

  o 2007 — *The History of Your Bible: Proving the King James to be the Perfectly Preserved Words of God* by Terence D. McLean

  o 201 3— *Which Bible Would Jesus Use? The Bible Version Controversy Explained and Resolved* by Jack McElroy

- The following authors comment more extensively on how Matthew 5:17-18 relates to or establishes the doctrine of preservation:

  o 1970 — *Which Bible?* Edited by David Otis Fuller

    - "The power and providence of God are displayed in the history of the preservation and transmission of His Word, in fulfillment of the promise of the Son of God, "For verily I say unto you, till heaven and earth pass, one jot or one tittle shall in no wise pass from the law till all be fulfilled" (Matt. 5:18). Our Lord was not given to exaggeration, and God's holy Law was not confined to the commands of Sinai but is set forth in all that He inspired His prophets and apostles to write." (Fuller, 5)

- 1999 — *Myths about the Modern Versions* by David W. Cloud. Regarding Matthew 5:18 and Matthew 24:35 Cloud states the following:

  - "As we see from the above Scriptures, the Lord Jesus Christ is very specific in His teaching about the preservation of Scripture. He teaches that man must have the very words of God, and He promises that His WORDS will not pass away. In Matthew 5:18, He says the very JOTS AND TITTLES of God's Word will not pass away! That is certainly verbal preservation." (109)

- 2003 — *In Awe of thy Word: Understanding the King James Bible Its Mystery & History Letter by Letter* by Gail Riplinger

  - This book is an expansion of Riplinger's earlier book from 1998 titled *The Language of the King James Bible: Discover Its Hidden Built-In Dictionary*. While I have not been able to locate in these volumes the specific use of Matthew 5:17-18, they both demand verbatim identicality as the standard of preservation to the very letter and word order.

  - In 2011, in commemoration of the 400th anniversary of the KJB, Riplinger published an essay titled *Settings of the King James Bible* in which she derided non-British spellings in the English Bible. American printings that changed the spelling of a word like "musick" to "music" were viewed as introducing careless errors into the KJB.

- 2006 — *Defending the King James Bible 3rd Ed.* by D.A. Waite

  - "Not "one jot" nor "one tittle" — that is Bible preservation, isn't it? Now, He's talking about the Old Testament, and I'm sure by extension we can carry that on to the New Testament as well. . . The Lord Jesus said that not one jot or tittle would pass away until all would be fulfilled. So, the Lord Jesus believed in Bible preservation, didn't He? There is good evidence that a tittle is the smallest Hebrew vowel which is a dot." (10-11)

- 2009 — *Glistering Truths: Distinctions in Bible Words* by Matthew Verschuur (Bible Protector)

- "That every jot and tittle in our pure English Bible is necessary for giving the exact sense." (Title Page)

- "In fact, the King James Bible has been called the best translation in the world. If we look at this Bible, that is, at the proper edition of it—the Pure Cambridge Edition—we find that every word is right and good. "(4)

- "Let no man presume that he can improve upon our English Bible as it now stands, pure and perfect. No matter what word, to alter it in any way is to violate the Scriptures' teaching concerning its own certainty and perfection. . . Certainly the King James Bible has gone through the "purified seven times" process to arrive to where it is at now. But this is not license for further changes, updates or alterations once this process has been completed. . . Rightness and exactness of words can be a matter of life and death. The very spelling of Bible words should be observed with the fear of God. . . In order to give the sense accurately, the exact words and letters and punctuation are required." (8)

- "Let us be perfectly clear, changing so much as the word order, spelling or punctuation is destructive." (13)

- "That a change as small as a minor point of punctuation is dire, if not obviously, at least puts in jeopardy the doctrine of the reliability of its jots and tittles." (16)

- The above list does not claim to be exhaustive of every use of Matthew 5:17-18 by King James Only advocates supporting the notion of plenary verbal preservation. Only indexed works were searched, I did not read every line in every work ever written on this topic. That being said, I am confident that the above sampling is indicative of how Matthew 5:17-18 is used by the majority of King James Only advocates.

CONCLUSION

- Matthew 5:17-18 — these verses are clearly referring to the Old Testament scriptures originally given to the nation of Israel.

- Jewish scribes knew they were duplicating God's word, so they went to incredible lengths to prevent error from creeping into their work. The whole process of copying the Bible was controlled by strict religious rituals, and the scribes carefully counted every line, word, syllable, and letter to ensure accuracy.

- The earliest surviving copies of the Hebrew Masoretic Text, the text supporting the King James Old Testament, date from around 900 A.D. Discovered in 1947, the Dead Sea Scrolls date from around 150 B.C. roughly one thousand years earlier. When compared with the Masoretic Text for the book of Isaiah, the Dead Sea Scrolls were found to be word for word identical in over 95% of the text. The remaining 5% variation consisted of obvious slips of the pen and variations in spelling. Dr. Randell Price stated the following in his book on the Dead Sea Scrolls:

  - "Once a comparison was made between the text of the *Isaiah Scroll* and the Masoretic Text, it was evident that, except for minor details (such as spelling) that do not affect the meaning of the text, the two were **almost identical**. Even though the Qumran text was more than six centuries older than the text of the Masoretes, it confirmed the accuracy with which the scribes had carefully preserved and transmitted the biblical text through time." (Price, 127)

- This is historical confirmation of the Biblical promise of Preservation. Yet, even with its high degree of precision, there is not *verbatim identicality*. The use of Matthew 5:17-18 by King James Only advocates demanding *verbatim identicality* or "jot and tittle" precision as the standard for preservation goes too far and demands more than can be historically proven.

- In the next Lesson, we will look at the use of Matthew 5:17-18 by those critical of the King James Only position.

WORKS CITED

Cloud, David W. *Myths About the Modern Bible Versions*. Oak Harbor, WA: Way of Life Literature, 1999.

Fuller, David Otis. *Which Bible?* Grand Rapids, MI: Institute for Biblical Textual Studies, 1970.

Price. Randall. *Secrets of the Dead Sea Scrolls*. Eugene, OR: Harvest House Publishers, 1996.

Verschuur, Matthew. *Glistering Truths: Distinctions in Bible Words*. Bible Protector, 2009.

Waite, D.A. *Defending the King James Bible*. Collingswood, NJ: The Bible For Today Press, 2006.

Webb, Gary C. "Not One Jot or One Tittle Matthew 5:17-18" in *Thou Shalt Keep Them: A Biblical Theology of the Perfect Preservation of Scripture*. El Sobrante, CA: Pillar & Ground Publishing, 2003.

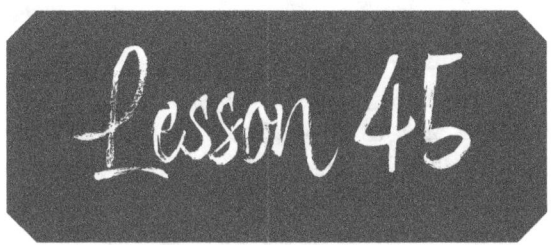

JOT AND TITTLE PRESERVATION, MATTHEW 5:17-18 (PART 2)

INTRODUCTION

- Last week in Lesson 44 we looked at the use of Matthew 5:17-18 by King James Only Advocates. In doing so we observed that many King James defenders use Matthew 5 to establish their insistence upon verbatim identicality as the standard for preservation.

- In this lesson, we want to look at the use of Matthew 5:17-18 by those critical of the King James Only position.

- In conclusion, I will offer my own thoughts on how these verses should be properly understood.

USE OF MATTHEW 5:17-18 BY THOSE CRITICAL OF THE KING JAMES ONLY POSITION

- In Lesson 44 we used Gary C. Webb's essay "Not One Jot or One Tittle Matthew 5:17-18" from *Thou Shalt Keep Them: A Biblical Theology of the Perfect Preservation of Scripture* as a means for framing the discussion.

- In like manner, in this lesson, we will use William C. Combs' essay "The Preservation of Scripture" as framework for structuring our study.

- Combs commences his discussion of Matthew 5:17-18 by noting that the passage "is one of the most commonly referenced passages used to support the preservation of Scripture." Moreover, he identifies the "jot" and "tittle" as follows:

  ○ Jot — "It is universally agreed that the "jot" (ἰῶτα *iota*) refers to the Hebrew (or Aramaic) letter ◌ (*yôd*), the smallest letter in the Hebrew alphabet." (Combs, 21)

  ○ Tittle — "The "tittle" (κεραία *keraia*) literally means "horn," that is, a "projection" or "hook." This is often been understood to refer to small parts of letters, especially to small strokes distinguishing Hebrew letters." (Combs, 21)

- When taken at face value Combs concedes that the phrase "could be understood to teach an absolutely perfect preservation of the "Law." (21) Combs then cites Richard Flanders' essay "Does the Bible Promise Its Own Preservation" as a case in point. Flanders wrote:

  ○ "Some say that this promise refers only to the fulfillment of scripture and not to its preservation. But notice that it says the text of the Bible (to the very letter) will not "pass" in the sense that "heaven and earth" shall one day "pass." The Greek word used here for "pass" is *parelthe*, and it refers to the physical extinction of the thing that shall pass. It can also be translated "perish." Just as God's creation will pass someday, God's Words will never pass! The actual existence of the original text of scripture will continue eternally, just as the physical existence of heaven and earth will not continue." (Quoted in Combs, 21)

- Mark well the nature of Flanders' position. He makes two important assertions: 1) "the text of the Bible, the very letter will not pass" and 2) "the actual existence of the original text of scripture will continue eternally." How is this accomplished according to Flanders? By preservation, of course. If this is not a statement arguing for *verbatim* preservation, I am not sure what is.

- Combs is quick to jump on this point in his comments following the Flanders quote.

    o "Flanders's interpretation is just how Matthew 5:18 is commonly understood from the KJV/TR viewpoint. Cloud explains: "In summary, the Bible promises that God will preserve His Word in pure form, including the most minute details (the jots and tittles [sic], the words), and that this would include the whole Scriptures, Old and New Testaments. The biblical doctrine of preservation is verbal, plenary preservation...." Waite describes this as the "inerrant preservation of the Words of the Bible." But, in fact, these advocates of KJV/TR position do not actually take Matthew 5:18 literally, even though they claim to do so. If not one "jot" or "tittle" is to be changed, then they should insist on using only the 1611 edition of the KJV since "jot" and "tittle" certainly involve spelling, and there have been thousands of spelling changes since 1611." (Combs, 21-22)

- In my opinion, Combs has just pointed out something that the King James Only advocates have not dealt with honestly. If they are going to demand *verbatim identicality* to every "jot and tittle," which edition of the KJB exactly reproduced the original autographs? As we will see below, even Flanders is forced to hedge on this point later in his essay.

- Now Combs has the King James Only advocates positioned right where he wants them in order to deliver what he thinks is a final deciding factual blow.

    - "There are two things to be said about the KJV/TR interpretation of Matthew 5:18. First, it is an *incontrovertible fact*, obvious to anyone who has examined the manuscript evidence, that we do not now possess the words of the autographs in an absolutely inerrant state. This assertion is most significant since it flatly contradicts the whole thesis of the KJV/TR position. I will demonstrate the truth of this assertion later in this essay. Second, Jesus is not teaching in this verse the "inerrant preservation of the Words of the Bible."" (Combs, 22)

Discussing Combs' Statement on the Use of Matthew 5:17-18 by King James Advocates

- Let us now dissect Combs' statement. First, Combs is correct, we cannot know for certain what the words of the original were; if one demands *verbatim identicality* as their standard for preservation and inerrancy. Moreover, he is correct that this fact alone causes the King James Only notion that Matthew 5:17-18 is teaching exact identicality of wording (the very jots and tittles) as the standard for preservation to suffer damage. Even within the Byzantine Text, the textual tradition that King James Advocates favor as the preserved text line, there is not *verbatim identicality* of wording. The same could be said for the printed editions of the TR as well as the various editions of the KJB itself. In this way, the King James Only position is unscriptural because it demands more from the doctrine of preservation than what the Bible asserts.

- Second, what is Combs' standard for speaking about "an absolutely inerrant state?" It is none other than the standard of *verbatim identicality* in wording. While Combs is correct in his criticism of the King James Only position, on the other side of the spectrum he is arguing for the absolute inerrancy of the original autographs that no longer exist and which no one alive has ever seen. What verse of scripture teaches you to believe that God confined His inspired and inerrant word to some non-existent pieces of parchment?

- In this way, both sides are making unscriptural assumptions and talking past each other with the issue of *verbatim identically* being the great mount impassible that divides them. Recall from Lesson 40 that the language "in the original autographs" was added to Protestant doctrinal statements in the latter half of the 19th century as a means of answering the German Higher Critics and Rationalists. In this way, Protestant Christians reworked their position on the Bible based upon terms set by their opponents. This reworked Bibliology became the new orthodoxy in Fundamental and Evangelical circles in the 20th century. In the same way that Protestant scholars in the 19th century overreacted to the forces of liberalism; believers in the 20th century overreacted to the new "Originals Only" orthodoxy by overstating their case in the opposite direction. Therefore, cordial, and productive dialogue on this topic has proved elusive. Both sides are separated by the same thing (the false assumption that preservation requires *verbatim identicality* of wording), do not realize it, and are therefore talking past each other.

- The position I am arguing for in this class is both scriptural as well as logical and in line with the historical and textual facts. The scriptures assert their own inspiration and preservation which means we must have more than the non-existent originals. They do not, however, teach *verbatim identicality* as the standard for preservation.

- Above we saw that Combs quoted Richard Flanders' article "Does the Bible Promise Its Own Preservation" to buttress his point regarding the use of Matthew 5:17-18 by some King James advocates. A deeper look at the Flanders article will prove instructive. Flanders offers the connection between the Dead Sea Scrolls and the Hebrew Masoretic Text as historical proof of the promise of preservation as well as the existence of the Traditional Hebrew supporting the KJB from before the time of Christ (50 BC). Flanders quotes Drs. Gleason Archer and Randall Price to support his conclusion:

- Archer — "... the Hebrew University Isaiah Scroll [of the Dead Sea Scrolls] . . . corresponds **almost letter for letter** with the [traditional text] . . . and yet dates from 50 B.C." (Reproduced from Flanders)

- Price — "Once a comparison was made between the text of the Isaiah Scroll and the Masoretic Text [the traditional Hebrew text], it was evident that, **except for minor details (such as spelling)** that <u>do not affect the meaning of the text</u>, the two were **almost identical** . . . It confirmed the accuracy with which the scribes had carefully preserved and transmitted the biblical text through time." (Reproduced from Flanders)

• Please note that Flanders' quotes do not quite support his position. Above we quoted Flanders as saying the following with respect to Matthew 5:17-18, "But notice that it says the text of the Bible (to the very letter) will not '"pass" in the sense that "heaven and earth" shall one day "pass."'" But then later in the same essay, when seeking to furnish historical proof of "jot and tittle" preservation Flanders quotes two scholars who stop short of the *exact identicality* in preservation that Flanders had previously used Matthew 5:17-18 to argue for.

• Next, note the underlined portion of the quote from Price. Price admits that one does not need *verbatim identicality* for the text to convey the exact same meaning without possessing the exact same words.

• Without realizing the inconsistencies in his argumentation, following the quotes by Archer and Price, Flanders goes on to highlight a very interesting point in the opposite direction. Consider what he says about the nature of textual variants:

  - "To my friend, however, and many scholars like him, the most significant find at the Dead Sea in regard to the Bible's text was the existence of variant texts! The principles of modern textual criticism are based on the assumption that the **exact preservation** of the original text of an ancient document is extremely unlikely." (Flanders)

- This statement on the part of Flanders highlights precisely why modern textual critics adopt a reconstructionist approach to the text. They do not believe in the promise of preservation on account of the fact that it did not occur with *exact identicality*.

- At this point it might be good to remind everyone regarding the definition of the English word preservation. Noah Webster defined the word as follows in *American Dictionary of the English Language*:
  - *Preservation*—the act of preserving or keeping safe; the act of keeping from injury, destruction or decay; as the *preservation* of life or health; the *preservation* of buildings from fire or decay; the *preservation* of grain from insects; the *preservation* of fruit or plants. When a thing is kept entirely from decay, **or nearly in its original state**, we say it is in a high state of *preservation*.

- Even according to the English dictionary, something does not have to be in an *identical* state or condition in order to qualify as having been preserved.

Combs and Glenny on the Correct Understanding of Matthew 5:17-18

- Having rejected how many King James advocates utilize Matthew 5:17-18 in their argumentation, Combs offers the following alternative:
  - "Matthew 5:18 is first of all an example of hyperbole, "a conscious exaggeration or a type of overstatement in order to increase the effect of what is being said." In a graphic way, then, this text makes a point similar to Isaiah 40:8—if "not the smallest letter or stroke shall pass from the Law until all is accomplished," the "Law" is immutable; it "stands forever." "No part of the law, not the most insignificant letter, was to be set aside"; "the law is

unalterable." But unlike Isaiah 40:8, this text is more directly tied to Scripture since "Law" in verse 18 is at least a reference to the Torah, more probably the entire OT. But again, this is not to be taken literally, as though Jesus were promising that no Hebrew manuscript could be changed or that no copyist could make an error. This is simply a hyperbolic way of saying that God's written revelation cannot be changed.

If the Scripture cannot be changed, then it obviously remains valid, with full authority. Thus, the emphasis in Matthew 5:18 is more on the *authority* and *validity* of the OT, not primarily its preservation. As Moo observes: "Probably, then, we should understand v. 18 to be an endorsement of the continuing 'usefulness' or authority of the law." Thus, this verse makes no *direct* affirmation concerning preservation; however, the emphasis on the continuing authority of the Scriptures can *by implication* be used to argue for the preservation of those same Scriptures." (Combs, 22-23)

- In summation, Combs views the passage as dealing more generally with the authority and validity of the Old Testament than with the exact preservation of every word of scripture.

- W. Edward Glenny writing in 1997, a few years before Combs, took a similar yet somewhat different understanding of Matthew 5:17-18.

    o "Matthew 5:18 is clearly speaking of the fulfillment in Christ of OT ethical (3:15) and prophetic (1:23; 2:15; 4:14; etc.) texts. When Matthew writes in verse 18 "Till heaven and earth pass, one jot or one tittle shall in no wise pass from the law, till all be fulfilled," it must be read in light of its context. Verse 17 says, "Think not that I am come to *destroy* the law, or the prophets; I am not come to destroy, but to *fulfill*." The point of the verse is that Jesus did not come to destroy (or to perpetuate for that matter) the OT Law. He is the one whom all the OT points to (Luke 24:25-27, 44-46) and He came to fulfill all that was prophesied about Him in it. Ryrie comments in his study notes that "The Lord's point is that every letter of every word in the O.T. is vital and will be fulfilled." This passage is not speaking about the preservation of the exact words found in the autographa; it is declaring that all the prophecies in the OT which pointed to Christ will be fulfilled down to the smallest detail. In addition, the context makes it clear that Jesus is speaking about the fulfillment of every detail in the OT text. Matthew 5:18 does not ever refer to the NT text, let alone speak of its perfect supernatural preservation." (Glenny in *The Bible Version Debate*, 87)

- In a nutshell Glenny is saying that Matthew 5:17-18 are asserting that even the smallest details of the Old Testament are going to be fulfilled.

CONCLUSION

- In the past I believed that Matthew 5:17-18 taught jot and tittle preservation. When I taught the series *Final Authority: Locating God's Word in English* here at the church in 2010, I used Matthew 5:17-18 to assert the notion that preservation took place with *exact identicality*. Now in the light of further research and study I would no longer hold to my former position on Matthew 5:17-18. This does not mean, however, that I do not believe in the fundamental promise of preservation.

- Matthew 5:17-18 is simply teaching that no detail of the Law is going to go unfilled by the Lord Jesus Christ. He was the perfect fulfillment of the righteous requirements of the law.

- Given that the passage is not asserting that the Old Testament was preserved with *exact identicality* there is no reason to argue by extension that Matthew 5:18-19 is teaching the *verbatim* preservation of the New Testament. This is a King James Only argument used to buttress their position of perfect or verbal plenary preservation.

- As I said in Lesson 28:
  - God promised to preserve His word.
    - Psalms 12:6-7; 119:111, 152, 160; Isaiah 30:8; 40:8; Matthew 4:4; 24:35; I Peter 1:23-25
  - God did not see fit to preserve His word by preserving the originals.
    - This is self-evident because the originals no longer exist.

The Historical Development of Protestant Bibliology

Protestant Bibliology Before 1860

- *Inspiration*—Divine Dictation accepted descriptor for how inspiration was accomplished; not limited to the original autographs and extended to vernacular languages via translation. Translations = the word of God (Westminster Confession of Faith)
- *Preservation*—believed in the promise of preservation: "... being immediately inspired by God, and, by His singular care and providence, kept pure in all ages, are therefore authentical ..." (WCF)
- *Inerrancy*—no formal doctrine of inerrancy; the scriptures were believed to be inerrant because they are the word of God; the Holy Spirit bears witness with the believer's spirit that the scriptures are infallible. (WCF)
- *Textual Criticism*—began with the notion the scriptures were the inspired word of God and of Divine origin; what God gave by inspiration was preserved and "kept pure in all ages" and was available to be translated into the vernacular languages of the nations.

Protestant Bibliology Is Attacked

Between 1860 and 1900 the Protestant view of the Bible was attacked and rewritten in response to the following forces: 1) Evolution, 2) Liberalism/Modernism, 3) German Higher Criticism, and 4) Rationalism. The attackers point out the existence of *variant readings* in the manuscript copies as part of their attack on Protestant Bibliology. The existence of *variant readings* leads to a confining of inspiration, infallibility, and inerrancy to the nonexistent original autographs. It was widely thought by defenders of the Bible at the time that the scriptural standard for preservation required "verbatim identicality." This understanding combined with the undeniable existence of a multitude of *variant readings* in the body of manuscripts became Mt. Impassable for those wishing to hold to historic Protestant Bibliology.

Protestant Bibliology Is "Revised" After 1860

Instead of holding the line in the face of attack, Protestant Theologians "revised" Protestant Bibliology according to terms set by their opponents. In an attempt to address the existence of *variant readings* noted above were altered in the following ways:

- *Inspiration*—was limited to the nonexistent original autographs; Divine Dictation is dropped and ridiculed as a descriptor for how inspiration was accomplished.
- *Preservation*—the promise of preservation was dropped from doctrinal statements.
- *Inerrancy*—formal doctrine developed that limited inerrancy to the nonexistent original autographs; took shape in a logical syllogism that meet the German Higher Critics on their own terms.
- *Textual Criticism*—was completely reworked starting with the rationalistic/naturalistic notion that the Bible is like any other book and should be treated in like manner to any work of antiquity. Replaced the text of the Reformation (TR) with a "new and improved" Greek text. Modern Textual Criticism is built on top of the Rationalistic suppositions of Westcott & Hort.

These "revised" points became the new Protestant Orthodoxy on the Bible and were carried forward into the 20th century by Fundamentalists in their doctrinal statements.

FROM THIS GENERATION FOR EVER | VOL. 2

Option 1: Originals Only Position

Developed in the late 19th and early 20th centuries as a reaction against the German Higher Critics and Rationalists. During this time doctrinal statements were rewritten to include the language "in the Originals Only" and dropped all references to preservation. This position confines inspiration and Inerrancy to the nonexistent original autographs as a means of dealing with the *variant readings*. Has led some to deny that the scriptures promise their own preservation. Advocates argue that it is their job to reconstruct the Biblical text. Position is nonscientific and non-falsifiable, in the absence of the originals how does one know whether they have accurately reconstructed the text. Modern Versions existed since the Revised Version of 1881 but did not succeed in replacing the widespread use of the KJB by American Christians. After WWII the Neo-Evangelical movement grew in popularity and heavily promoted the new Protestant Orthodoxy on the Bible ("Originals Only") as well as Modern Versions. Position is of no practical consequence and cannot be maintained by faith in God's word.

Option 2: Faith for Faith's Sake Position

Formed in the late 1960s and early 70s as a reaction against Option 1 and the sudden popular use of Modern Versions, and their divergent readings from the traditional King James text. Just as Option 1 was forged as a reaction to the attack on Protestant Bibliology in the late 19th century, Option 2 is a reactionary position against Option 1. By the time one gets to Option 2 they are two steps removed from the Protestant Bibliology that existed before 1860 as outlined at the top of the chart. This position pretends like *variant readings* don't exist and insists upon plenary verbal preservation or the notion the preservation occurred with "verbatim identicality" of wording. Some incorrectly insist that God re-inspired His word in English between 1604 and 1611 as a means of providing the "verbatim identicality" of wording this view of preservation demands. Has the correct starting point, is consistent with the fideistic (believing) approach to Scripture; but carries the corollary between preservation and inspiration too far. Refuses to acknowledge the textual/historical facts that no two Greek manuscripts (even Byzantine); editions of the *TR*, or printings of the KJB are exactly the same.

Option 3: Biblically Amended Position on Preservation (The Solution)

In light of the internal and theological problems created by Options 1 & 2 an amended position is necessary. Drops "verbatim identicality" as the standard for preservation. If one allows the KJB to teach them about the *nature of preservation* they will conclude that demanding "verbatim identicality" as the standard for preservation was overreaching to begin with. There are at least four Scriptural proofs found within the KJB that support this conclusion:

1) How the OT quotes OT
2) How the NT quotes the OT
3) How the NT quotes the NT
4) Comparison between II Kings 19 & Isaiah 37 (See notes for Lesson 43)

Observing these realities allows one to maintain their belief in the promise of preservation without overstating the facts. This Biblically revised position can still be maintained by faith in God's word without abandoning the fideistic (believing) approach to Scripture. Maintaining this position allows one to hit a RESET button so to speak and return to a position on inspiration and preservation that is more in line with the Protestant Bibliology enunciated before 1860. This position is true to the Protestant doctrine of *sola scriptura* and rids the discussion of unscriptural rationalistic presuppositions.

Pastor Bryan Ross – Grace Life Bible Church – Grand Rapids, MI

- - God did not supernaturally over-take the pen of every scribe, copyist, or typesetter who ever handled the text to ensure that no differences of any kind entered the text.
    - Differences exist at every level of this discussion.
  - If the standard for preservation is "plenary" or "pristine" identicality, why did God not just preserve the originals and thereby remove all doubt?
- If God intended to preserve His word with *verbatim identicality*, we would have historical/textual evidence that preservation occurred with that level of precision. No such evidence exists.
- This does not mean that one must abandon belief in the promise of preservation in the face of variant readings. Rather, it means that one must amend their understanding of preservation to match what the Bible teaches about the matter. Please consider the following chart titled "The Historical Development of Protestant Bibliology" designed to capture in graphic form the major ideas expressed in Lessons 41-45.
- To be clear, I do believe in a perfect Bible if, by "perfect," one means the following:
  - I believe in *"perfect preservation"* if, by "perfect," one means the existence of a pure text that does not report information about God, His nature or character, His doctrine, His dispensational dealings with mankind, history, archeology, or science that is false. In short, God's promise to preserve His word assures the existence of a text that has not been altered in its "character" or "doctrinal content" despite not being preserved in a state of *"verbatim identicality."*

WORKS CITED

Combs, William W. "The Preservation of Scripture?" in *Detroit Baptist Seminary Journal*. Fall 2000.

Flanders, Richard. Does the Bible Promise its Own Preservation.

Glenny, W. Edward. "The Preservation of Scripture" in *The Bible Version Debate: The Perspective of Central Baptist Theological Seminary*. Minneapolis, MN: Central Baptist Theological Seminary, 1997.

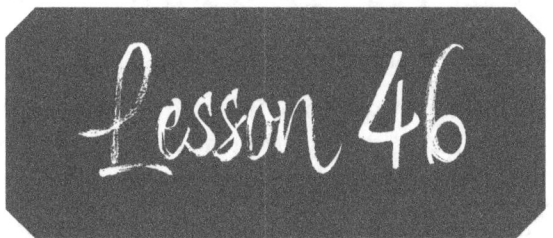

FINAL THOUGHTS ON THE COROLLARY AND THE EXTENT OF PRESERVATION

INTRODUCTION

- Last week in Lesson 45 we finished our two-part discussion of Matthew 5:17-18 and its impact upon the doctrine of preservation. In conclusion, we observed:

  o Matthew 5:17-18 is simply teaching that no detail of the Law is going to go unfilled by the Lord Jesus Christ. He was the perfect fulfillment of the righteous requirements of the law.

- o Given that the passage is not asserting that the Old Testament was preserved with exact identicality, there is no reason to argue by extension that Matthew 5:18-19 is teaching the verbatim preservation of the New Testament. This is a King James Only argument used to buttress their position of perfect or verbal plenary preservation.
  - o If God intended to preserve His word with verbatim identicality we would have historical/textual evidence that preservation occurred with that level of precision. No such evidence exists.
  - o This does not mean that one must abandon belief in the promise of preservation in the face of variant readings. Rather, it means that one must amend their understanding of preservation to match what the Bible teaches about the matter.

- To be clear, I do believe in a perfect Bible if, by "perfect," one means the following:
  - I believe in "perfect preservation" if, by "perfect," one means the existence of a pure text that does not report information about God, His nature or character, His doctrine, His dispensational dealings with mankind, history, archeology, or science that is false. In short, God's promise to preserve His word assures the existence of a text that has not been altered in its "character" or "doctrinal content" despite not being preserved in a state of "verbatim identicality." (Lesson 45)

- In Lessons 41 and 42 we considered whether preservation was the corollary of inspiration. We concluded that a corollary between the two doctrines does exist in a general sense but that there is an inherent danger in overstating the connection. We concluded that the corollary is carried too far when one demands that preservation occurred with *verbatim identicality*. In Lesson 43 we looked at four categories of scriptural proof demonstrating that it was excessive to demand *verbatim identicality* as the standard for preservation in the first place: 1) how the Old Testament quotes the Old Testament, 2) how the New Testament quotes the Old Testament, 3) how the New Testament quotes the New Testament, and 4) II Kings 19 and Isaiah 37.

- Having considered how Matthew 5:17-18 fits into this discussion we are ready to conclude our discussion of the corollary and the extant of preservation. To accomplish this task, we will look at the following points in this lesson:
    - The Argument from Authority
    - Final Thoughts on the Extent of Preservation

THE ARGUMENT FROM AUTHORITY

- Once again, Dr. William W. Combs of Detroit Baptist Seminary raises this point in his essay "The Preservation of Scripture." Combs states:
    - "Closely tied to the argument for preservation based on a correlation between inspiration and preservation is another corollary between the *authority* of Scripture and preservation." (Combs, 29)

- Essentially this argument is based upon the notion that for the scriptures to possess any *authority* they must have been preserved in some sense. Combs quotes Harold Stigers's essay "Preservation: The Corollary of Inspiration" to illustrate this secondary use of the corollary.
    - "The preservation of the Scriptures is bound up with their authority so that the two are really indissoluble. The former is a most necessary outgrowth of their inspiration." (Stigers, 217)

- In essence Stigers is arguing that ". . . since the Scriptures are authoritative, an authority that comes from inspiration (2 Timothy 3:16), the Scriptures can have no continuing authority unless they are preserved." (Combs, 29) In other words, the scriptures possess their authority precisely because they were given by inspiration of God. Likewise, if the words given by inspiration were not preserved, the scriptures would not retain their authority. This is a different approach to the corollary than what we have seen thus far in our study of the concept based upon *verbatim identicality* of wording.

- In his 1973 essay "Autographs, Amanuenses, and Restricted Inspiration" Greg L. Bahnsen states the following regarding "dependable" preservation:

  o "It is certainly legitimate for us to maintain that God in His sovereignty has preserved His Word in dependable form for all generations. To be a Christian *requires* the possession of God's words as a basis for faith and direction in life...and men in all generations are *responsible* to be Christians." (Bahnsen, 110)

- Concerning the *authority* of scripture, Dr. Wayne Grudem stated the following in his popular *Systematic Theology*:

  o "The authority of Scripture means that all the words in Scripture are God's words in such a way that to disbelieve or disobey any word of Scripture is to disbelieve or disobey God." (Grudem, 73)

- This type of authority is found in the fact that these words were given by inspiration of God (II Timothy 3:16-17). The purposes for which scripture is profitable–namely, doctrine, reproof, correction, and instruction in righteousness-cannot be fulfilled unless the scriptures are preserved. This is where Combs sees the impact of texts such as Matthew 5:17-18 and John 10:35 upon the doctrine of preservation.

  o "This is where Matthew 5:17–18 and John 10:35 also tie into the doctrine of preservation. Since both passages teach a continuing authority for Scripture, as we have demonstrated, they indirectly support a doctrine of preservation. But the same can be said for numerous texts that command the believer's obedience. If these texts are essential to the believer's sanctification, and they are, they must have been preserved." (Combs, 30)

- In this way Combs and others maintain a belief in the promise of preservation in a general sense. Preservation must have occurred or else the scriptures would have no enduring authority. In this way preservation is the corollary of inspiration.

FINAL THOUGHTS ON THE EXTENT OF PRESERVATION

- It is only when one demands that preservation requires the same precision as inspiration i.e., *verbatim identicality* that the corollary runs into trouble. Lessons 42 through 45 were devoted to highlighting this point.

- When discussing the extant of preservation, one must clearly identify what they mean by the words "perfect," "pure," and "error." By perfect most commentators on both sides of the issue mean *verbatim identicality*. Consider the following statements made by Dr. Combs:

    o "How pure have the original words of the biblical writings been preserved? It is an indisputable fact, proven by the manuscripts and versional evidence, that God has not perfectly (that is, without error) preserved the Scriptures throughout their long history of transmission. There is no single manuscript, printed text, or version that can be shown to be error free. This is patently obvious to anyone who is at all familiar with the transmission history of the Scriptures. First, we should note that no two Greek manuscripts of the New Testament agree exactly; these thousands of manuscripts all differ from one another to some degree. No one has ever suggested, even within the KJV/TR camp, that a particular one of these manuscripts is a perfect copy of the autographs — that it is error free. This conclusively demonstrates that God has permitted errors to enter the transmission process, which is the inevitable result of providential preservation." (Combs, 49-50)

- Mark well that for Combs an "error" constitutes a textual variant of any kind. In this way he is assuming *verbatim identicality* as the standard for preservation. When one Biblically amends their position on preservation (See Lessons 42 and 43) and thereby realizes that preservation did not occur with *exact identicality*; it brings the entire discussion on the extant of preservation into focus. On this amended view of preservation, an "error" would constitute a variant that substantively alters the doctrinal content of the Bible. Variants that constitute a different way of saying the same thing are not "errors" because they are substantively equivalent.

- According to this Biblically adjusted view of preservation, the terms "pure" and "perfect" do not demand *exact identicality* of wording but simply substantively equivalent meaning. I have no problem speaking about "pure" or "perfect" preservation if by "perfect" one means

    o "The existence of a pure text that does not report information about God, His nature or character, His doctrine, His dispensational dealings with mankind, history, archeology, or science that is false. In short, God's promise to preserve His word assures the existence of a text that has not been altered in its "character" or "doctrinal content" despite not being preserved in a state of "*verbatim identicality*."

- If preservation did not occur with this level of "perfection" or "purity" then how could the scriptures have any authority as identified in point one?

- Combs is correct to point out that the textual facts do not seem to matter to most King James Only advocates, "So we see that the evidence of manuscripts, texts, and versions means nothing to those in the KJV/TR camp." (Combs 35) Most are content to double down on faith for faith's sake in the promise of preservation. After quoting statements regarding the need for faith in God's word by

King James advocates David Cloud and Jack Moorman; Combs states the following:

> o "In one sense Moorman is absolutely correct. What the Bible teaches about its own preservation is to be accepted by faith. But that can be said of everything the Bible teaches — everything the Bible teaches is to be accepted by faith. This argument from faith or "the logic of faith," as Hills likes to call it, actually boils down to faith in the KJV as the perfectly preserved Word of God, in spite of all the evidence to the contrary. This is not faith, at least not in the biblical sense, but pure presumption.
>
> The fundamental fallacy in KJV/TR position can be traced to the faulty premise that the Scriptures themselves teach a perfect and inerrant preservation of the actual words of the autographs. We saw this earlier in Flanders's statement that "the actual existence of the original text will continue eternally...." It is not enough to hold a Bible in one's hand, even a King James Bible, and say this is the Word of God; the KJV/TR position insists that one must be able to say that these are the *Words* of God. Anything else, according to Waite, is "an apostate, heretical, modernistic, and liberal position." (Combs, 36)

- Combs is correct that faith in "the perfectly preserved Word of God" cannot be maintained by faith in God's word if by "perfect" one means matching the original autographs with *exact identicality*. That is a presumption because the word of God teaches no such doctrine.

- Before we are too hard on the likes of Cloud, Waite, and Moorman, it needs to be made clear that the Originals Only position is equally guilty of making unbiblical rationalistic presumptions. There is no verse of scripture that teaches that inspiration, infallibility, and inerrancy are confined to the non-existent original autographs alone. Therefore, this position cannot be held by faith in God's word either. It was a position forged as a rationalistic response to German Higher Criticism and Rationalism during the latter half of the 19th century. It was largely on account of the existence of textual variants that inspiration, infallibility, and inerrancy were confined to the original autographs.

- Once again, both positions are forged by taking an equally presumptuous approach to how to account for the lack of *verbatim identicality* in the surviving manuscript copies. Differences in wording are not inherently a problem so long as they do not report information that is false or contradictory. This is where we must recognize the difference between 1) a different way of saying the same thing, and 2) substantive differences in meaning. I know from personal experience that this distinction is lost on many King James Only advocates. For many King James Only advocates such as Waite, any difference of any kind constitutes a situation where one is forced to declare which reading is the word of God.

  o "Thus one cannot honestly, according to Waite, say that the NASB is the Word of God. He complains that if one holds "his King James in his hand and the New American Standard in his hand with 5,604 differences in their Greek texts in the New Testament alone, how can they both be the 'Word' of God? 'Word of God' could not mean the 'Words of God' because of these differences in the Words.'" (Quoted in Combs, 36)

- Waite fails to distinguish between the nature of these differences. I reject the Critical Text and the NASB because many of these 5,604 differences are substantive: not merely different ways of saying the same thing. But mark well that is not what Waite is saying, he is making the categorical statement that any differences of wording of any kind is an attack on the word of God. The problem here is one of consistency. The printed editions of the KJB contain different wording yet Waite is not willing to identify which edition of the KJB got all the words "perfect."

Concluding Thoughts from Combs

- Professor Combs concludes his section on "The Extent of Preservation" with the following paragraph:

  o "The true situation is this: God has preserved his Word to this day, but because of the means he has chosen to use to accomplish this preservation — providentially, through secondary causation — the words of the autographs have not been inerrantly preserved. Instead, God has chosen to allow for variations to occur — variants within the Hebrew, Aramaic, and Greek copies of the autographs. God has providentially provided all these copies in order to preserve the Scriptures. So it is proper to say that preservation has taken place in the totality of manuscripts. Because God chose this method of preservation, it was not possible to provide a perfectly pure text with no variations (errors). It was sufficient for God's purpose to preserve his Word in copies of the autographs whose exact wording contains some variation. This level of purity is sufficient for God's purposes." (Combs, 37)

- In the end, Combs is partly right and partly wrong. Combs doubles down in the opposite direction of Waite. He insists that "the words of the autographs have not been inerrant preserved" because he is assuming *verbatim identicality* as his standard for *inerrant* preservation. Therefore, inerrancy is only applicable to the original autographs. Combs' insistence upon *exact identicality* of wording is reiterated in his statement that "it was not possible to provide a perfectly pure text with no variations." For Combs the mere presence of textual variants negates prefect/inerrant preservation because of how he is using those words.

- I also disagree with his conclusion that preservation occurred in the "totality of manuscripts." This is not possible since some of the manuscript copies do possess substantive differences in meaning and some, in certain readings, teach opposite information.

- In contrast, I believe Combs to be correct with respect to the following statements:

    o "God has preserved his Word to this day."

    o "God has chosen to allow for variations to occur."

    o "It was sufficient for God's purpose to preserve his Word in copies of the autographs whose exact wording contains some variation. This level of purity is sufficient for God's purposes."

- Next week we will begin discussing the method of preservation by looking at whether "providential" is an appropriate descriptor to utilize when discussing how preservation occurred.

WORKS CITED

Bahnsen, Greg L. "Autographs, Amanuenses and Restricted Inspiration," in Evangelical Quarterly 45 (April-June 1973).

Combs, William W. "The Preservation of Scripture?" in *Detroit Baptist Seminary Journal.* Fall 2000.

Grudem, Wayne. *Systematic Theology.* Grand Rapids, MI: Zondervan, 1994.

Stigers, Harold. "Preservation: The Corollary of Inspiration" in *Journal of the Evangelical Theological Society* 22 (September 1979).

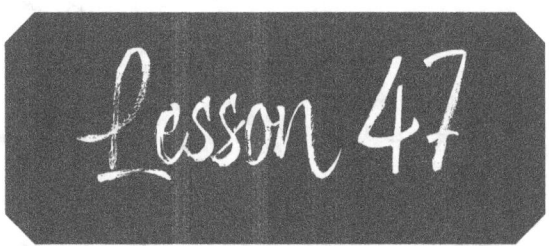

THE METHOD OF PRESERVATION: PROVIDENTIAL OR MIRACULOUS?

INTRODUCTION

- In Lessons 28 and 29 we began the second term of the class with an Introduction to Preservation. After reviewing some key points regarding inspiration from the first term, we took stock of the following facts exhibited on this chart:

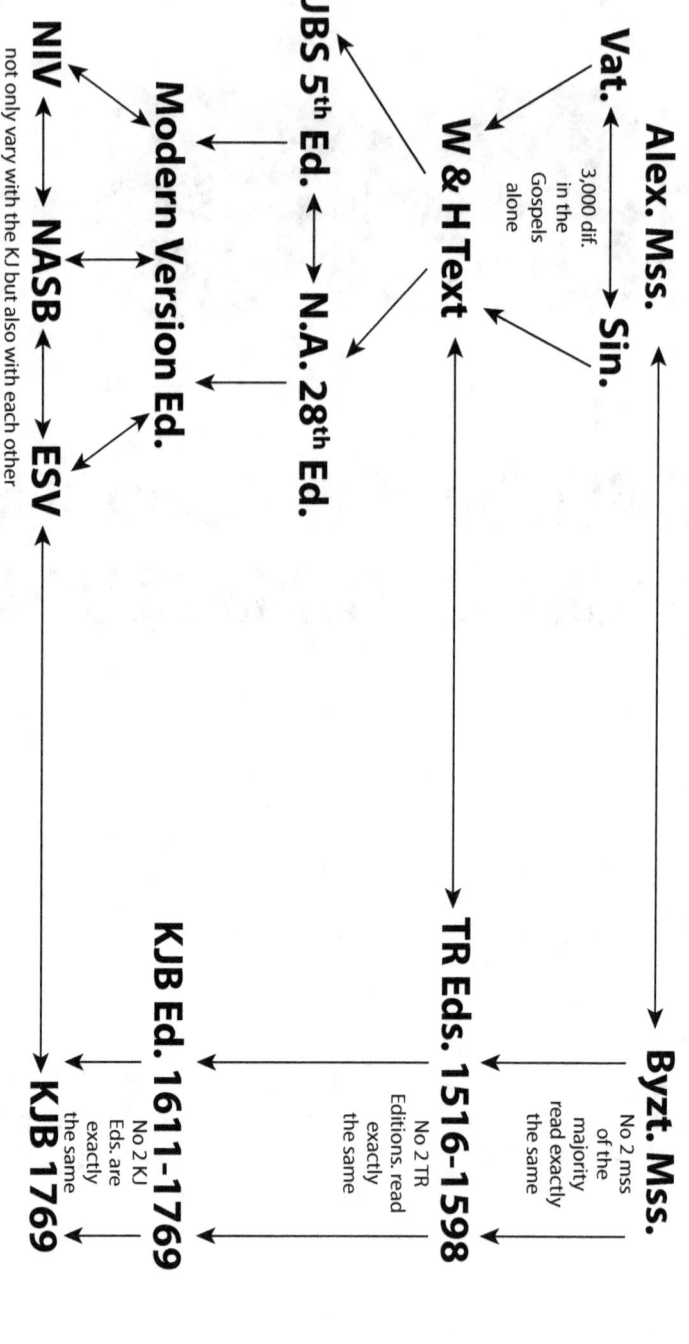

- Summary Statement:

  - "If the preservation of the Word of God depends upon exact preservation of the words of the original documents, then the situation is dire. No two manuscripts contain exactly the same words. No two editions of the Masoretic Text contain exactly the same words. No two editions of the *Textus Receptus* contain exactly the same words. No two modifications of the King James Version contain exactly the same words and the Bible nowhere tells us which edition, if any, does contain the exact words of the originals. These are not speculations, these are plain facts." (Bauder, 155)

- In Lesson 29 we used the Book of Jeremiah as a case study to prove that God could preserve His word without preserving the original autographs.

- In Lesson 30, after discussing the Core Issue of Preservation versus Restoration, we studied how the textual facts presented in Lessons 28 and 29 have given birth to the following three views on the doctrine of preservation:

  - View 1 — Denial of a Doctrine of Preservation
  - View 2 — Preservation in the KJV/TR/MT Tradition
  - View 3 — Preservation in the Totality of Manuscripts

- With these three views in mind, Lessons 31 through 38 were devoted to determining whether the scriptures teach their own preservation.

  - Psalm 12:6-7 (Lessons 31 & 32)
  - Psalm 119: 111, 152, 160 (Lesson 33)
  - Isaiah 30:8; 40:8; I Peter 1:23-25 (Lessons 34 & 35)
  - Matthew 4:4 (Lessons 36 & 37)
  - Matthew 24:35 (Lesson 38)

- Lesson 39 brought closure to our study of the relevant passages and concluded that the scriptures do promise their own preservation. This conclusion was arrived at through a consideration of the following four points:

    o Preservation: The Bible's Claim for Itself

    o Preservation: God Keeps His Promises

    o Preservation: The Superiority of the Fideistic Approach

    o Preservation: The Historic Position of the Reformers

- In Lesson 40 we studied "Why Preservation Matters" by looking at how Protestant Bibliology was revamped during the latter half of the 19th century. Moreover, we considered the agnosticism of Bart Ehrman as an example of the logical conclusion of the reworked Bibliology and its removal of the promise of preservation.

- More recently, Lessons 41 through 46 covered the corollary between preservation and inspiration as well as the extant of preservation. These lessons presented the notion that preservation did not occur with *verbatim identicality* and that some have carried the corollary too far and used it to make unscriptural assertions regarding preservation.

- In this Lesson we want to begin a consideration of the method of preservation. We will begin this study by looking at whether "providential" is an appropriate descriptor to describe the method of preservation.

Preservation: Miraculous or Providential?

- First, we saw in Lessons 31 through 39 the scriptures do teach their own preservation.

- Psalm 12:6-7; 119:111, 152, 160; Isaiah 30:8; 40:8; Matthew 4:4; 24:35; I Peter 1:23-25

- Given that preservation is the Bible's claim for itself, it must have occurred, or else God would have failed to keep his promise (Numbers 23:19; Titus 1:2). This means that the Godhead was active in some way, shape, manner, or form to ensure the fulfillment of the fundamental promise of preservation. The question is how does one explain/understand how the Godhead accomplished the preservation of scripture?

- Before there was a textual or King James Only controversy, the Protestant Reformers elected to describe preservation as "providential" in their early doctrinal statements. The following language from Chapter I Article VIII from *The Westminster Confession of Faith* (1646) was repeated in the *Savoy Declaration of Faith and* Order of 1658, London Baptist Confession of 1689, and Philadelphia Baptist Confession of 1742.

  - "The Old Testament in Hebrew (which was the native language of the people of God of old), and the New Testament in Greek (which, at the time of the writing of it, was most generally known to the nations), being immediately inspired by God, and, **by His singular care and providence, kept pure in all ages**, are therefore authentical; so as, in all controversies of religion, the Church is finally to appeal unto them. But, because these original tongues are not known to all the people of God, who have right unto, and interest in the Scriptures, and are commanded, in the fear of God, to read and search them, therefore they are to be translated in to the vulgar language of every nation unto which they come, that, the Word of God dwelling plentifully in all, they may worship Him in an acceptable manner; and, through patience and comfort of the Scriptures, may have hope."

- Consequently, there has been a long-standing precedent within Protestantism to not only affirm belief in the promise of preservation but to do so using the term "providence" as a descriptor for how preservation occurred.

- Therefore, one should not be surprised to find Edward F. Hills, a Presbyterian defender of the Traditional Text in the 20th century, using the term "providential" to describe how preservation occurred. As a graduate of Westminster Theological Seminary, Hills viewed himself as a defender of the historic position enunciated by the *Westminster Confession of Faith*. We have already observed the following statement from Hills' 1956 work *The King James Version Defended* regarding "providential preservation" in Lesson 8.

    - "If the doctrine of divine inspiration of the Old and New Testament Scripture is a true doctrine, the doctrine of the **providential preservation** of the Scriptures must also be a true doctrine. It must be that down through the centuries God has exercised a **special providential control** over the copying of the Scriptures and the preservation and use of the copies, so that trustworthy representatives of the original text have been available to God's people in every age. God must have done this, for if He gave the Scriptures to His Church by inspiration as the perfect and final revelation of His will, then it is obvious that He would not allow this revelation to disappear or undergo any alteration of its fundamental character.

        Although this doctrine of the **providential preservation** of the Old and New Testament Scriptures has sometimes been misused, nevertheless, it also has been held, either implicitly or explicitly, by all branches of the Christian Church as a necessary consequence of the divine inspiration of these Scriptures." (Hills, 2)

- Elsewhere in *The King James Bible Defended*, when discussing the minor differences that exist in the various editions of the *TR*, Dr. Hills recognizes a difference between what he calls "providential" and "miraculous" preservation.

    - "The texts of the several editions of the *Textus Receptus* were God-guided. They were set up under the leading of God's **special providence**. Hence the differences between them were kept to a minimum. But these disagreements were not eliminated altogether, for this would require not merely **providential** guidance but a **miracle**. In short, God chose to preserve the New Testament text **providentially** rather than **miraculously**, and this is why even the several editions of the *Textus Receptus* vary from each other slightly." (Hills, 222-223)

- We have already seen in Lessons 41 through 46 that using *verbatim identicality* as the standard for preservation is overreaching. In order to accomplish preservation in a state of *Xeroxed identicality* God would have had to supernaturally, i.e. miraculously, overtaken the pen of every scribe, copyist, typesetter, and printer who ever handled the text to ensure that no differences of any kind ever entered the text. That God did not choose to accomplish preservation in this manor is apparent because there are slight differences even in the manuscripts comprising the Byzantine Text Type not to mention the various editions of the *TR*.

- That being said, the question at hand in Lesson 47 is how does one explain how this was accomplished? Hills looks at the historical data and concludes that preservation could not have been "miraculous" because of the existence of textual variants. These statements by Hills ought to make one wonder how he is using the term "miraculous." The first definition for "miraculous" offered by the *Oxford English Dictionary* is ". . . not explicable by natural laws; supernatural."

- In recent conversation regarding these matters our beloved Brother David Reid stated the following:

    o "I am not sure that preservation was not miraculous as the term is properly defined. Miraculous means "not explicable by natural laws, supernatural." We critique modern textual theory when it treats the Bible the same as any other book and fails to account for its unique character. Did God inspire His word and then simply leave it to natural human processes with zero involvement by God as to whether and to what extent His word was preserved? The answer has to be no. God did and does something because He has promised to preserve His word, and He is going to make sure that it happens. That something that God does is beyond common human processes and is therefore supernatural, i.e. miraculous.

- o I think the appropriate analogy is the preservation of the Jews. Personally, I would say that God's preservation of the Jews throughout time has been miraculous even though there has been great loss of life of individual Jews. Something can be miraculous even if man can point to examples where there was not "perfect preservation" as theologians have defined the term. God «failed,» so to speak, to prevent the Holocaust and the individual destruction of millions of Jews, but He nonetheless has preserved the Jews because they would no longer exist at all if God had not often acted miraculously as for example in the book of Esther. So it is with the word of God. God permitted textual variants to occur within the universe of manuscripts, but God nonetheless has acted to preserve His word, otherwise Satan would have destroyed the entire Received Text tradition. It is a miracle that the word of God can be found at all given Satanic and human attempts to destroy it. Preservation wasn't "miraculous" as theologians use the term because they make the unscriptural assumption that miraculous preservation would not allow for the existence of any textual variants. However, using the dictionary definition of the word "miraculous," i.e. not explicable by natural laws, supernatural, it is obvious that God has miraculously preserved his word." (Reid, email dated 1/23/17)

- Hills' use of terminology appears confused because of his insistence that "miraculous" in this case would equate with zero textual variants. The question remains whether or not it was providential? What does one mean when they use the terminology providential?

- Dr. William W. Combs of Detroit Baptist Theological Seminary addresses this issue in his essay "The Preservation of Scripture." Regarding whether preservation was "miraculous" or "providential" Combs states the following:

  - o "As far as the method of preservation is concerned, there are only two options. Scripture must be preserved either directly, by miraculous intervention in the transmission process, and/or indirectly, through secondary causation — "through the actions of human wills," as Sproul reminded us earlier. It is generally agreed that God's normal method of preservation has been indirect, through secondary causation. This method has usually been termed providential, though, as we previously noted, providence simply has to do with God carrying out his design for the universe, regardless of whether that is done directly or indirectly. But in discussions of preservation the term providential is used to signify that though God miraculously inspired his Word, he has normally chosen to preserve it via secondary causation, that is, through ordinary human means. And because preservation has been by ordinary human means, the transmission process has inevitably resulted in the introduction of errors." (Combs, 30)

- First, note that Combs equates all textual variants with "errors" i.e., he does not distinguish between the nature of the variants: 1) substantively equivalent variants, or 2) substantive differences in meaning. He does this because he is assuming *verbatim identicality* as the standard for preservation.

- Second, it is important to note how Combs defines "providence." He defines it as "secondary causation—through the actions of human wills" or "ordinary human means." In other words, according to Combs, there is nothing supernatural about preservation at all; it is a completely "ordinary" process. God was content to use secondary causation i.e., men copying the text by "ordinary human means" to accomplish the preservation of His word. Once again it is important to note that Combs holds this position because of the existence of variant readings and the fact that the copies do not possess "verbatim identicality."

- Regarding these comments by Combs, Brother Reid stated the following:

    o "Because textual variants exist, Combs concludes that God's method of preservation must have been providential and used "ordinary human means." Combs reasons that if God had used miraculous means to preserve His word then there would be no textual variants. But this hardly follows.

    God never promised to preserve Shakespeare or Aristotle, so their writings have been preserved through ordinary human means. Whether what we have today is an accurate reflection of what they originally wrote, no one knows. But God has promised to preserve His word, and He therefore obligated himself to ensure that it happened. To think that God took no personal action whatsoever to facilitate preservation while Satan has been actively attempting to corrupt and destroy the word of God since Genesis 3 seems to me the height of naiveté.

As normally defined, miraculous and providential are not direct antonyms. Rather, they have been defined by the participants in this discussion as antonyms because of the shared pernicious assumption that miraculous preservation would prevent textual variants from existing. This seems reminiscent of the Calvinism v. Arminianism debate. Both sides start with a flawed understanding. They then, frame the terms of the discussion while laboring under that misunderstanding and insist that people pick a side. The appropriate response is not to pick a side but to reject both flawed positions. Similarly, the proper response to the miraculous v. providential debate is to choose neither side because the debate has been framed in a manner that is unscriptural, confusing and contrary to the natural meaning of words. Since God didn't feel the need to put a label on the manner in which He chose to accomplish preservation, it doesn't seem profitable for man to invent one." (Reid, email dated 1/23/17)

- It is difficult to see how the preservation of the "precise wording" demanded by many King James Advocates could be accomplished via the ordinary human means of secondary causation. Yet many King James Only (KJO) advocates view the use of "providential" as a means of avoiding some of the more outlandish enunciations of the KJO position. Combs is quick to point this out in the next paragraph.

    o "As we have observed earlier, because advocates of the KJV/TR position commonly claim to believe in providential preservation through ordinary human means, they generally wish to distance themselves from the idea of a miraculous re-inspiration of manuscripts or versions. However, providential preservation via secondary causation cannot produce the kind of product this position claims to possess—an error-free TR and/or KJV. Speaking of the TR, Waite says:

o It is my own personal conviction and belief, after studying this subject since 1971, that the words of the Received Greek and Masoretic Hebrew texts that underlie the King James Bible are the very words which God has preserved down through the centuries, **being the exact words of the originals themselves**. As such, I believe they are inspired words.

o . . . No matter whether one uses the miraculous language of inspiration to describe preservation, or simply calls it providential, the Bible the KJV/TR position claims to possess — an infallible and inerrant Bible — requires a continuous chain of miracles throughout the transmission process." (Combs, 31-32)

- Combs is correct if one demands *verbatim identicality* as the standard for preservation. The only way the text could have traversed the seas of time and history in a state of *Xeroxed identicality* is for the Godhead's involvement in the process of preservation to have been of the sort that no variations of any kind ever entered the text. The fact that there are textual variants in the very Greek manuscripts (Byzantine) that KJO advocates maintain are the most accurate proves that historically this *type* of miraculous preservation did not occur.

- These points highlight why dropping *verbatim identicality* as the standard for preservation is such a crucial move. As Brother Reid pointed out above, "the pernicious assumption that perfect preservation would avoid textual variants" has led to extremely poor uses of terminology by those on both sides of the preservation/textual debate.

- All this highlights a potential problem with using the term "providential" at all as a descriptor for how preservation was accomplished. Most notably, the Bible never uses the term "providential" to describe how preservation would occur.

- Acts 24:2 — the word "providence" only occurs one time in your Bible, and it is not in a context having anything to do with preservation. The underlying Greek word only occurs one other time in the Greek text supporting the KJB.

- o Romans 13:14 — "provision"

- According to *Strong's Concordance* the Greek word rendered as "providence" and "provision" is the word *pronoia* which means: 1) forethought, providential care, and 2) to make provision for a thing.

- The *Oxford English Dictionary* (*OED*) defines "providence" as follows:

  > 1. a. Foresight; anticipation of and preparation for the future; prudent management, government, or guidance.
  >
  > b. Regard for future needs in the management of resources; thrift, frugality.
  >
  > 2. In full **providence of God** (also **nature,** etc.)**, divine providence.** The foreknowing and protective care of God (or nature, etc.); divine direction, control, or guidance.
  >
  > 3. That which is provided; a supply, a provision.
  >
  > 4. The action of providing something; provision, preparation, arrangement. Chiefly in **to make providence.**
  >
  > 5. a. An act or instance of divine intervention; an event or circumstance which indicates divine dispensation.

  - **special providence**, a particular act of direct divine intervention.

- Notice that the two uses of the Greek word *pronoia* correspond to the following English uses which have nothing to do with "an act or instance of divine intervention."

  > 1. a. Foresight; anticipation of and preparation for the future; prudent management, government, or guidance.
  >
  > 3. That which is provided; a supply, a provision.

- Based upon the Biblical use of "providence", one could only call preservation "providential" in that God, in his foresight, provided a mechanism through which preservation would be accomplished namely, the copying process. It says nothing, though, about how that copying process would be conducted.

- Secondly, things get confused when one uses words that the scriptures do not. The theological uses of "providence" exhibited by definitions 2 and 5.a. certainly imply some sort of direct divine intervention that conjures meanings more along the lines of the "miraculous" than secondary causation by ordinary human means.

- Note the *OED*'s sub entry under 5.a. for "special providence" or "a particular act of direct divine intervention." Once again this speaks of a particular "miraculous" act more so than the secondary causation notion of "providence" outlined by Combs above in his essay.

- With this definition work in mind, notice how confused the second Hills quote actually is. He uses the terminology "special providence" in the middle of arguing for why preservation was not "miraculous."

    o "The texts of the several editions of the *Textus Receptus* were God-guided. They were set up under the leading of God's **special providence**. Hence the differences between them were kept to a minimum. But these disagreements were not eliminated altogether, for this would require not merely providential guidance but a miracle. In short, God chose to preserve the New Testament text providentially rather than miraculously, and this is why even the several editions of the *Textus Receptus* vary from each other slightly." (Hills, 222-223)

- When one lays aside the "no textual variants" presumption, there really is no difference between "miraculous" and "special providence" as described by Hills.

- In short, it seems that the use of the word "providence" in this theological sense muddies the waters with respect to the methodology of preservation. For these reasons, I recommend that one not use the term as a descriptor for explaining how preservation occurred. There is nothing to be gained from using such a loaded and confused term.

- Even if I cannot explain the exact mechanics and methodology, I know that God must be active in the preservation process somehow. After all, he promised that he would preserve his word. Consider the following words of wisdom from Brother David W. Reid:
    - "The Bible tells us what God wants us to know. It doesn't tell us all the things that God does, which are innumerable (John 21:25), and most significantly, God doesn't tell us how he does what he does. Often, we would like to know how God does certain things so that we can then leverage that mechanism to accomplish what we want without having to rely upon God. However, that knowledge is hid from us. Instead, what we must do is believe what God has chosen to reveal and trust God to administer the details to accomplish the good pleasure of His will, whether we know the details or not (Eph. 1:5, Isa 46:10)."
        - Job 5:9 — "**Which doeth great things and unsearchable**; marvellous things without number:"
        - Job 9:10 — "**Which doeth great things past finding out**; yea, and wonders without number."
        - Job 33:13 — "Why dost thou strive against him? for he giveth not account of any of his matters."
        - Ecclesiastes 3:11 — "He hath made every *thing* beautiful in his time: also he hath set the world in their heart, **so that no man can find out the work that God maketh from the beginning to the end.**"
        - Isaiah 40:28 — "Hast thou not known? hast thou not heard, *that* the everlasting God, the LORD, the Creator of the ends of the earth, fainteth not, neither is weary? ***there is* no searching of his understanding.**"
        - Romans 11:33 — "O the depth of the riches both of the wisdom and knowledge of God! how unsearchable *are* his judgments, and **his ways past finding out!**"
        - Romans 11:34 — "**For who hath known the mind of the Lord?** or who hath been his counsellor?"

- o An example may help. In II Kings 6:4-7, God caused an axe head to swim, obviously a miracle. But how did God do that? Did God decrease the density of the axe head temporarily so that it rose to the surface of the water? Or did God increase the density of the water around the axe head so that the axe head floated? Or perhaps God without altering the density of any object created a powerful upward current in the water that caused the axe head to rise? Or perhaps something altogether different occurred. We do not know because scripture is silent on this matter as it so often is in describing the mechanics of how God accomplishes His will. Evidently, God has chosen to reveal to man the end result of what God has chosen to accomplish while leaving out the details of how it was actually performed. So it would seem with the innumerable unknown acts God has performed throughout history to preserve His word." (Reid, email dated 1/23/17)

- During the dispensation of grace, God works primarily in His saints through the written word of God and the power of the indwelling Holy Spirit.

  - o Ephesians 3:20 — God's power is at work in the believer's inner man during the current dispensation.

  - o Philippians 2:13 — once again God is at work today during the dispensation of grace but it is primarily an inward work.

  - o I Thessalonians 2:13 — this working of God is accomplished in the believer's inner man through "the word of God."

- It seems that God chose to preserve His word through Bible believing saints. As we will study in future lessons, in Time Past with respect to the Old Testament this was accomplished through the nation of Israel. Today during the dispensation of grace, preservation was accomplished through Bible believing saints who knew they had God's word, and faithfully copied the text to the best of their ability without the aid of direct supernatural/miraculous intervention.

- At the end of the day here is what we can know for sure.

    o God promised to preserve His word.

        - Psalms 12:6-7; 119:111, 152, 160; Isaiah 30:8; 40:8; Matthew 4:4; 24:35; I Peter 1:23-25

    o God did not see fit to preserve His word by preserving the original autographs.

        - This is self-evident because the original autographs no longer exist.

    o God did not supernaturally i.e., miraculously over-take the pen of every scribe, copyist, or typesetter who ever handled the text to ensure that no differences of any kind entered the text, if by miraculous one means exact identicality.

        - Differences (textual variants) exist at every level of this discussion.

    o If God intended to preserve His word with *verbatim identicality* (plenary verbal preservation) we would have historical/textual evidence that preservation occurred with that level of verbatim precision.

        - No such evidence exists.

    o If the standard for preservation is "plenary" or "pristine" identicality, why did God not just preserve the originals and thereby remove all doubt?

- I Corinthians 1:25-29; 2:5 — I believe that the reason God chose to do it this way is because He wanted us to stand by faith in the power and wisdom of God and not in the wisdom and ability of man.

- This is why I am so excited about the revised understanding of preservation (Reset Button) that we have presented in Lessons 41 through 46. One can maintain it by faith in God's word alone without the need to insert rationalistic suppositions to rescue the enterprise.

- In short, the Bible does not use the term "providential" to describe how preservation was accomplished, therefore, it is not helpful for us to do so either.

WORKS CITED

Bauder, Kevin T. "An Appeal to Scripture" in *One Bible Only? Examining the Exclusive Claims for the King James Bible*. Grand Rapids, MI: Kregel Publications, 2001.

Combs, William W. "The Preservation of Scripture?" in *Detroit Baptist Seminary Journal*. Fall 2000.

Hills, Edward F. *The King James Version Defended*. Des Moines: IA, Christian Research Press, 1956.

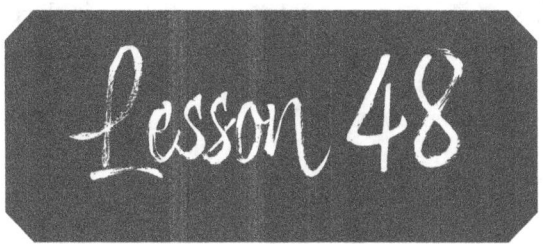

THE PROCESS OF PRESERVATION: THE MULTIPLICITY OF COPIES

INTRODUCTION

- Last week in Lesson 47 we began a consideration of the *method* of preservation by looking at the question of whether "providential" was an adequate descriptor to describe how preservation occurred.

- We determined that it was better to not use the term for the following reasons: 1) the scriptures themselves never use the term "providential" to describe how preservation occurred, and 2) the meaning and usage of the term is widely varied and therefore has been the source of much confusion.

- We know that God was/is active in the preservation of His word on account of the fact that He promised He would preserve it. Our inability to describe everything about it does not negate God's promise or His trustworthiness to see that it was accomplished.

- While we cannot know everything about the process, the scriptures do provide more information about the process of preservation than one might have heretofore realized.

- God's design was to preserve His word in a multiplicity of accurate reliable copies that are just as authoritative as the original autographs. The goal of this lesson is to begin laying out the Biblical case for how preservation was accomplished.

REVIEW OF LESSONS LEARNED FROM THE BOOK OF JEREMIAH

- In Lesson 29 we used the book of Jeremiah as a means of framing the discussion of preservation as our study of the topic was commencing. To begin our discussion of the *method* of preservation, I would like to review that information.

- We need to not ascribe more importance to the original autographs than God does. Nor should we demand more from the doctrine of preservation than God does in His word. I want to use the book of Jeremiah to illustrate both points.

- Jeremiah 36:1-4 — Baruch writes from the mouth of Jeremiah the original manuscript of Jeremiah 1-36 (Original #1).

- Jeremiah 36:20-24 — Jehoiakim and Jehudi destroy the original manuscript of Jeremiah. Note that the text explicitly states in verse 24 that "they were not afraid." Do they not know that they just destroyed an original autograph?

- Jeremiah 36:27-32 — God re-inspires Jeremiah in chapters 1 through 36 and adds "many like words" to what was destroyed in the fire by Jehoiakim (Original #2).

- Jeremiah 45:1 — these additional words comprise chapters 45 through 52 at a minimum, and possibly chapters 37 through 41 as well.

- Jeremiah 51:61-63 — Jeremiah writing at the bidding of God the Holy Spirit tells Seraiah to destroy Original #2 by tying a stone to it and throwing it into the Euphrates River after it is read in Babylon. God Almighty orders the destruction of Original #2. Why would God do this? Did God not know that a bunch of Fundamentalists in the 20th and 21st century would be looking for the originals?

- Daniel 9:2—over 70 years later Daniel comes to understand, by reading the book of Jeremiah, that the captivity was supposed to last 70 years. How is that possible if Original #2 was destroyed? Copies were made prior to the captivity. Once the copies were made, God did not care what happened to the original. The original contents of Original #2 were preserved via the copying process. Daniel had access to the inspired word of God through the copy he had in front of him.

- Matthew 2:17-18 — contains a quotation from Jeremiah 31:15. First, how did Matthew have access to what Jeremiah said over 470 years (70-year captivity + 400 years of silence) later if God had not preserved His word? So, God secured the contents of the book of Jeremiah despite directing Jeremiah to have Original #2 thrown into the Euphrates River.

- This seems to suggest that modern attempts to search for, find, and/or reconstruct the originals are out of step with how the Bible would teach you to think about things.

    o *Searching for the Original Bible* by James Price

    o *The Quest for the Original New Testament* by Philip Comfort

- Second, notice that Jeremiah 31:15 and Matthew 2:18 do not possess identical or *verbatim* wording i.e., they are not *identical* even within the KJB. Before reading Matthew 2:18 it is important to note the wording of verse 17:

    o "Then was fulfilled that which was spoken by Jeremy the prophet, **saying**,"

- Verse 18 is not a free quotation of the book of Jeremiah but a precise quotation of Jeremiah 31:15

Jeremiah 31:15	Matthew 2:18
Thus saith the LORD; A voice was heard in Ramah, lamentation, *and* bitter weeping; Rahel weeping for her children refused to be comforted for her children, because they *were* not.	In Rama was there a voice heard, lamentation, and weeping, and great mourning, Rachel weeping *for* her children, and would not be comforted, because they are not.

- These facts demonstrate that demanding *verbatim identicality* as the standard for preservation is excessive and reaches beyond how the Bible would teach you to think about the matter. Necessitating "plenary verbal preservation" or "identical preservation" demands that the words be preserved exactly as they were given under inspiration without any wording differences of any kind. This standard cannot even be sustained within the text of the KJB itself—the very text that King James Only advocates claim is perfect.

- While these two verses (Jeremiah 31:15 and Matthew 2:18) do not exhibit identical wording, they are "substantively equivalent" with each other i.e., they possess a "doctrinal equivalence." They say/teach/communicate the exact same doctrinal content without using the exact same individual words. Put a different way, they constitute a different way of saying the same thing, NOT a substantive difference in meaning.

- So, from the example of Jeremiah outlined above, we can conclude the following:

    o The promise of preservation does not require the perpetual existence of the original autographs. According to God the Holy Spirit, faithful copies are a sufficient means of fulfilling the promise of preservation.

    o God the Holy Spirit does not require *verbatim identicality* as the standard for preservation.

THE APOSTLE PAUL ON INSPIRED COPIES

- I want to show you some things about II Timothy 3 that we did not consider during the first term when we were studying the doctrine of inspiration.

- II Timothy 3:16—all scripture is given by inspiration of God. It is God-breathed. The words literally came out of the mouth of God. Jesus said that man lives by every word that "proceedeth out of the mouth of God" (Matthew 4:4) God dictated the words out.

- II Timothy 3:15—how is it that Timothy knew the "holy scriptures" from his childhood? Did Timothy possess the original autographs for the entire Old Testament? No. What did Timothy and his family possess? Copies. If Timothy had known the Holy Scriptures from his childhood, as the text plainly asserts, then his mother and his grandmother possessed copies of the word of God and they taught it to him.

- First, note that God the Holy Spirit calls the copies that Timothy possessed "holy scripture." This is not my opinion or the opinion of some other man.

- Second, notice that verse 15 comes before verse 16. Verse 16 says that the copies that Timothy was taught from were inspired. Inspiration and preservation go hand in hand in the primary text used to teach inspiration. The scriptures in verse 16 are clearly qualified by the scriptures of verse 15, and it is a reference to copies of the Old Testament. They did not have the original manuscripts, but they had copies. The point here is not that the copies were themselves inspired directly by God as were the original autographs but that the contents of the inspired originals were carried forward to the copies i.e., the copies were of equal weight and authority as the original autographs themselves, according to God the Holy Spirit.

- In other words, God the Holy Spirit makes no distinction between what was originally breathed out by God and the copies that Timothy's family possessed. They are both called scripture by God the Holy Spirit.

- In the context, when Paul said, "All scripture *is* given by inspiration of God," that is a reference to a real tangible thing that Timothy could hold in his hands. It was not a reference to some nebulous thing in the past that nobody ever saw at one time. Verse 16 is not a reference to something that Timothy could not find, but it is a reference to copies of the scriptures.

- Always remember that the original autographs were never at any point in history gathered and compiled together into a completed Bible like you have in front of you.

- I have critical commentaries on my bookshelf at home which maintain that II Timothy 3:15 is referring to the Septuagint (LXX), a Greek translation of the Old Testament allegedly made in 250 B.C. If Paul is referring to the Septuagint in verse 15, then that means he calls a translation of the Old Testament the inspired word of God in verse 16. If this is the position of the scholars, why then do they get so upset when someone holding an English translation says, "This is the inspired word of God?" Do you see what a double standard that is?

- II Timothy 3 is a fantastic passage. One cannot separate the promise of preservation via the copying process from the primary text used to teach inspiration. Inspiration and preservation are inextricably linked. It is unfortunate that the two have been confounded by some and the corollary overstated. Likewise, it has been equally detrimental to the body of Christ to limit inspiration, infallibility, and inerrancy to the original autographs alone on account of the presence of variant readings in the manuscript copies.

- The issue of preservation is not merely a philosophical necessity; it is a Biblical fact. It is not a philosophical necessity for me to say that God had to have done it because logic tells me. I believe in preservation because God says that He is going to preserve His word. You need to be aware of a proper estimation of what God's word is – it is the issue of inspiration plus preservation.

AUTHORITATIVE COPIES: THE PROCESS OF PRESERVATION

- John 10:34-35 — Jesus Christ is referring to the word of God that these people possessed. My point is that they do not have the original autographs. They have copies of the word of God just like you and I have a copy of the word of God today. Jesus Christ says to them, "The copy is what God says to you, and it is what was written down, and it cannot be broken. It is the word of God, and it cannot be destroyed."

- Matthew 22:3 1— they did not have original manuscripts. They had copies of the word of God. They had copies that they were reading; and Jesus said, "You can pick that copy up, and when you read that thing, you are reading what God said to you." That tells me that God's design is to preserve His word in copies. Do not forget that! The process of preservation is going to be preserving the word in a multiplicity of copies – the multiplying of copies of the bible.

- The original manuscripts are not the only issue with God. Do not misunderstand me; they are an issue because God has to write it down to start with. Inspiration has to do with the original manuscripts, and they wrote them down. But that is not the only issue either in inspiration or in preservation. It is certainly not the only issue with God. God designed to preserve what was written down in the original manuscripts in copies of those original manuscripts, and the copies are the issue with God.

- The original manuscripts are not the only issue. They are lost, and we do not have any of them. In fact, there has never been a time in human history where there was one bible collected together at one time made up of nothing but original manuscripts. So, if you must have original manuscripts, then you are in trouble. God has a more important plan than just trying to preserve one copy of the bible with that one copy being the original manuscript.

- In Grace School of the Bible, Pastor Richard Jordan said the following about the "original manuscripts" and textual criticism's quest to reconstruct the original text.

- o "The original manuscripts are not the issue with God. In fact, the term "original manuscripts" is just a catch phrase developed by scholars to discredit the word of God.

  There is a system, an epistemology of thought and teaching, called "textual criticism." You need to be familiar with that term. Textual criticism is simply a bunch of fellows trying to reconstruct the original text. They are trying to reconstruct and recreate and decide what the original manuscripts looked like…

  When men try to reconstruct the original text, it results in having no absolute and final authority except for the scholars.

  … When you hear about the older manuscripts and the original manuscripts, there is really a lot of phoniness about that. The older manuscript issue is a hoax. The International Standard Bible Encyclopedia on page 2955 has a very interesting admission. They say that the older manuscripts are not in every case the better reading. That is an interesting admission for the scholars to make because it is exactly true. Just because a manuscript is older that does not mean that it is best. It might just be an old corruption.

  In this class, you want to learn that the original manuscripts are not the only issue with God, but rather, he has a plan and a purpose to preserve his word in copies. His plan has never been to preserve the original manuscripts down through history, because that has not happened. In his word, it is very clear that the way he has designed to preserve his word is in a multiplicity of copies." (Jordan, *MSS 101*—Lesson 10)

- Exodus 32:15-16 — God did not even use a man to write these. These are the "original" originals. They were not even written by Moses, but they were written by God Himself. You cannot get much more original than that.

- Exodus 32:17-19 — Moses had the "original" originals and destroyed them before anyone even had a chance to read them.

- Exodus 34:1-2, 27-28 — God re-inspires original number 2.

- Deuteronomy 10:1-5 — Moses brings original number 2 down from the mountain and places it in the ark. Do we still have access to the contents of these tablets of stone? Yes. How? Because we have access to the original tablets? No. Because the contents of those tablets were copied.

- The scenario here with Moses and the giving of the Law is very similar to our example from the book of Jeremiah. In both cases the original was destroyed. In both cases God re-inspired a second original. In both cases original number 2 was either lost or destroyed. Yet, we have access to what God told Moses in the Mount and what God said through the pen of Jeremiah in the absence of the original autographs. How are we granted this access? Through the process of the scriptures being copied.

- You need to understand that God's design is not to preserve the originals. God's design is to preserve His word through copies of the originals. It is not that the original must be preserved in itself, but rather that copies of the original autographs are made that are just as authoritative as the originals.

- We will see that process in the next few lessons in detail. The issue is not just the original manuscripts, but God has preserved His word in the form that He intends you and me to have it in, and He will do that no matter what – original manuscripts or no original manuscripts. The originals can be destroyed, and it does not affect the effectiveness of the preservation of the word of God for us today.

WORKS CITED

Jordan, Richard. Grace School of the Bible, Manuscript Evidence 101, Lesson 10.

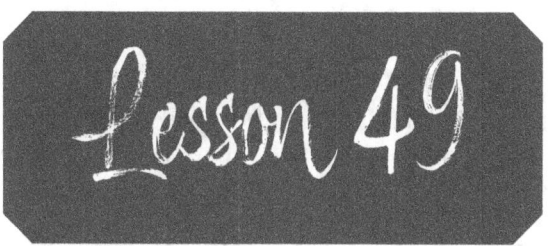

THE PROCESS OF PRESERVATION: THE MULTIPLICITY OF COPIES, PART 2

INTRODUCTION

- In Lesson 48 we began looking at the Process of Preservation. In doing so we considered the following points:
  - Reviewed lessons learned from the book of Jeremiah
    - The promise of preservation does not require the perpetual existence of the original autographs. According to God the Holy Spirit, faithful copies are a sufficient means of fulfilling the promise of preservation.

- - God the Holy Spirit does not require *verbatim identicality* as the standard for preservation.

- The Apostle Paul on inspired copies
  - II Timothy 3:15-16 — God the Holy Spirit makes no distinction between what was originally breathed out by God and the copies Timothy's family possessed. They are both called scripture by God the Holy Spirit.
  - Authoritative Copies: The Process of Preservation
    - Began looking at Biblical texts highlighting the fact that the Original Autographs are not nor have ever been the issue with God in preservation.

- In Lesson 49, we want to pick up where we left off two weeks ago and continue looking at the Process of Preservation.

AUTHORITATIVE COPIES: THE PROCESS OF PRESERVATION

- Exodus 32:15-16 — God did not even use a man to write these. These are the "original" originals. They were not even written by Moses, but they were written by God Himself. You cannot get much more original than that.

- Exodus 32:17-19 — Moses had the "original" originals and destroyed them before anyone even had a chance to read them.

- Exodus 34:1-2, 27-28 — God re-inspirers original number 2.

- Deuteronomy 10:1-5 — Moses brings original number 2 down from the mountain and places it in the ark. Do we still have access to the contents of these tablets of stone? Yes. How? Because we have access to the original tablets? No. Because the contents of those tablets were copied.

- The scenario here with Moses and the giving of the Law is very similar to our example from the book of Jeremiah. In both cases the original was destroyed. In both cases God re-inspired a second original. In both cases original number 2 was either lost or destroyed. Yet, we have access to what God told Moses in the Mount and what God said through the pen of Jeremiah in the absence of the original autographs. How are we granted this access? Through the process of the scriptures being copied.

- You need to understand that God's design is not to preserve the originals. God's design is to preserve His word through copies of the originals. It is not that the original must be preserved in itself, but rather that copies of the original autographs are made that are just as authoritative as the originals.

- Deuteronomy 31:9, 24-26 — the ark is called "the ark of the testimony" over and over again in the Bible. The reason it is called "the ark of the testimony" is because the word of God, the testimony of God, was placed in the box.

- Turn to Deuteronomy 17 and let's notice how they make copies of the contents of that box for the people and for the kings. God Almighty wants them to preserve His word. He sets up a mechanism where it is written and preserved in their midst, and they do not just carry it around in the ark. They keep the original autographs in the box for safekeeping, but that is not the only place that the word of God was. They are not just carrying that box around without anybody having access to its contents. They are making copies of what is in that box and people have those copies.

- Deuteronomy 17:14-18 — in other words, he goes in there and gets that testimony (that original manuscript) and he is to write himself a copy of the word of God. When he sits on the throne, he is to have his own personal copy of God's word to Israel.

- II Kings 11:12

- Deuteronomy 17:19-20 — the king is to have his own copy of the word of God. It is the copies that are important. If the original manuscripts were all that was important to God, He would have told him to get the original manuscripts, which were available at that time. If the original manuscripts were the issue, He would have said, "Preserve that original manuscript and when the king comes, give them to him." But the copies are the issue. God Almighty wants His word copied and distributed.

  o "The copies of those original manuscripts are just as reliable as the originals. They are in no way inferior to the originals. Deuteronomy 17:19-20 makes it very clear that God Almighty will bless the king for following the copy, because the copy is as much the word of God as the original. When he follows the copy, he is keeping all the words of this law. So, the copies are in no way inferior to the original manuscripts. God wanted the copies made and the copies were made." (Jordan, *MSS 101*)

- Deuteronomy 6:6-9 — the common ordinary Israelite had the word of God; and he was required to memorize it, and to learn it, and to teach it to his children. They all had copies. Every Israelite did not have his own personal copy – maybe there was one copy per family. But, the king had his own personal copy.

- Psalm 19:7-9 — David is reading copies of the word of God; he is not reading the bible in its original manuscripts. He says that it is perfect; it is sure; it is right; it is pure, true, and righteous altogether. It is pure. That is some testimony for a bunch of copies!

- Proverbs 25:1 — God preserved His word in copies, and the copies are just as reliable and authoritative as the originals.

- There are two things that you want to remember.

  o God wants His word copied. He wants copies made of His word. Psalm 68:11 – The Lord gave the word: great *was* the company of those that published *it* (put it out)." They spread it abroad. God wants His word published abroad.

- o God's design is to preserve His word in copies. The issue is not just that he wants everybody to have it, but that it is the copying process and method and mechanism whereby He will preserve it. These copies are accurate and reliable.

- Daniel 9:1-2 — we have already seen that Daniel had copies of the book of Jeremiah while in captivity.

- Daniel 9:11-12 — Daniel has the words that God wrote to him through Moses. He has a copy of that Mosaic Law. He has copies of the books of Genesis to Deuteronomy. Do you see the importance he puts on it? He said, "And he hath confirmed his words." Daniel assumed that the very words that he was reading were right and that they were God's words.

- Zechariah 1:1-2 — Zechariah was a companion of Ezra who first went back to the land after the Babylonian Captivity. Zechariah records God's message to Israel after the Captivity.

- Zechariah 1:5-6 — Zechariah is saying, "Your fathers and the prophets are all dead and gone, but my words live forever." The words do not just live forever, but they are among the people; i.e., the people have them in their possession. Individual Israelites, like Daniel, had copies of what the prophets said, and the copies have the same authority as the original words. Those words and copies take hold of the fathers and these people, and it has happened to them just like the original said it would happen to them. The final absolute authority that is in the originals is maintained in the copies that they have, and the copies are out among the people.

- When God talks about preserving His word, he is not talking about preserving it in heaven in a copy that nobody has access to. He is talking about preserving it in a physical existence in the earth where people can hold it.

- Matthew 24:15-16 — we just read about Daniel the prophet in Daniel 9. Daniel the prophet lives in approximately 600 BC (550 BC or something like that). In Matthew 24:15 standing in the shadow of the cross some 483 years later, the Lord Jesus tells Israel that when they see something come to pass that was written down hundreds of years earlier that they need to flee into the wilderness. Jesus Christ is saying, "You can read what Daniel the prophet wrote down in 550 or 600 BC right now when I am here with you in 30 AD." But, that is not all. There will be some people three and a half years into the tribulation that will also read the same thing, so God Almighty has to preserve His word up until that time for someone to read Daniel 9 and understand what they are reading. He is talking about preserving His word through time and through history into the future out there in the ages to come.

- Jesus Christ's attitude about it was that God Almighty was going to provide the word of God for people to read, not to hear about, not to understand the content of the message, but to read the words on the page of Daniel 9 in the tribulation period, which has to be out there in the future from today. That is preservation in copies. The word of God is preserved in copies because it says in Matthew 24, "(whoso readeth, let him understand:) Then let them which be in Judaea flee into the mountains." He is talking to a whole bunch of people that are reading this. Nobody has the original manuscript of Daniel 9. The only other way to figure that out is that somebody will discover the original manuscript during the tribulation, and they will start reading it then. If you believe that, is it not a whole lot easier for you to believe that God will preserve His word in copies?

- Luke 4:21 — in this verse Christ is talking about what is written down on the page. He is reading a copy of the book of Isaiah, and he calls it scripture; and he says, "It is fulfilled in your ears." If the original manuscripts were the only issue, Jesus Christ would not be telling the truth in this verse. The contents of the copy Christ held in his hand could be fulfilled in their ears, which means the very words of God are being fulfilled there. The authority, and the accuracy, and the infallibility of the bible extend far past the originals. These issues extend beyond the original autographs into generations of copies, which is why Christ can hold it in His hand and call it "scripture." What is scripture according to the bible definition? The scripture is "God breathed." It is the words God dictated to be written down on a page. According to Christ in Luke 4, the words He just read were scripture. The copy Christ read from was just as accurate and authoritative as the original autographs.

- Acts 8:32, 35 — twice in this passage God the Holy Spirit calls the copy of the book of Isaiah that the Eunuch has in his chariot scripture.

- Acts 15:21 — notice in Acts 15 that there are copies of the word of God in every city in the territory. Moses is read every Sabbath day in every city in the region. There are copies of the word of God scattered all over the territory, and those copies are scripture. They are considered authoritative by Jesus Christ, and by Philip, and by the Holy Spirit, and by the Apostle Paul.

- Acts 17:2

- Acts 18:2 — the scriptures are down in North Africa (Acts 8), Nazareth (Luke 4), Greece (Acts 17), and Asia Minor (Acts 18). These scriptures are spread throughout the Mediterranean world of the 1st century. As Paul travels, he encounters people who possess and know the scriptures. Apollos travels all around, and he is mighty in the scripture. The scriptures are all over that territory, via a multiplicity of copies.

- Daniel 10:20-21 — the angel's statement about the scriptures in verse 21 is that they are "the scripture of truth," meaning the writings do not have any errors in them. There is no error in truth i.e., they do not report any information that is false. This is the same terminology; the "scripture" is used throughout the Bible to refer to copies that are in use across historical time periods and geographic settings.

- The modern notion that inspiration, infallibility, and inerrancy apply to the original autographs alone is not a scriptural idea. No one who holds this position does so by faith in God's word. They do so based upon rationalistic presuppositions. Throughout the Bible God the Holy Spirit uses the same word "scripture" (*graphe*) to refer to what was directly given under inspiration and the manuscript copies of the originals.

- God's purpose and intent was to preserve His word via a multiplicity of accurate and reliable copies that were just as authoritative as the original autographs themselves. In the next lesson we will study some things about how that process functioned in the Old Testament.

WORKS CITED

Jordan, Richard. Grace School of the Bible, Manuscript Evidence 101, Lesson 10.

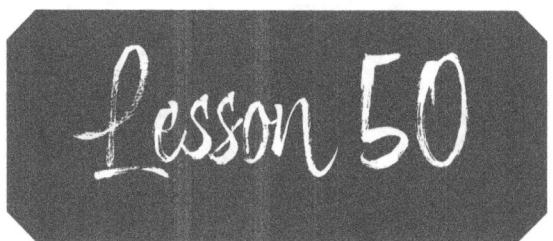

THE PROCESS OF PRESERVATION: THE PEOPLE OF PRESERVATION IN THE OLD TESTAMENT

INTRODUCTION

- In Lessons 48 and 49 we observed that God's design was to preserve His word in a multiplicity of accurate reliable copies that were just as authoritative as the original autographs. According to God's word, it was never His design to preserve His word by preserving the original documents.

- In Lesson 50 we want to look at the details of how this preservation would occur during the Old Testament. In order to accomplish this task we will be looking at the following three points:

- o Israel: The Institution for Preservation in the Old Testament
- o Importance of the Words "Keep" and "Preserve"
- o The Means of Preservation Within the Nation
  - The Role of Individuals and Families
  - The Role of the Levites and Scribes

ISRAEL: THE INSTITUTION FOR PRESERVATION IN THE OLD TESTAMENT

- Thus far, we have learned that God has promised to preserve His word. We have seen that the promise of preservation was accomplished through a multiplicity of accurate, reliable copies that are just as authoritative as the originals themselves. In this lesson, we will discuss the people God used in time past to accomplish the preservation of His word.

- God has always had an appointed group of people to copy and preserve His word. When it comes to the preservation of the Old Testament, there was a distinct group of people that were charged with the responsibility of preserving and copying the word of God in time past, specifically, the nation of Israel.

- Romans 3:1-2 — according to Paul, the word of God was given to the nation Israel. One of the reasons, purposes, and functions for which God chose the nation of Israel was to have a vehicle through which He could give and preserve His word. In time past God entrusted His word to that nation.

  - o Acts 7:38
  - o Romans 9:3-5

- In an essay titled "Israel, the Means of Preservation in the Old Testament", Dr. Kent Brandenburg identifies the nation of Israel as the "institution" whereby God accomplished the preservation of the Old Testament. Regarding the matter, Dr. Brandenburg states in part:

    o "God spoke to mankind in the Old Testament through the leadership of Israel. From the New Testament, there is the clear sense that the Jews considered the Law and the Prophets to be given to them for the keeping. Israel was God's depository and repository for His Words in the Old Testament." (Brandenburg in *Thou Shalt Keep Them*, 105)

- We have seen that God has always taken the initiative with respect to preservation. God gave Moses the commandments, and Moses destroyed them. Then, God Almighty took the initiative to reproduce them by re-inspiring original number two. God is the one who took the initiative in preservation. Preservation is not something that God leaves for man to do because man wants to do it. Rather, it is God's design, His purpose, and His plan.

IMPORTANCE OF THE WORDS "KEEP" AND "PRESERVE"

- Psalm 12:6-7 — we already established back in Lessons 31 and 32 that these verses are talking about the preservation of God's word, not the people. Verse 7 contains two Hebrew words that are significant to our discussion this morning in Lesson 50 regarding the process of how preservation occurred.

    o *Shamar* — or "keep" in Psalm 12:7

    o *Natsar* — or "preserve" in Psalm 12:7

- *Shamar* — "is used with the meaning of "to hedge about, guard, protect, attend to, or exercise great care over." *Shamar* appears in Genesis 3:24 as the activity of the Cherubim in protecting or guarding the Garden of Eden after God had evicted Adam and Eve. Other locations give this same sense of guarding against intruders with reference to gatekeepers (Is. 21:11) or to watchmen (Song 5:7). In Genesis 2:15 *shamar* is used for Adam's activity in taking care of or tending to the things of the Garden of Eden. In this way it is also used for the keeping of a flock (Gen. 30:31) or a house (II Sam. 15:16). In Proverbs 6:24, *shamar* characterizes the guardianship of a young man from the strange woman, in essence, the instruction of a parent protecting his moral purity. Cain in Genesis 4:9 asked, "Am I my brother's keeper?" This use of *shamar* applies to the defending or attending to someone for his safekeeping." (Brandenburg in *Thou Shalt Keep Them*, 98-99)

- *Natsar* — "has the understanding of "protect, maintain, obey, and preserve." Proverbs 27:18 clearly uses it in the sense of protecting or preserving an item of agriculture, saying, "Whoso keepeth the fig tree shall eat the fruit thereof; so he that waiteth on his master shall be honoured." *Natsar* was used to communicate the function of protecting military or agricultural properties (Job 27:18; Nah. 2:1), and those employed in this activity were called watchmen (Jer. 31:6; II Kin. 17:9; 18:8). In Psalm 141:3 *natsar* decries the ethical maintenance of one's mouth or vocal mechanism (Prov. 13:3). The same use of *natsar* related to the preservation of one's heart (Prov. 4:23), tongue (Ps. 34:14), and path of life (Prov. 16:17)." (Brandenburg in *Thou Shalt Keep Them*, 98)

- "Both of these words as witnessed in their usage, contain the strong sense of "guarding, protecting, tending, preserving, or maintaining." Any object toward which these two verbs might direct their action would receive this same essential trust. How these verbs are used with objects other than "words" or some synonym of "words" should be applied to their understanding when they are used with "words" or some synonym of "words." (Brandenburg in *Thou Shalt Keep Them*, 99)

- Psalm 119 brings together the use of the Hebrew verbs *shamar* and *natsar* along with a bunch of synonyms for the "words." As we saw in

Lesson 33, throughout Psalm 119 a host of different yet synonymous words are used interchangeably to refer to the scriptures. Please note that the number in parenthesis indicates that number of times that the word or phrase occurs in Psalm 119.

- o Psalm 119:1 — "law of the Lord" (24 times)
- o Psalm 119:2 — "testimonies" (22 times)
- o Psalm 119:3 — "his ways" (6 times)
- o Psalm 119:4 — "thy precepts" (21 times)
- o Psalm 119:5 — "thy statutes" (22 times)
- o Psalm 119:6 — "thy commandments" (21 times)
- o Psalm 119:7 — "righteous judgements" (18 times)
- o Psalm 119:9, 11 — "thy word" (38 times)

- Virtually every verse in Psalm 119 contains a reference to the words of God. There are 176 verses in the Psalm and 172 of them contain one of the words identified above. As the preeminent chapter regarding the word of God in all of scripture, Psalm 119 combines these synonyms for scripture with the two Hebrew verbs in question. Unless otherwise noted, the verb in each of the following verses is *shamar*.

    - o Psalm 119:2 (*natsar*), 4, 5, 8, 17, 22 (*natsar*), 33 (*natsar*), 34 (*natsar*), 55, 56 (*natsar*), 57, 60, 63, 67, 69 (*natsar*), 88, 100 (*natsar*), 101, 106, 115 (*natsar*), 129 (*natsar*), 134, 136, 145 (*natsar*), 146, 158, 167, 168

- Psalm 12:6-7 — God has seen to the keeping, guarding, protecting, and preservation of His words because He promised that He would (see also Psalm 146:5-6). God has His part in the preservation process and ensures it. That being said, the way God executes the process is through the cooperation of believing men. Simply stated, what God is keeping He wants men keeping. God ensures the keeping but He uses men to do it. "No one should doubt that God will keep His Words, but this does not take away from the responsibilities that man has in preservation. Repeatedly, God instructs man to keep His Words."

- Exodus 15:26; 20:5-6 — "keep" = *shamar*
- Leviticus 18:4-5 — "keep" = *shamar*
- Deuteronomy 4:2; 11:22; 29:9 — "keep" = *shamar*
- Joshua 22:5 — "keep" = *shamar*
- I Kings 2:3 — "keep" = *shamar*
- II Kings 17:13 — "keep" = *shamar*
- I Chronicles 29:19 — "keep" = *shamar*
- II Chronicles 34:31 — "keep" = *shamar*
- Nehemiah 1:9 — "keep" = *shamar*
- Psalm 78:7 — "keep" = *shamar*
- Ecclesiastes 12:13 — "keep" = *shamar*
- Ezekiel 11:20 — "keep" = *shamar*
- Daniel 9:4 — "keep" = *shamar*

- Some might argue the word "keep" is essentially a synonym for "do" or "obey;" according to Dr. Kent Brandenburg there are several reasons why that is not true.

    - First is the meaning or usage of *natsar* and *shamar*. These words do not mean "do" or "obey." They do mean "keep, protect, preserve, or guard."

    Second, there are Hebrew words for "do" and "obey." Deuteronomy 12:1 uses "do" with reference to God's Word when it says, (quotes verse) . . . There is more to *natsar* and *shamar* than just "doing" or "obeying.

    Third, there are several verses which highlight a difference between "keep" and "do" or "obey" in the same verse.

    - Leviticus 25:18 — "keep" = *shamar*; "do" = *asah*

- Deuteronomy 13:4 — "keep" = *shamar*; "obey" = *shama*
- Ezekiel 36:27 — "keep" = *shamar*; do = *asah*
- Ezekiel 37:24 — "observe" = *shamar*; "do" = *asah* (Brandenburg in *Thou Shalt Keep Them*, 102-103)

- In summation of this point Dr. Brandenburg writes:
  - "The word "keep" (*natsar* or *shamar*) is not used as a synonym for "do" or "obey." Instead, it has its own meaning that was used to distinguish a particular activity with reference to His Words.

    God's Words, all and each of them, are kept by more than just doing or obeying them. "Keep" elevates the task beyond solely "obeying" or "doing." God's Words are preserved by His people through their believing, preaching, teaching, practicing, and defending them (in addition, I would say by copying them). Every one of these tasks is taught in God's Word and they are all interrelated. Belief leads to teaching and practice. Teaching leads to belief and practice. Practice leads to belief and teaching. If Scripture is lost because it is not defended, then it cannot be believed, taught, or practiced. God's word is defended by believing, teaching, and practicing it. . . When Scripture becomes less valued or important because of wrong belief, teaching, and practice, then Scripture will be ignored and lost by the ones responsible for keeping it. Vigilance in keeping (*natsar* and *shamar*) requires more than just doing or obeying; it involves all of the activities that will allow God's Word to be passed down from one generation to the next for the glory of the Lord." (Brandenburg in *Thou Shalt Keep Them*, 103)

THE MEANS OF PRESERVATION WITHIN THE NATION

- The "keeping" or preservation of the scriptures in time past was both a corporate and individual charge. This is observable by noting the use of both singular and plural personal pronouns with "to keep."

- o Psalm 119:17 — the individual believer is responsible for the preservation of Scripture.
- o Leviticus 26:3 — the entire nation of Israel was also responsible for the preservation of Scripture.

- We see therefore that the job of preserving God's word was both individual and corporate. Individual families played a role in keeping/preserving God's word as did the God ordained religious hierarchy of the nation.

The Role of Individuals and Families

- "Part of the continuation of any aspect of Israel's worship was dependent on the practice of individual families as led by their fathers. Worship at the temple only continued when fathers preserved it by bringing their animals to that location for sacrificial offerings. Passing down God's Word relied upon the diligent transfer to the children. As the nation was God's preserving institution, the family accomplished this task on the most fundamental level." (Brandenburg in *Thou Shalt Keep Them*, 106)

  - o Deuteronomy 6:6-9
  - o Deuteronomy 11:18-21

- "When parents keep God's Words themselves, and pass them down to their children, then nations also keep and pass them on." (Brandenburg in *Thou Shalt Keep Them*, 106)

The Role of the Levites and Scribes

- Deuteronomy 31:24-26 — Moses took the initial section of the word of God when it was completed there, and he put it in the ark for keeping. He committed that text that he began to write to the priest, (the Levites). Those Levites were charged with the responsibility of keeping the book.

- Moses did not put the word in the ark because he no longer wanted it. He was not trying to get rid of it. Neither did Moses put the word in the ark because he knew he would die, and he wanted it kept safe. If Moses was just worried about the fact that he would die, what do you think he would have done with it? Who would he have given it to? He surely would have given it to Joshua because Joshua would be his successor. But, Moses did not give it to Joshua, rather, he put it in the ark, and he committed it to the Levites to take care of. Moses put the word in the ark because God's design was not just that Joshua had the word, but that there would be a group of people selected out and charged with the responsibility of taking care of His word. In time past the Levites were charged with the care and oversight of God's word.

- Deuteronomy 10:1-9— God said to put the word in the ark, and then He raises up an entire group of people to take care of the ark. God sets up an entire tribe of people to do the job of preserving His word. It is important that you see that. The Old Testament is to be preserved by the tribe of Levi, especially the issue of the priesthood. One of their primary functions has to do with preserving the word of God and teaching the word of God. God never designed to preserve His word by writing it and putting it up on a library shelf somewhere, just like they did not put the word in the ark just to put it away.

- Deuteronomy 31:9-12, 19—the idea is that the word is to be copied, and it is to be taught to the people. There is a group of people, an entire tribe in Israel (the Levites), chosen by God and separated from all of their brethren and given the responsibility, among other things, of keeping that book, and copying that book, and preserving that book, and teaching that book to the nation.

- We will continue our discussion of this point in Lesson 51.

WORKS CITED

Brandenburg, Kent. "Israel, the Means of Preservation in the Old Testament" in *Thou Shalt Keep Them: A Biblical Theology of the Perfect Preservation of Scripture.* El Sobrante, CA: Pillar & Ground Publishing, 2003.

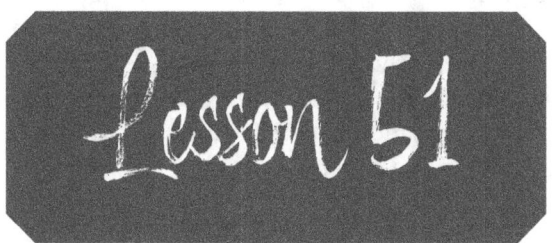

THE PROCESS OF PRESERVATION: THE PEOPLE OF PRESERVATION IN THE OLD TESTAMENT, PART 2

INTRODUCTION

- In this lesson, I want to continue our study of preservation in the Old Testament by finishing what we began last week.

- Last week in Lesson 50 we looked at the Process of Preservation in the Old Testament. In doing so, we observed that the word of God was committed to the nation of Israel in time past. One of the purposes that God had in forming the nation Israel, in raising the nation up, and preserving her throughout time past was to have a vehicle through which He would write and preserve His word.

- In Lesson 50 last week we studied the Hebrew verbs *shamar* ("keep" in Psalm 12:7) and *Natsar* ("preserve" in Psalm 12:7) and how they relate to the fundamental promise of preservation. We observed how these Hebrew verbs are used interchangeably with various synonyms for the "law of the Lord" i.e., God's word to Israel in Psalm 119 ("law of the Lord" (24 times); "testimonies" (22 times); "his ways" (6 times); "thy precepts" (21 times); "thy statutes" (22 times); "thy commandments" (21 times); "righteous judgements" (18 times); "thy word" (38 times).

    o Psalm 119:2 (*natsar*), 4, 5, 8, 17, 22 (*natsar*), 33 (*natsar*), 34 (*natsar*), 55, 56 (*natsar*), 57, 60, 63, 67, 69 (*natsar*), 88, 100 (*natsar*), 101, 106, 115 (*natsar*), 129 (*natsar*), 134, 136, 145 (*natsar*), 146, 158, 167, 168 (*natsar*).

- Furthermore, we considered the following three reasons for why the verb "keep" is not a synonym for "do" or "obey."

    o First is the meaning or usage of *natsar* and *shamar*; these words do not mean "do" or "obey." They do mean "keep, protect, preserve, or guard."

    Second, there are Hebrew words for "do" and "obey." Deuteronomy 12:1 uses "do" with reference to God's Word when it says, (quotes verse) . . . There is more to *natsar* and *shamar* than just "doing" or "obeying.

    Third, there are several verses which highlight a difference between "keep" and "do" or "obey" in the same verse.

    - Leviticus 25:18 — "keep" = *shamar*; "do" = *asah*
    - Deuteronomy 13:4 — "keep" = *shamar*; "obey" = *shama*
    - Ezekiel 36:27 — "keep" = *shamar*; do = *asah*
    - Ezekiel 37:24 — "observe" = *shamar*; "do" = *asah* (Brandenburg in *Thou Shalt Keep Them*, 102-103)

- Since "keep" and "do/obey" are not synonymous, they are not dependent upon each other. Israel's inability to "obey" the law does

- not hamper her ability to preserve it. If this were the case, there would not have been copies of the Old Testament available during the earthly ministry of Christ. Yet throughout the Old Testament, Israel demonstrated time and again that she was incapable of obeying and fulfilling the righteous requirements of the law.

- Previously when we ran out of time, we had been looking at how preservation would be accomplished within the nation of Israel. In doing so, we had identified the role of individuals and families and had just begun to discuss the role of the Levites and scribes.

- Now I would like to finish our discussion of preservation in the Old Testament before beginning a study of the New Testament next week.

THE MEANS OF PRESERVATION WITHIN THE NATION

- The "keeping" or preservation of the scriptures in time past was both a corporate and individual charge. This is observable by noting the use of both singular and plural personal pronouns with "to keep."

    o Psalm 119:17 — the individual believer is responsible for the preservation of Scripture.

    o Leviticus 26:3 — the entire nation of Israel was also responsible for the preservation of Scripture.

- We see, therefore, that the job of preserving God's word was both individual and corporate. Individual families played a role in keeping/preserving God's word as did the God ordained religious hierarchy of the nation.

The Role of Individuals and Families

Karl Brandenburg states the following:

- o "Part of the continuation of any aspect of Israel's worship was dependent on the practice of individual families as led by their fathers. Worship at the temple only continued when fathers preserved it by bringing their animals to that location for sacrificial offerings. Passing down God's Word relied upon the diligent transfer to the children. As the nation was God's preserving institution, the family accomplished this task on the most fundamental level." (Brandenburg in *Thou Shalt Keep Them*, 106)

- Deuteronomy 6:1-9 — this passage highlights both the individual and corporate aspects of preservation.
  - o Verses 1-5 — are corporate in that they refer to the entire nation and utilize *shamar* twice in verses 2 and 3.
  - o Verses 6-9 — are individual. It follows therefore, that one way the nation was to keep the statutes was at the local level of the home in verses 6 through 9.

- Deuteronomy 11:18-22 — the individual activity of verses 18 through 21 have a cumulative effect in verse 22; note the "ye." When each family acted in accordance to verses 18 through 21, the net impact in verse 22 is that the nation kept the law.
  - o "When parents keep God's Words themselves, and pass them down to their children, then nations also keep and pass them on." (Brandenburg in *Thou Shalt Keep Them*, 106)

The Role of the Levites and Scribes

- Deuteronomy 31:24-26 — Moses took the initial section of the word of God when it was completed there, and he put it in the ark for keeping. He committed that text that he began to write to the priest (the Levites). Those Levites were charged with the responsibility of keeping the book.

- Moses did not put the word in the ark because he no longer wanted it. He was not trying to get rid of it. Neither did Moses put the word in the ark because he knew he would die, and he wanted it kept safe. If Moses was just worried about the fact that he would die, what do you think he would have done with it? Who would he have given it to? He surely would have given it to Joshua because Joshua would be his successor. But, Moses did not give it to Joshua, rather, he put it in the ark, and he committed it to the Levites to take care of. Moses put the word in the ark because God's design was not just that Joshua had the word, but that there would be a group of people selected out and charged with the responsibility of taking care of His word. In time past, the Levites were charged with the care and oversight of God's word.

- Deuteronomy 10:1-9 — God said to put the word in the ark, and then He raises up an entire group of people to take care of the ark. God sets up an entire tribe of people to do the job of preserving His word. It is important that you see that. The Old Testament is to be preserved by the tribe of Levi, especially the issue of the priesthood. One of their primary functions has to do with preserving the word of God and teaching the word of God. God never designed to preserve His word by writing it and putting it up on a library shelf somewhere, just like they did not put the word in the ark just to put it away.

- Deuteronomy 31:9-12, 19 — the idea is that the word is to be copied, and it is to be taught to the people. There is a group of people, an entire tribe in Israel (the Levites), chosen by God and separated from all of their brethren and given the responsibility, among other things, of keeping that book, and copying that book, and preserving that book, and teaching that book to the nation.

- II Chronicles 15:3 — the purpose of the priesthood was to teach the people. They taught them doctrine out of the word of God just as they had conducted and presided over the sacrifices. All those things taught doctrine to the people. Eventually, the priests forgot the doctrine and kept the ritual.

- Malachi 2:4-7 — do you see what the function of the priest was? That priest's lips should keep knowledge. If you wanted knowledge from God, and if you wanted to know what the word of God says, that priest's job was to preserve that and have it ready for you when you needed it.

- In addition to the Levites, God chose men within Israel as a whole to spearhead the stewardship of the Words of God. These unique individuals were the scribes.

- Micah 3:8-12 — people do things for fame, and for money, and for position, and for reputation, and yet they are always real pious to say, "Is not the Lord among us?" That is what these guys are doing in Micah. These priests became a part of Satan's policy of evil against the word of God. They became a part of Satan's policy of corruption – corrupting the word of God. You can see his policy of corruption in operation there when you see the judges of the people doing it for money, and the priests teaching for money, and the preachers preaching for money, not for the Lord.

- Isaiah 36:22, 37:1-2 — notice that Hezekiah had faithful scribes with him.

- Proverbs 25:1 — these faithful scribes copied the word of God for King Hezekiah as part of the job.

- Jeremiah 36:12, 21-22 — contrast the functioning of Hezekiah's scribes with the conduct and activity of Jehoiakim's scribe, Elishama.

- Jeremiah 8:4-9

- Deuteronomy 28 — they should have known what was coming based upon what God told Israel would come upon them in the law.

- These verses highlight the fact that God's promise to preserve and the adversary's attempt to corrupt/destroy the word of God are occurring at the same time.

- Ezra 7:6 — Ezra was down in Babylon for seventy years and had the word of God with him in Babylon. Recall from a previous study that Daniel had access to the book of Jeremiah while in captivity in Babylon.

- Ezra 7:10-12, 21, 27 — God Almighty had scribes. He had His faithful men to preserve His word, and the job got done.

- Nehemiah 8:5, 8-9 — from these passages we observe that within the nation the scribes were charged with the responsibility of preserving/copying God's word. The scribes would copy, read, and teach God's word.

- In other words, I am trying to get you to see that God's word was preserved through the dynamic of people handling it, not in one copy sitting on a bookshelf for 500 or 1000 years. That is not the way God preserves His word. He preserves His word by it being in the hands of a certain kind of people, and those people are charged with the responsibility to execute God's purpose.

THE FALL OF ISRAEL

- When you come to the New Testament, you have a unique problem that you do not have when you are dealing with the Old Testament. Today, living during the dispensation of grace, the nation of Israel has fallen from her favored time past status. Therefore, God is no longer using that nation the same way He did in time past.

- Much of the pro-King James literature suffers from not having the correct dispensational framework from which to evaluate preservation in the New Testament.

- With the fall of Israel, did everything change? What happened with God's design? What happened to His procedure for preserving His word now that the people that He used in time past had been set aside?

- With the fall of Israel, the special group of people God uses to preserve his word changes. But, the process itself does not change. The design stays the same; however, the group of people changes.

- It is important to understand that the process remains the same even though the people God uses to preserve His word changed. Israel fell and God set them aside, yet He did not set aside His design to preserve His word through a multiplicity of copies. The people changed, but the process and design stayed the same.

- We will begin to study these matters next week.

WORKS CITED

Brandenburg, Kent. "Israel, the Means of Preservation in the Old Testament" in *Thou Shalt Keep Them: A Biblical Theology of the Perfect Preservation of Scripture*. El Sobrante, CA: Pillar & Ground Publishing, 2003.

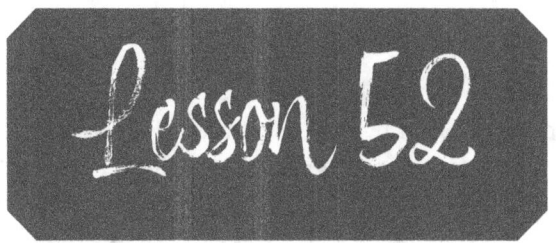

THE PROCESS OF PRESERVATION: PRESERVATION AND THE NEW TESTAMENT

Since Lesson 47 we have been looking at the Method and Process of preservation. The process that we have been discussing, which is clearly laid out in the scripture, demonstrates that God's design was to preserve His word in a multiplicity of accurate reliable copies. According to the word of God, these copies were just as authoritative and reliable as the original autographs themselves. These copies were distributed among the people to be read, studied, and memorized.

In Lessons 50 and 51 we studied how the Process of Preservation occurred in the Old Testament. In order to accomplish this purpose, we considered the following three points:

- o Israel: The Institution for Preservation in the Old Testament

- o   Importance of the Words "Keep" and "Preserve"
- o   The Means of Preservation Within the Nation
  - The Role of Individuals and Families
  - The Role of the Levites and Scribes

We concluded Lesson 51 by discussing the fall of Israel and its potential impact upon the doctrine of preservation. In doing so we concluded that with the fall of Israel, the special group of people God used to preserve His word changed, but the process itself did not change. The design stayed the same; however, the group of people changed.

With this in mind we want to begin a consideration of the Process of Preservation in the New Testament.

PRESERVATION AND THE NEW TESTAMENT

- When discussing the preservation of the New Testament we are faced with a unique challenge. There are not any scriptures written after the New Testament from which one can demonstrate that the New Testament was preserved.

- One of the ways I demonstrated to you that the Old Testament was preserved was by looking in the New Testament and seeing that they had copies of the Old Testament. It was not just that God said that He was going to preserve His word. If Jesus can go into Nazareth and open up a copy of the book of Isaiah and read from it and call it scripture, then I know the book of Isaiah had been preserved until 30 AD when Jesus read it in Luke 4. But we do not have anything like that for the New Testament. There is no way to go to any later scripture to authoritatively identify the fact that the New Testament has been preserved like you can with the Old Testament. Therefore, you must understand the doctrine of preservation as outlined in the scriptures and stand upon it by faith as a Biblical fact.

- When we come to the New Testament, we are placed in a position where we must walk by faith and not by sight. We are required to understand the promise of preservation as set forth in scripture. By this time, you certainly should understand it. If you have studied through your bible, you should certainly understand the doctrine of preservation, and the process involved; the fact that God designed to preserve His word through a process of copying and that He entrusted that task to a particular group of people. When you come to the New Testament, you no longer need that demonstration. You can rest upon the bible fact that what God can preserve before our dispensation, He can preserve during the dispensation of grace so that we can have it.

- The reason we know that God preserved the New Testament is because we have demonstrated beyond doubt from the word of God that God promised to preserve the Old Testament and observed its historical reality by looking at the New Testament. It follows therefore, that God would do the same for the New Testament.

- In this lesson, by looking at six to eight passages, I want you to see that during the lifetime of Paul and the apostles who wrote the New Testament (Mark and Luke were not apostles, but Paul, James, Peter, John and Jude were apostles), copies of their writings, i.e. the New Testament books, were being made. The New Testament books were collected and distributed among the saints as they were being written. These books were being studied as scripture during the lifetime of the New Testament apostles. They were authoritatively recognized as scripture. They were not recognized as scripture hundreds of years later by the decrees of some apostate church council, but they were recognized as scripture during the lifetime of the men who wrote the New Testament.

- If you can understand the design that God followed to preserve His word, it is not strange when you come to the New Testament and find that copies of the word of God were readily available, and they were recognized as scripture while the New Testament was still in the process of being written.

1ST CENTURY COPIES OF THE NEW TESTAMENT

- II Peter 3:1-2 — when we looked at that verse previously, I pointed out to you that Peter's attitude towards the books that he was writing was that they are just as authoritative as what the Old Testament prophets wrote.

- II Peter 3:15-16 — do you see Peter's estimation of what Paul wrote? Peter said that they take Paul's epistles, and they twist them as they do the other scriptures.

- The Apostle Peter obviously considered the epistles of Paul to be scripture. Notice that Peter had all of Paul's epistles that were written at that time, according to II Peter 3:16.

- It is interesting that Peter had all of Paul's epistles, and he had them for some time. It was not just Peter that had Paul's epistles because folks were studying them to the point that some were already wresting with them during the first century.

- By the way, these epistles were not written to Peter, nor were any of Paul's epistles written to the Jerusalem church. Paul's epistles were written to the Gentile churches, and then copies were made, and Peter had copies of them down in Palestine. Peter was not the only one that had copies; all the people to whom Peter is writing possessed copies as well. They were studying them, and they were getting confused doctrinally by not rightly dividing the word of truth.

- When Paul says to rightly divide the word, the saints of the first century had access to the scriptures. Part of what they had access to was the prophetic program and part it was the mystery program (Paul's epistles), and they had to rightly divide it. The scriptures were being written, copied, and placed into the hands of the people. Then those copies were being distributed far and wide, and they were recognized, at that time, as being the word of God. Peter calls the copies of Paul's epistles scripture i.e., of equal authority to the originals. The only way that could happen is just to have a bunch of people with copies of Paul's epistles and copies of the rest of the word of God. They had copies and none of them possessed the original manuscripts. If one thinks that Peter is referring to the original manuscripts then Peter, a circumcision apostle, would have needed to have stolen the Gentile church's epistles in order to have them in his personal possession.

- The subject of verse 16 is "as also in all *his* epistles." People were studying them and twisting them like the other scriptures. "His epistles" in verse 16 are clearly considered to be scripture. Peter has them and the people that Peter is writing to in the Jewish church have them, and they have had them for some time because they had had them long enough to have been studying them.

- I Timothy 4:13-16 — notice the instructions that Paul gave to Timothy in verse 13 - "Till I come, give attendance to reading, to exhortation, to doctrine." What is Timothy supposed to read? From what is Timothy supposed to exhort the people? From where does his authority come? Paul is telling Timothy to read the scripture. He is to exhort the people from the scripture. He is to teach them doctrine from the scripture. Paul expects Timothy to have the scripture to teach, and to preach, and to read to these people. When he says in verse 15, "Meditate upon these things; give thyself wholly to them; that thy profiting may appear to all," Paul is telling Timothy to pay attention to his own personal study. Paul is telling Timothy to be a student.

- I Timothy 5:17 — "To labor in the word" is to spend time studying the scriptures. According to this passage, there were people who had been studying the book and teaching it to others. Paul is instructing them to look out among themselves and to take notice of those elder(s) that are studying their bibles and teaching it to the saints. They were already doing this before they received this epistle from Paul, and that is my point. Paul is not telling them to study this epistle (I Timothy) and preach this epistle, but Paul is telling them to look out among themselves and find the men who were already studying the scriptures before Timothy received the epistle. Thus, they have scripture other than I Timothy that they had been studying. Timothy is instructed to give double honor to these men who were laboring in the word.

- I Timothy 5:18 — in other words, these people that Paul is writing to have the word of God. Paul quotes Deuteronomy, but he also quotes Luke. Paul says, "The scripture says that." Do you know what Paul is doing? Paul is saying, "Go look it up for yourself." Those people had the book of Deuteronomy, so they could look it up, but they also had access to the book of Luke. They had the Old Testament, and they already had portions of the New Testament. What they did not have was the original autographs.

- Acts 1:1-2 — notice the phrase "the former treatise." It is obvious that there is a former book and that its existence is known during the 1st century. The people at Ephesus, where Timothy was pastoring, had copies of the book of Luke. Luke was a traveling companion to the apostle Paul, and he was a close friend of both Paul and Timothy. These people did not have the original manuscript of the book of Luke. Theophilus had the original manuscript of the book of Luke, and these people had copies of the book of Luke. All of this is incidental to what is being taught in the text. The subjects of these passages are something else, but as you read the passages you pick up on the fact that these people had the New Testament scriptures in their hands. These scriptures were being collected together, copied, distributed among the people, and were just as authoritative as the original autographs. According to God the Holy Spirit, the copies of the book of Deuteronomy, for example, were just as much "God-breathed" as what Moses placed in the ark at the end of Deuteronomy.

- II Timothy 2:15 — as previously mentioned, to have the ability to rightly divide the word of truth; they needed to have access to the word of truth in order to rightly divide it. There is not any other reasonable/logical conclusion one can reach. These first century saints must have had the scriptures; they had some books containing the prophetic program and some books containing the kingdom program. Just as you and I today, they had to rightly divide between prophecy and mystery. However, there were some people at that time who were not doing such a good job of rightly dividing the word.

- II Timothy 1:15 — we see here the apostasy from the doctrine that Paul had given already. Hence, Paul exhorts Timothy to study to be approved of God, rightly dividing the word. Paul said, "Do not make the mistake of mixing the two together like these other men."

- II Timothy 4:1-2 — they are to take the book and preach the word. The reference is obviously not just to the Old Testament, but to Paul's epistles as well. Paul wants them to preach the doctrine committed to His trust. When Paul says, "Preach the word," he is not just telling them to go out and preach any part of the bible, especially not after II Timothy 2:15.

- II Timothy 1:13 — I submit to you that Paul's epistles present to you that "form of sound words" which are to be preached today. Paul's epistles are what equip the man of God in II Timothy 3:16, 17 "unto all good works."

- Acts 20:28-32 — is Paul talking about the Old Testament? No, Paul is not talking about the Old Testament. The Old Testament is not what we are to teach in this age, and it is not what Paul commends them to teach. The Old Testament is not called "the word of his grace" in the scriptures. The word of his grace is that word that is committed to Paul.

- Ephesians 3:2 — that is what was committed to Paul. Thus, when Paul says, "I commend you to the word of his grace," he is talking about the word of God that had been written down by him. Paul wrote the book of Galatians, I Thessalonians, II Thessalonians, I Corinthians, II Corinthians and the book of Romans by the time Acts 20:1-3 took place. They had a considerable amount of the word of God written down, collected, and in their hands.

- Colossians 3:16 — the word of Christ is that word that the Lord Jesus Christ, from heaven's glory, committed to him through the apostle Paul. Folks, it has to do with the word of God.

- Colossians 2:7 — Epaphras and these Colossians had copies of the word of God with them, and Epaphras could teach them, and they could go home and study.

- Ephesians 3:1-4 — before this writing, Paul wrote down some things about the mystery. He said, "I wrote them afore, whereby, when you read them." Well, where had he written them before? He wrote I Thessalonians, II Thessalonians, Galatians, I Corinthians,

II Corinthians, and Romans. Paul said, "When you read those things, you will understand." The implication is that these people at Ephesus had copies of those prior books. Now, these people are the same people in Acts 20:32 that he commends to the word of his grace. The elders from the church at Ephesus are the people that we just read about in Acts 20. The implication about the Ephesian church is that they had Paul's prior epistles. They read what he wrote earlier.

- I am simply trying to drive home the fact that these 1st century saints had copies of God's word. The New Testament text was being written down, copied out, collected, and distributed just like we studied with respect to the Old Testament. Thus, one can have faith that the same process that existed back in the Old Testament, demonstrated in the New Testament to have worked for 1500 or 2000 years, was also at work during the dispensation of grace.

- I Thessalonians 5:27 — this is one of the earliest epistles, if not the first, then the second epistle that Paul wrote. There is a possibility that Paul wrote the book of Galatians before he wrote Thessalonians. But in the earliest epistles that Paul wrote, he tells them that he expects them to see that this epistle is read and distributed among all the holy brethren. This verse makes it clear that Paul sees the design of preservation existing in copies of his epistles being made and distributed among the various churches.

- Galatians 1:1-2 — the book of Galatians was a circular letter. It was one letter written to several different churches in the region of Galatia. Now, you know what would have happened when it got to the church in Lystra before they sent it to the church in Iconium, don't you? You know good and well that someone made a copy of that epistle before passing it along to the next assembly. Paul intended the book to make the rounds and to be a norm and a standard for doctrine in those churches.

- Colossians 4:15-16 — Paul wants this epistle read, not just at Colosse, but at the Laodicean church as well. Colossians is one of the prison epistles, and it was one of the last books Paul wrote. Paul's design, from the very beginning to the very end, was that his epistles were to be read obviously by the people he wrote them to, but also in all the other churches too. Paul wants the information, and the doctrine, to get out to everybody everywhere.

CONCLUSION

- I Corinthians 5:9 — "I wrote unto you in an epistle not to company with fornicators." Where is the epistle that contains that information that Paul wrote? It was obviously prior to this epistle, but this is I Corinthians. Paul is saying that he wrote them a letter before this one. This epistle is I Corinthians in our bible, but Paul is saying that he wrote them a previous letter. If that is not bad enough, Paul says in II Corinthians 1, "I wrote you a letter between I Corinthians and II Corinthians." Thus, there are at least four letters that you can identify, but only two of them show up in your bible. Therefore, I know that there are many things that the apostle Paul wrote that were not the divinely inspired word of God. But, what was divinely inspired was being collected together and authoritatively identified as such. In the next lesson, we will study how they distinguished between one epistle and another and how they knew which one was the inspired word of God and which one was not. God had a group of people whose function in the church, at that time, was to authoritatively identify which epistles were the word of God. They identified which epistle was not the word of God. They identified the word of God and made authoritative copies of it and made sure it was distributed.

- There is one other thing that I want you to notice. Obviously, these people are collecting and sharing copies of the word of God. They are commanded to do so. In summation, the process of New Testament preservation was the same as the Old Testament process – through copies. God had a special group of people charged with the responsibility of seeing that the task was carried out. I wanted you to see in this lesson that the process was the same in the New Testament as it was in the Old Testament. You must base your faith on the fact that the New Testament has been preserved.

Lesson 53

THE PROCESS OF PRESERVATION: THE PRESERVATION OF THE NEW TESTAMENT, PART 2

INTRODUCTION

- A few weeks ago, in Lesson 52 we looked at how the process of preservation established in the Old Testament was continued in the New Testament despite the fall of Israel. The process is simply that God will preserve His word through a multiplicity of reliable,

- accurate copies of the original manuscripts. Copies of copies eventually were handed down to us, and they are reliable and accurate. That is how God has preserved His word.

- We have seen how God preserved His word in time past. He used a special group of people in the Old Testament — the nation Israel. Within the nation of Israel, He had the Levites (the priesthood) as well as scribes to preserve His word. We saw that process demonstrated in the Old Testament beginning with the books that Moses wrote, and then other books were continually added to the Torah.

- In our last lesson we saw that with the fall of Israel the process remained the same. In other words, God is still preserving His word through a multiplicity of copies, rather than just preserving one original manuscript or one copy of the original manuscript.

- But, with the fall of Israel, the following question arises: What about the people? Who are the ones responsible for preserving the New Testament? In the New Testament there was also a special group of people during the days of the apostles, people whose function (one of their functions) it was to identify, copy, and collect the word of God just as in the Old Testament. These are the folks who accomplished the copying and dissemination of the New Testament documents as we studied in Lesson 52.

ROLE OF THE NEW TESTAMENT PROPHET

- Ephesians 4:8, 11-12 — Paul is talking about Jesus Christ after His ascension, not prior to it. The earthly ministry of Christ takes place, then Christ dies on the cross, He spends the forty days on earth and then He ascends into heaven. The Holy Spirit comes on the day of Pentecost. Then the fall of Israel takes place in Acts 7 with the stoning of Stephan. The apostle Paul gets saved on the road to Damascus in Acts 9. Then the Lord Jesus Christ, from heaven's glory, reaches down, and not only saves Paul, but he commits to Paul a new system of knowledge and information – a new realm, a new program called the mystery.

- Paul says that He gave certain gifts to the body of Christ – apostles, prophets, evangelists, pastors and teachers. Christ ascended up on high, (and in the passage it is not necessarily His ascension after His resurrection, but is an ascension far above all heavens), which is where Christ is when Paul gets saved. He ascends far above all heavens, and from that position, He gives these offices to the church. The twelve apostles were made apostles before the crucifixion of Christ but there were men that were made apostles after the ascension of Christ; therefore, they are not one of "the twelve apostles."

- I am trying to point out that there are prophets that were given to the body of Christ. There are prophets that affect the ministry of the body of Christ during its infancy before the full revelation of the mystery was made known to the Apostle Paul.

- Ephesians 2:19-20 — the household is built on the foundation of the apostles and prophets. Thus, I know something about apostles and prophets. Apostles and prophets are "foundational" gifts. It is the function of an apostle and a prophet to lay the foundation of the house.

- I Corinthians 3:10 — the apostles and the prophets are foundational gifts to the body of Christ. They lay out the foundation upon which the ministry of the rest of the body was built upon. Now, one of the functions of a prophet in the Bible is to be God's spokesman. That was not a prophet's only function, but it was one of them. He speaks for God.

- Exodus 4:15-16 — Aaron was Moses' spokesman; he was Moses' mouthpiece. He spoke Moses' words.

- Exodus 7:1 — by comparing scripture with scripture, the definition of "a prophet" is "a spokesman." God puts His words in the prophet's mouth, who in turn speaks the word of God. One of the functions of a prophet is to identify the word of God.

- Ezekiel 3:17 — Ezekiel is to get God's word, know what it is, and then send it out to the people.

- Jeremiah 15:19 — the prophet Jeremiah is God's mouth piece.

- II Chronicles 36:12 — I am just trying to impress upon you the idea that a prophet is a man that speaks God's word.

- I Corinthians 14:23, 29-32 — God Almighty gave His word through these people; He gave revelation and information through the office of the New Testament prophets. These prophets have the capacity to identify what God is saying to the body of Christ. This gift of prophesy was one of the foundational gifts used in the establishing of the body of Christ. Paul was "the apostle of the gentiles" (Romans 11:13) and yet there were a number of other apostles in a secondary sense.

    o Acts 14:14—Barnabas was an apostle in a secondary sense. Barnabas does not directly receive information from Jesus Christ, but he receives it from Paul, and he is sent out in that sense.

    o Timothy and Silas, along with other men, are identified in the scripture as apostles. Epaphroditus is an apostle and he is identified as such in Philippians 2.

- One of the functions of the prophets given to the body of Christ during its infancy was to identify God's word. The prophets in those churches were the men in the local churches who actually did the copying of the epistles. When the prophets got a collection of letters together from a bunch of different churches, they would read those letters; and they would say, "This copy is the word of God; this is scripture. But, this other letter is not scripture." They would say, "This letter that Paul wrote, I Corinthians, is the second letter that Paul wrote to the Corinthians, but this is the word of God. The other letter, the first one that Paul wrote to the Corinthians, was just personal correspondence. The third letter Paul wrote to the Corinthians was not scripture; but the fourth one is, and it is II Corinthians, and it is to be in the Bible."

- There had to be somebody in the local assembly who had the capacity to identify what God's word was when that assembly received copies from different places. They were getting all of this information from all over the place and they indicated what was scripture and what was not.

- II Thessalonians 2:1-2 — there were phony letters floating around the churches that claimed to be from Paul. Therefore, when those churches received one of those letters, they had to know if it was scripture or not.

- Thus, God Almighty in the founding of the church gave some prophets so they could identify "Thus saith the Lord." It was not the only function of the prophets, but it was one of their functions. The evangelist, the pastor and teacher, took the copies and did the work of the ministry with them. They did not make the copies, but they used the copies. They preached the word from the copies that they had. But, the prophet's function was to say, "This is God's word." Then they made accurate, reliable copies of the word and distributed them. The apostles took them out to the various churches.

- I Corinthians 12:28 — God put prophets in the church. He put them in the local churches.

- I Corinthians 14:36-37 — in other words, are you the only people that received a copy of the word of God? Are you the only people that sent copies of the word of God out? Those people are receiving and sending copies of the word. There were people in the Corinthian church who were suppressing the gift and the function of the prophet, and they were trying to exalt other gifts above it. Thus, the work of the prophet was not getting done, and consequently the word was not getting out. Paul was rebuking them about that. Paul was rebuking these people for their frustration of the function of the prophet.

- I Timothy 6:3 — I am saying to you that "the scriptures of the prophets" are the scriptures that the prophets copied down. Those prophets in those New Testament churches (the Pauline churches) collected the word of God together. Matthew, Mark, Luke, John, Acts, Romans, Corinthians, Galatians, Ephesians, Philippians, Colossians, Thessalonians, Timothy, Titus, Philemon, Hebrews,

James, Peter, I John, II John, III John, Jude, and Revelation were the books that these prophets collected together. They said, "These are scripture." They identified them as what God Almighty said, and they authoritatively said, "These are the scriptures."

- According to II Peter 3, Peter had all of Paul's epistles. All of those people in Galatia that Peter wrote to had Paul's epistles. They had them because of the functioning and the activity of these prophets, who Christ gave as foundational ministries to the body of Christ to produce that book and to authoritatively identify it.

PRESERVATION AFTER THE PROPHETS: THE ROLE OF THE PAULINE GRACE CHURCHES

- God had a process to preserve His word through copies. He had a people to preserve His word. He had a people to identify the word of God, to collect it and to preserve it in the New Testament. But, these prophets died and there are no longer any prophets today. We enjoy the apostle's ministry and the prophet's ministry by having the written word of God. So, who preserves the word of God after the prophets have died out?

- Human viewpoint would say, "The prophets are gone so there are not any more authoritative copies of the word of God."

- I Timothy 3:14-15 — notice that Paul talks about the "house of God." That is the local church that Timothy is involved with. It is the church of the living God, which is the body of Christ. The body of Christ is the "pillar and ground of the truth." Folks, the word of God was committed to local assemblies for them to teach and distribute. This process of preservation works in the body of Christ on the idea of what the Protestants used to call "the priesthood of the believer." That means that in the Old Testament there was a "priesthood;" but God has done away with the Old Testament priesthood now, and every believer can go to God for himself. In the Old Testament, you needed a priest to go in and represent you, but now, you are a priest, and you can represent yourself.

- I Peter 2:9 — "the priesthood of all believers" is a bad term because they use this verse as a proof text. We understand that, dispensationally, that is not good terminology and yet the truth of the concept is real. You and I function today on a personal basis with God Almighty. We do not need any "go-betweens" or mediators (I Timothy 2:5); we go straight to God Almighty.

- Now, the one thing you want to guard against is this – please remember this! The issue in preservation is not an authoritative church but rather, an authoritative Bible. The Roman church will take what I am telling you and say this, "See, since the church has the responsibility of preserving the word of God, therefore, the church has the power to say what is right and what is wrong. The church can tell you what the Bible says."

- I Timothy 3:15 — the local assembly is the pillar and ground of the truth. What is the foundation of the truth? In the passage, it is the local assembly. The local assembly is responsible for the maintenance of the truth. Thus, it is the responsibility of the local assemblies, the bible-believing people, to teach and distribute the word of God today. God preserves His word through history in the hands of Bible-believing people that study the word of God, and that teach the word of God, and that preach the word of God from a believing viewpoint.

- Regarding the role of the believing church in preserving the scriptures, Dr. David Sorenson states the following in his book *Touch Not the Unclean Thing: The Text Issue and Separation*:

    o "...Some proponents of the critical text position will say that God may have preserved His Word, but He did not say how He would do so. To the contrary, the New Testament does provide insight into how God has promised to preserve His Word . . . (quotes II Timothy 3:15) . . . The Apostle makes it clear that the church is both the foundation as well as the support of the truth.

    The word translated pillar refers to an architectural support such as a load-bearing column. One illustration which comes to mind is that of a lighthouse. The structure of the light is that which upholds it and supports it. Is not this a careful illustration of the relationship of the church and the Word of God? The word translated "ground" refers to a foundation. The church is therefore that pillar which supports the truth. The church of Jesus Christ is both the foundation as well as the pillar of support which hold forth the truth...

The church, like a lighthouse, shines forth the light of the Word of God upon a dark world. Lighthouses serve two purposes: 1) to warn of danger or 2) to point to safety. The local church does both through the preaching of the Word. It warns of the danger of hell ahead. It also points to the safety of heaven through our Lord Jesus Christ. The connection of the local church to the truth of the Word of God should be only too apparent.

However, there very well may be a deeper truth. That is, the church is the structure which God has ordained to uphold the truth of the Word of God through the centuries. The view of the writer is that God has used the believing churches down through the ages as the primary structure by which the New Testament has been preserved. That certainly was true in the first century. The same remains true today. And as we shall see, it has been the case through the course of history. Thus, the contention of this writer is that the church is the pillar and the ground by which the truth of the Word of God has been preserved." (Sorenson, 58-59)

- The idea that the New Testament text was preserved via "the priesthood of all believers" shows up over and over in pro-King James literature. Those who are King James Advocates who also happen to be mid-Acts Pauline Dispensationalists have a unique problem with citing these writings to bolster their position on preservation because they are full of unsound dispensational reasoning and examples. For example, *Thou Shalt Keep Them: A Biblical Theology of the Perfect Preservation of Scriptures* contains an entire section on "God's Method of Preservation" containing four essays. The first essay titled "Israel, the Means of Preservation in the Old Testament" by Kent Brandenburg was quite good and was quoted in Lesson 50. Two of the remaining three essays are questionable from a dispensational/doctrinal standpoint.

- The fourth essay titled "Stewards of the Mysteries of God: I Corinthians 4:1-2" is worthy of consideration for any King James Advocate who also happens to be a mid-Acts Pauline Dispensationalist. Please consider the following excerpts from Gary La More's essay along with my commentary:

    o "First of all, in the light of the foolishness of worldly wisdom, Paul wanted his missionary companion, the church at Corinth, and him to be recognized as "ministers of Christ." He includes his audience, the church, with the use of the plural pronoun "us". This identifies Paul, his church-planting associates, and the Corinthian church. . . ." (La More *Thou Shalt Keep Them*, 123)

    In the context, I believe Paul is referring to himself, Apollos, and Timothy.

    "Secondly, Paul wanted the Corinthian church to see himself and themselves as "stewards" of the mysteries of God." The word "steward" carried with it the idea of a "custodian" of the mysteries of God. A steward was an administrator, a trustee, or an overseer of an estate. . . The word "steward" can also signify "overseer," "superintendent," or distributor." The apostles (Paul particularly) and comrades were responsible to God since they were charged with the task of disseminating the Divine message found in the Word of God. The message therefore is not of apostolic origin, but has God as its source. The Apostles were not responsible for the ultimate truth of it, but only for the fidelity with which they conveyed it." (La More in *Thou Shalt Keep Them*, 124)

    o I Timothy 1:11

    o Ephesians 3:3 — the mystery i.e., the body of truth pertaining to the body of Christ for the dispensation of grace was committed to the trust of the Apostle Paul.

    o "The "mysteries of God" and the Word of God are synonymous. The root of the word for "mystery" is *muein* meaning "to close" (the mouth, the lips). When a mystery is made known, instead of the mouth staying closed, it is now opened. What was not known is now known and what was not revealed is now revealed. Mysteries of God are known by special revelation... The mystery is disclosed by revelation, so that making it known is revelation. For this reason, mystery is very often used with the term for revelation (Rom 16:25-26; I Cor. 2:10; Eph. 1:9; 3:3, 5, 8; 6:19; Col. 1:26-27; 4:4) . . . In I Corinthians 4:1 the word "mystery" is plural. The plural intimates the Words or passages of scriptures, the various special revelations of God. Each mystery is important, and the faithful steward will put forth due diligence to lose none of them, but to faithfully keep them with the house given the authority by his Master to do so. The Master is the Lord Jesus Christ, the Head of the church, the house in which the stewards labor in keeping the mysteries." (La More in *Thou Shalt Keep Them*, 124-125)

- Ephesians 3:2 — this message was given to Paul so that he could give it to the body of Christ.

- Romans 16:26 — this message is for "all nations for the obedience of faith."

- Acts 20:32 — Paul commends the Ephesians elders unto the "word of his grace."

- I Timothy 3:15 — Timothy is the pastor of the church at Ephesus. It was the job of the Pauline assemblies to "keep" and "preserve" the scriptures during the dispensation of grace.

    o "Finally, Paul wanted to be known as a faithful man. Having designated himself as a steward of the mysteries of God in the preceding verse, Paul now sets forth the primary requisite for a steward—he must be "faithful," true and worthy of trust and confidence (I Tim. 1:12). Since his stewardship involved the mysteries of God, he accurately and aggressively proclaimed these truths." (La More in *Thou Shalt Keep Them*, 125)

    o II Timothy 2:1-2 — Paul wants the doctrine passed on from generation to generation. How is that going to happen?

- II Timothy 4:1-2 — by preaching the word. In order for Timothy, and those that follow after him to follow Paul's instruction, what are they going to need to have? The word of God.

- The primary job of preserving the word of God during the dispensation of grace is going to fall to Pauline grace believing and preaching assemblies. The very people whom the organized hierarchical sacramental church persecutes as heretics.

    o "Since the philosophy of heaven, the message for which the steward is held responsible, is nonsense to the unsaved world (I Cor. 1:18), he should not be interested in trying to please it. In fact, he must not concern himself in the least with what the world thinks of his stewardship. The faithful steward must please his Owner, God. Strong temptation exists for the steward, especially today and particularly on the issue of perfect preservation of God's Words, to please the academic crowd, which is most likely to reward his subjugation with a false label of scholarship. The seduction is a self-serving lure of intellectual pride. . . God did not commit this stewardship to textual critics. He works the best through stewards in His church who are faithful to His Word and its message. Paul knew that God had preserved His Word: otherwise he would not have written I Corinthians 4:1-2. The faithful members of the church today, like those members of the Corinthian church, are given the stewardship of the Words of God. This is the message of the Apostle Paul in this text. The members receive the Words, guard the Words, and pass on those very Words to the next generation of local church members." (La More in *Thou Shalt Keep Them*, 126-127)

- This is why what one believes is critically important in any discussion of preservation. In future Lessons we will demonstrate the historical veracity of this point by looking at the role the Paulicians played in the preservation of the New Testament text.

CONCLUSION

- The word of God is not preserved in a beautifully bound copy of a vellum scroll sitting on a library shelf in the Vatican. The word of God is preserved out there in the hands of soul-winning, bible-believing, bible-preaching people. That is where God's word is, because God the Holy Spirit in us bears witness to His word. Bible-believing people use God's word, and the copies of the word of God that they use get worn out. Thus, the necessity for faithful reliable copies to carry God's word from generation to generation.

WORKS CITED

Brandenburg, Kent. *Thou Shalt Keep Them: A Biblical Theology of the Perfect Preservation of Scripture.* El Sobrante, CA: Pillar & Ground Publishing, 2003.

Sorenson, David H. *Touch Not the Unclean Thing: The Text Issue and Separation.* Duluth, MN: Northstar Baptist Ministries, 2001.

THE PROCESS OF PRESERVATION: SIMULTANEOUS NATURE OF PRESERVATION AND CORRUPTION

INTRODUCTION

- Since Lesson 48 we have been considering the Process of Preservation. In doing so, we have observed from the scriptures that God's design was to preserve His work in a multiplicity of accurate reliable copies that are just as authoritative as the original autographs. God did not elect to fulfill the fundamental promise of preservation via preserving the original autographs. This is self-evident, or we would possess the autographs today. Lessons 48 and 49 were devoted to establishing this understanding.

- Review of lessons learned from the Book of Jeremiah (Lesson 48)
- The Apostle Paul on Inspired Copies (Lesson 48)
- Authoritative Copies: The Process of Preservation (Lessons 48 and 49)

- In Lessons 50 and 51 we studied the people God used in the Old Testament to accomplish the preservation of His word. In order to accomplish this task, we considered the following points:

  - Israel: The Institution for Preservation in the Old Testament (Lesson 50)
  - Importance of the Words "Keep" and "Preserve" (Lesson 50)
  - The Means of Preservation Within the Nation (Lesson 51)
    - The Role of Individuals and Families
    - The Role of the Levites and Scribes
  - The Fall of Israel (Lesson 51)

- At the end of Lesson 51 we discussed the impact of the fall of Israel upon the process of preservation. We noted that the process did not change but those responsible for oversight and execution of the process did. When Israel fell, the task of preserving the scriptures passed from the nation of Israel to the body of Christ. Lessons 52 and 53 were devoted to looking at the process of preservation in the New Testament. In summation, we considered the following points in Lessons 52 and 53:

  - Preservation and the New Testament (Lesson 52)
  - 1st Century Copies of the New Testament (Lesson 52)
  - Role of the New Testament Prophets (Lesson 53)
  - Preservation after the Prophets: The Role of the Pauline Grace Churches (Lesson 53)

- Now that we have considered the Process of Preservation, it is imperative for us to note that while the process was being executed, corruption of the text was also occurring simultaneously. In this Lesson we want to consider how the forces of preservation and corruption were functioning at the same time.

THE SIMULTANEOUS NATURE OF PRESERVATION AND CORRUPTION

- In his 2016 publication *In Defense of Textus Receptus: God's Preserved Word to Every Generation*, Dr. Jim Taylor states the following regarding this important matter,

    - "There are two very important facts to remember as we study the doctrine of preservation [A point which we have already studied in detail. See Lessons 31 through 39.]. The first is the fact that God has promised to preserve His Word. But secondly, we should note that there have also been those who would seek to corrupt the scriptures as well. And both of these facts are operating at the same time. And seeing these two forces are happening simultaneously, it is very important to have a good understanding of preservation so that we can come to the proper conclusions." (Taylor, 47)

- Recall from Lesson 2 that Satan was the first destructive critic of God's word. Genesis 3 outlines the adversary's policy of evil against the word of God. Satan seeks to assail the final authority of God's word through the following five tactics:

    - Tactic 1 — Question God's word (Genesis 3:1)
    - Tactic 2 — Subtract from God's word (Genesis 3:2)
    - Tactic 3 — Add to God's word (Genesis 3:3)

- o Tactic 4 — Water down God's word (Genesis 3:3)
- o Tactic 5 — Deny God's word (Genesis 3:4)

- Sin, on planet earth, began with an attack on God's word in Genesis 3. There is a satanic policy of evil against the word of God clearly laid out in the scripture, and the design is simply to destroy the final authority of your Bible. Satan wants to take the word of God and make it less than the final authority.

- Now, how does the adversary seek to accomplish this strategy? Well, if you have a written authority, the tactic is to bring up another authority alongside of it and give it equal weight with the first. Well, then how does one decide which is right? When you have two competing authorities, who decides which is right? A third authority decides – you do, or somebody else does.

- So, Satan's attempt is to get rid of that final authority that God has placed in His word by putting up a competing authority. Satan does not want you to have the capacity in your hands to know what God said.

SCRIPTURAL EXAMPLES OF 1ST CENTURY CORRUPTION

- The question before us in this lesson is the following; is there any scriptural evidence to suggest that the New Testament text was being corrupted while it was still being written?

- II Corinthians 2:17 — "For we are not as many, which **corrupt** the word of God: but as of sincerity, but as of God, in the sight of God speak we in Christ."

- First, the verb translated "which corrupt" is in the present tense and the active voice. This means that while Paul was writing II

Corinthians (present tense) people were actively engaged in seeking to "corrupt the word of God" (active voice).

- Second, there is controversy concerning the translation of "corrupt" in the KJB. Many modern versions read some form of "peddle" in verse 17.

    o NIV — "... we do not **peddle** the word of God for profit."

    o ESV — "... **peddlers** of God's word ..."

    o NASV — "... **peddling** the word of God ..."

    o Footnote on verse 17 reads, "Or corrupting."

- *Strong's Concordance* defines the underlying Greek verb *kapēleuō* as follows:

    o to be a retailer, to peddle

    o to make money by selling anything

    o to get sordid gain by dealing in anything, to do a thing for base gain

    o to trade in the word of God

    o to try to get base gain by teaching divine truth

    o to corrupt, to adulterate

    o peddlers were in the habit of adulterating their commodities for the sake of gain

- There is no reason to change the King James Bible's rendering of *kapēleuō* as "corrupt." Whether one says "corrupt" or some form of "peddle", the bottom line is the same; the word of God whether written or spoken is being "adulterated" for the sake of gain. Coupled with the present tense and the active voice it is clear that Paul viewed "corruption" of God's word as a present reality that he was facing in the first century.

- Third, this was not an isolated problem. Paul explicitly states in verse 17 that "many" people were involved in this process. Dr. Jim

Tayler states the following regarding the circumstances outlined in II Corinthians 2:17:

- o "It would appear that even in the first century, there were those who were bent on presenting a corrupted message. Presumably, this would be both verbally as well as in written form." (Taylor, 50)

- II Thessalonians 2:1-2 — "Now we beseech you, brethren, by the coming of our Lord Jesus Christ, and *by* our gathering together unto him, That ye be not soon shaken in mind, or be troubled, neither by spirit, nor by word, **nor by letter as from us**, as that the day of Christ is at hand."

- In his essay, -*First Century Textual Attack*- Kent Brandenburg states the textual attack exhibited by II Thessalonians 2:2"

  - o "The false teachers shook and troubled the Thessalonian believers through three different means, swaying the beliefs of church members and then affecting them emotionally. Firstly, deception came by means of "spirit," supposed prophetic revelation or supernatural communications that were concocted by the deceivers. Secondly, distortion of Scriptural truth came by "word," probably sermons they preached which contained their false teachings. Lastly, deceiving counterfeiters of the Apostle Paul penned bogus letters in his name." (Brandenburg in *Thou Shalt Keep Them*, 133)

- Not only was Paul dealing with those who sought to "corrupt" the word of God (I Corinthians 2:17) but we learn in II Thessalonians 2:1-2 that he was also dealing with a forgery problem. People had written a false letter to the Thessalonians posing as the Apostle Paul. It is clear from the context, that this letter was filled with false doctrine regarding the timing of the catching up of the saints (rapture) and the resumption of the prophetic program.

- That this false/forged letter had a psychological impact upon the saints at Thessalonica is evident from verse 2: "That ye be not soon shaken in mind or be troubled." It was troubling for these saints who had rejoiced in the truth of I Thessalonians 4:13-18 to read a spurious letter claiming they had missed the event.

- This passage in II Thessalonians 2 provides tangible evidence of the culture of "corruption" that Paul was speaking about in II Corinthians 2:17. As soon as his epistles began to be circulated in the first century, they were met with opposition from those who opposed Paul's message and apostleship.

  o "When 2 Thessalonians was written in the middle of the first century, Satan already was using men to purposefully attack Scripture. Certainly this particular attack altered the text even more than changes made to single paragraphs, sentences, or words, by adding to the Scripture an entire epistle. However, it does reveal the existence of textual variants in the first century. Forgers who would add an entire epistle would not scruple to make smaller changes with canonical books." (Brandenburg in *Thou Shalt Keep Them*, 133)

- In a footnote (#223), Dr. Brandenburg states the following regarding the textual variations found in the book of I Thessalonians,

  o "A major variation such as the addition of an entire epistle was obviously very damaging to the eschatological belief of the church at Thessalonica. The variations of I Thessalonians in the CT [Critical Text] continue to significantly affect eschatology (1:10; 2:11, 12, 15; 3:2; 4:8, 13; 5:27). Those changes alter eschatological understanding even before 2 Thessalonians." (Brandenburg in *Thou Shalt Keep Them*, 133)

- While II Thessalonians 2 does not indicate who these forgers/false teachers were, we have a clue in II Timothy 2. In II Timothy 2:16-18 Paul identifies two men (Hymenaeus and Philetus) who were teaching that the "resurrection is past already" and thereby "overthrow the faith of some." Ill-intended men such as these would not have hesitated to alter legitimate scripture and/or forge scripture in order to accomplish their corrosive purposes, "their word will eat as doth a canker." We know from history, and will demonstrate in a future Lesson on transmission, that heretics altered the Biblical text in various ways so as to conform it to their heretical teaching.

- This culture of corruption prompted Paul to take steps to ensure the authenticity of his epistles.

    o   II Thessalonians 3:17

    o   Galatians 6:11

    o   Philemon 19

- II Corinthians 4:1-2 — "Therefore seeing we have this ministry, as we have received mercy, we faint not; But have renounced the hidden things of dishonesty, not walking in craftiness, **nor handling the word of God deceitfully**; but by manifestation of the truth commending ourselves to every man's conscience in the sight of God."

- We see from this verse that "there were those who corrupted the scriptures as well as others who mishandled the scriptures." Given what we have already seen in this section, this deceitful handling of the word of God would have no doubt taken the form of false verbal teaching such as tampering with the text of scripture.

- Galatians, I and II Thessalonians, as well as I and II Corinthians were some of the first epistles written by Paul. Written before Acts 20, these books were drafted between 54 and 60 AD, according to most commentators. These facts established the reality that the adversary was already seeking to corrupt the New Testament text while it was still being written.

- II Corinthians 11:3 — what means did the serpent use to beguile Eve? He used "any means" necessary, up to and including tampering with God's word. We see the results of this "any means" strategy in verse 4 where we see that false teachers were presenting a false Christ, by a false spirit, through another gospel.

IMPLICATIONS OF SCRIPTURAL OBSERVATIONS

- The above Pauline texts established that a culture of corruption with respect to the scriptures existed during the first century while the New Testament was being written. This culture of corruption includes the following minimum components:

- Corrupting the word of God (II Corinthians 2:17)

    o Forging the word of God (II Thessalonians 2:2)

    o Handling the word of God deceitfully (II Corinthians 4:2)

    o Any means strategy (II Corinthians 11:1-4)

- Please note that all of these components of corruption imply intentionality on the part of the corruptor. Once again, those holding to unsound doctrine would have ample motivation for tampering with the text so as to hide the heretical nature of their teaching.

    o "There are many reasons why men would desire to change God's words. In many cases, the changes are affected as a result of a desire to adhere to some false teaching. Since the scriptures condemn their heresies, some go so far as to change the scriptures in order that the heresies can go undiscovered." (Taylor, 52)

- The scriptures anticipate this situation by issuing three strategically placed warnings against tampering with the word of God.

    o Deuteronomy 4:1-2

    o Proverbs 30:5-6

    o Revelation 22:18-19

- The presupposition of Westcott and Hort that the shorter reading is to be preferred over a longer reading is not based upon scripture. According to the word of God, it is just as easy for someone with ill intentions toward the scripture to take away words as it would be for them to add them. The very fact that there are upwards of 3,185 differences in wording between the Critical Text and the Traditional Text (*TR*) implies God's scriptural warnings noted above need to be taken seriously.

- We have already established that God promised to preserve His word. If we do not believe this, then any discussion concerning the two texts become a matter of personal preference based upon man's intellect or will. But since we firmly believe that God has made good on His promise and preserved His word, we must conclude that one text or the other has been corrupted. This is not based upon the false standard of "verbatim identicality" of wording but upon the fact that the two texts differ substantively from each other i.e., they report contradictory information. They do not agree regarding what verses should and should not be included in scripture.

- Put another way, if we believe that God has preserved what He initially gave by inspiration, then we are forced to conclude that one text or the other is corrupt. Both texts cannot be pure because they differ from each other substantively.

    o "The only other option would be to conclude that our understanding of plenary-verbal inspiration is somehow flawed. And there are those who believe just that way. They contend that even though God promised to preserve each word, He never said that it would all be in the same text. But it is a very confusing and complex position because we are left with nothing to guide us into what is the pure reading and what is corrupt. How is a person to know? Again, rather than having concrete, scripturally based evidence, we are left to our own intellect, opinions, theories, and suppositions. Any variant in readings become subject to human reasoning and choice based upon everything but the promises of God." (Taylor, 56)

- As we have seen above there are numerous reasons why and how the text became corrupted. At this point, the reason why corruption exists is not the real issue. The reality that the two texts differ substantively is plain for all honest observers to see. The facts of the case are in reality simple.

- o God promised to preserve His word.
- o The two texts differ substantively.
- o Only one of them can unequivocally qualify as the preserved word of God.

CONCLUSION

- "Biblical principles and promises are the basis of a Scriptural Bibliology. No verses in Scripture teach a theory that the oldest manuscripts are the best, . . . [the passages considered above] reveal intentional corruption of the New Testament text in the first century. The Scriptures themselves denounce the theory of "oldest is best." These passages all indicate that the Bible was intentionally changed in the first century." (Brandenburg in *Thou Shalt Keep Them*, 135-136)

- "Those who weigh manuscripts using criteria such as age believe that people today should labor at restoring the text of the New Testament to a condition closer to that of the originals. This ongoing process of textual criticism does not represent the Biblical doctrine of the perfect preservation of Scripture. The contention that "oldest is best" is at best a rationalistic speculation. . . The Bible contains no verses espousing the "oldest is best" criterion. Instead, it teaches early and often that textual attack will come from Satan and his human instruments (Gen. 3:1-6; Matt. 4:1-11). (Brandenburg in *Thou Shalt Keep Them*, 131)

- "Bible believers maintain a distinctive bias toward what Scripture teaches. Scripture says God will preserve every word. Scripture declares God will use His ordained institution, Israel in the Old

Testament and churches in the New Testament, to preserve every word. Knowing that God says this, believers assume the He will do what He says. They trust Scriptural criteria and not human reasoning. It might make sense in man's thinking that old, rarely used manuscripts are superior to newer, often-used ones." (Brandenburg in *Thou Shalt Keep Them*, 131-132)

- The "oldest is best" mantra of the Critical Text position is repeated simplistically as if it is a universal truth. In reality it is not. Oldest is only best if all other things are equal which they hardly ever are. Blind commitment to the mantra does not, however, work for a book claiming to be of divine origin such as the scriptures. A divinely inspired book such as the Bible needs to be approached in the manner stated therein.

  o "Pure manuscripts and readings were embraced while others were rejected [This was one of the functions of the New Testament prophet in the early church.]. This behavior stemmed from authoritative warnings concerning tampering with Scripture. The Bible establishes clearly that there were corruptions of first century manuscripts by means of purposeful textual attack. . ." (Brandenburg in *Thou Shalt Keep Them*, 132)

- Through the ministry of the New Testament prophets, the Holy Spirit guided the churches to reject corrupt manuscripts and readings as well as to copy and distribute authentic ones. This ministry set the body of Christ on the firmest possible ground once the gift of prophecy ceased. Believers, who had convictions about preservation of scripture, were careful to make their copies as accurately as possible. Meanwhile, manuscripts that were deemed spurious were either discarded or destroyed along with old/worn out copies of authentic manuscripts.

  o "It was not uncommon among Jews to copy an Old Testament manuscript, and after having verified that the copies were accurate, to destroy the original manuscript. Since the Jews made up a segment of the New Testament churches, it is possible that they followed already established practices and did the same thing with the original autographs." (Taylor, 60)

- All that the age of a manuscript can tell us is that it existed. It does not tell us anything about whether or not it was in use in the churches.

- In the next Lesson we will discuss the matter of availability as we begin to wrap up our study of the doctrine of preservation.

WORKS CITED

Brandenburg, Kent. "First Century Textual Attack: 2 Peter 3:15-17 and II Thessalonians 2:2" in *Thou Shalt Keep Them: A Biblical Theology of the Perfect Preservation of Scripture*. El Sobrante, CA: Pillar & Ground Publishing, 2003.

Taylor, Jim. *In Defense of the Textus Receptus*. Cleveland, GA: Old Path Publications, 2016.

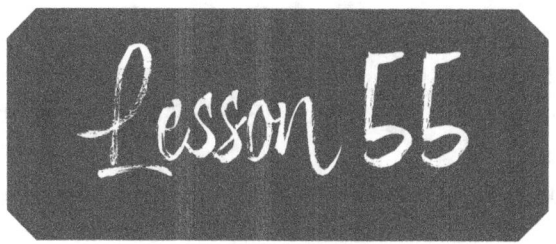

THE PROCESS OF PRESERVATION: THE QUESTION OF ACCESS AND AVAILABILITY

INTRODUCTION

- Last week in Lesson 54 we looked at the simultaneous nature of preservation and corruption. We saw that both were occurring during the first century when the New Testament was being written.
- Since Lesson 48 we have been studying the Process of Preservation. In summation, we have observed the following from scripture:
    - God promised to preserve His word.

- o Preservation was accomplished not by the preservation of the original autographs but through a multiplicity of accurate reliable copies that are just as authoritative as the originals themselves.
- o In the Old Testament the nation of the Israel was the custodian of the words of God. During the dispensation of grace, the body of Christ and local churches are the pillar and the ground of the truth.
- o In the Old Testament the copying process was overseen by the tribe of Levi. During the early part of the dispensation of grace the office of the New Testament prophet identified, copied, and distributed the scripture. Once the gift of prophecy ceased, the job of preserving/copying the text fell to Bible-believing Pauline grace assemblies.
- o Preservation and corruption were occurring at the same time.

- From this we conclude that the word of God is not preserved in a beautifully bound copy of a vellum scroll sitting on a library shelf somewhere. Rather, the word of God is preserved in the open hands of soul-winning, bible-believing, bible-preaching people. Bible-believing people use God's word, and the copies of the word of God that they use get worn out. Thus, the necessity for faithful reliable copies to carry God's word from generation to generation.

- This preservation model implies that God's word was available and accessible to God's people not hidden away in the desert sand, under a rock, in a cave, or in an inaccessible library.

- Over the next couple of Lessons, we will conclude our discussion of preservation for this term by looking at the issues of availability and accessibility.

THE QUESTION OF AVAILABILITY AND ACCESSIBILITY

- In this section we will once again use Dr. William W. Combs' essay from the Fall 2000 issue of the *Detroit Baptist Seminary Journal* titled "The Preservation of Scripture" to frame the discussion. The pertinent portion is a section titled "Is Public Availability a Necessary Component of Preservation?" that is toward the end of the essay.

- Before proceeding further, it is important to notice the circumscribed limits that Combs has placed upon the discussion.

- Dr. Combs begins this section by noting that many King James/ *Textus Receptus* Advocates "argue that the doctrine of preservation also includes the idea of public availability of the true text of Scripture." (Combs, 41) As proof of the notion, Combs offers the following quotations from Dr. Edward F. Hills:

  - "It must be that down through the centuries God has exercised a special, providential control over the copying of the Scriptures and the preservation and use of the copies, so that trustworthy representatives of the original text **have been available to God's people in every age**." (Hills, 2)

  - "He must have preserved them not secretly in holes and caves but in a public way in the usage of His Church." (Hills, 86)

- According to Dr. Combs the sentiments expressed by Dr. Hills were first expressed by Dean Burgon in the late 19th century after the publication of the Westcott and Hort Greek Text (W&HT) as well as the Revised Version in 1881. Burgon stated the following in *The Traditional Text of the Gospels* in 1896:

  - "I am utterly unable to believe, in short, that God's promise has so entirely failed, that at the end of 1800 years much of the text of the Gospel had in point of fact to be picked by a German critic out of a waste-paper basket in the convent of St. Catherine; and that the entire text had to be remodeled after the pattern set by a couple of copies which had remained in neglect during fifteen centuries, and had probably owed their survival to that neglect; whilst hundreds of others had been thumbed to pieces, and had bequeathed their witness to copies made from them." (Burgon, 12)

- In other words, according to the textual model embraced by Drs. Westcott and Hort, Burgon reasoned that "... God kept hidden from the church the true text of the Word of God from sometime around the ninth century until the discoveries of the Codex Sinaiticus and Vaticanus in the nineteenth century." (Combs, 42)

- While I personally find the reasoning of both Hills and Burgon to be sound given the parameters of the debate, Dr. Combs not surprisingly takes exception to it. Firstly, Combs views the expression "true text" as "loaded language" that "distorts the view of those who do not believe that either the TR or MT is necessarily the closest text to the autographs." (Combs, 42) Dr. Combs maintains that the TR, MT, and W&HT all accurately convey the message of the autographs. Therefore, the TR, MT, W&HT as well as the more recent editions of the Nestle-Aland Text and the United Bible Societies' Text can all rightly be called the "true text" because they "accurately convey the message of the autographs." According to Combs there are no substantive differences between the various Greek texts listed above that affect doctrine.

    o "It has already been argued that doctrinal differences among Christians do not stem from differences in Greek texts or English versions. Many of us simply prefer the more recent editions of the Greek New Testament because we honestly believe that they present a text that is somewhat more accurately representative of the autographs." (Combs, 42)

- If Combs believes that "more recent editions of the Greek New Testament" are better representatives of the autographs, then he must by default believe that there are verses in the TR/KJB that should not be there. How the presence of extra verses does not affect doctrine is beyond my ability to comprehend. The notion that the debate over the inclusion or exclusion of Mark 16:9-20 does not affect any doctrine is wishful thinking on the part of Combs.

- Consequently, Combs' first objection to the notion that preservation includes the idea of "public availability" is a moot point. The verses and readings that Combs thinks are the best representation of the originals were not made available to the body of Christ until the late 19th century according to the critical theory. Therefore, the objections to the critical theory and its implications voiced by Burgon and Hills on the grounds of "public availability" still stand.

- Combs' second objection to the notion that preservation requires "public availability" centers on the fact that scriptures make no such proclamation.

    o "Second, the belief that God must have made the Scriptures publicly available at all times has no basis in Scripture itself or in the transmission history of the text." (Combs, 42)

- While it is true that there is no single verse in which God explicitly states, "I will preserve my word by making it publicly available;" the totality of verses that we have looked at regarding the process of preservation imply not only availability to God's people but also use by them.

- Combs states the following to buttress his point from above:

    o "In fact, Scripture itself records an instance where part of the Old Testament was not available for a period of probably more than fifty years. When the temple was being repaired in the eighteenth year of the reign of Josiah (622 B.C.), we read of the finding of "the book of the law" by Hilkiah the high priest (2 Kings 22:8-10; 2 Chr 34:14-18). Though it is not clear whether "the book of the law" is a reference to the entire Pentateuch or just the book of Deuteronomy, it is undeniable from the reaction of Josiah (vv. 11ff.) that there had been general ignorance of the Law for some time (Josiah says "our fathers have not obeyed the words of this book," v. 13). According to Deuteronomy 31, Moses wrote down the Law and gave it to the Levites to "place it beside the ark of the covenant" (v. 26). It is probable that normal access to the Scriptures was through copies since the ark, and presumably the Law, was placed in the most holy confines of the temple. But during the reign of Manasseh (697–642 B.C.) true Israelite religion was practically wiped out, and **it may well be** that all copies of the Law were destroyed, thus explaining the general ignorance of the Law until it was discovered during the reign of Josiah." (Combs, 42-43)

- First, note how Combs inadvertently advocates for the process of preservation we have outlined in the class. He acknowledges that original autographs were placed in the Ark of the Covenant in the holy of holies, first in the tabernacle and then later, in the temple. He then states that "normal access to the Scriptures was through copies." While it is true that under the reign of Manasseh Israel did not fare well spiritually; there is a big difference between "practically wiped out" as Combs acknowledges and entirely wiped out. Therefore, his statement "**it may well be** that all copies of the Law were destroyed" is complete speculation. Does Combs actually believe that the only copy of the book of the Law in all of Israel was the one found by Hilkiah the priest during the reign of Josiah? Just because the word of God may have been absent from the priests and the king for a period of time does not mean it was unknown or unavailable to believers within Israel.

- Romans 11:4 — the reign of Ahab was another terrible time for the truth of God's word in Israel's history. Yet Paul says that as many as 7,000 Israelites had "not bowed the knee to the image of Baal." It is nothing but pure speculation on the part of Combs that II Kings 22:8-10 and II Chronicles 34:14-18 mean that God's word was not available to anyone outside of what was found in the temple. In fact, I would argue that it would be contrary to God's purpose in preservation to allow His word to be diminished to only one available witness.

    o Psalms 68:11

Daniel B. Wallace on Public Accessibility

- Dr. Combs is not the only author to take acceptation with the notion that "accessibility" is critical in the Process of Preservation. In the 1990s Dr. Daniel B. Wallace published a series of essays in scholarly journals in which he challenged the "corollary of accessibility." (Wallace *The Majority-Text Theory*, 188) In his 1994 essay "The Majority-Text Theory: History, Methods and Critique" Wallace argues that "accessibility" is "inferred" by those supporting the Majority Text position.

    o "Hence the MT position is based on a corollary (accessibility) of a corollary (preservation) of a particular dogmatic stance (verbal inspiration)." (Wallace TMTT, 201)

- Wallace's comments from 1994 were preceded by his 1992 essay titled "Inspiration, Preservation, and New Testament Textual Criticism" in the *Grace Theological Journal*. In this essay Dr. Wallace quotes Dr. Edward F. Hills and offers the following comment in response:

    o " 'God must preserve this text, not secretly, not hidden away in a box for hundreds of years or mouldering unnoticed on some library shelf, but openly before the eyes of all men through continued usage in his church.' (Hills, 31) Preservation is therefore linked to public accessibility." (Wallace, IPNTTC, 30)

- The same essay contains an entire section titled "Public accessibility of a pure text is a theological necessity." In this section, Dr. Wallace argues against the notion of "accessibility" on the following general grounds: 1) the majority text was not available until 1982, 2) the *Textus Receptus* differs from the majority text in "almost 2,000 places," 3) no one had access to anything other than the majority text for 350 years between 1516 and 1881, and 4) the majority text was not readily available in Egypt for the first four centuries. (Wallace, IPNTTC, 30)

    o See Appendix A to read this section authored by Dr. Wallace.

- It is important to note that many of Dr. Wallace's comments are directed at Dr. Wilbur Pickering's and the Majority Text position. It is also instructive to note that Dr. Wallace points out that "many" of the differences between the Majority Text and the *Textus Receptus* "are theologically significant." (Wallace, IPNTTC, 30) Yet we are expected to buy into the notion that there are no theological differences at all between the Critical Text and the *Textus Receptus*. The double standard is quite glaring.

CONCLUSION

- Deuteronomy 30:11-14 — "11) For this commandment which I command thee this day, it *is* not hidden from thee, neither *is* it far off. It *is* not in heaven, that thou shouldest say, Who shall go up for us to heaven, and bring it unto us, that we may hear it, and do it? Neither *is* it beyond the sea, that thou shouldest say, Who shall go over the sea for us, and bring it unto us, that we may hear it, and do it? But the word *is* very nigh unto thee, in thy mouth, and in thy heart, that thou mayest do it."

- Dr. Kent Brandenburg wrote an entire chapter on this passage for the book *Thou Shalt Keep Them: A Biblical Theology of the Perfect Preservation of Scripture*. Regarding these verses Brandenburg writes in part:

    o "These words, in their context, teach the doctrine of the general availability of all the Words of Scripture for every generation. . .Every generation of Israel needed the Words for the purpose of reviewing, remembering, believing, and practicing them. In Deuteronomy, they were told to remember them fourteen times, and ordered not to forget His Words nine times." (Brandenburg in *Thou Shalt Keep Them*, 85-86)

- Verses 11 through 13 are negative and tell the reader what the commandment is not.

- o "Negatively, the commandment is not hidden, nor is it far off. The Hebrew words translated "not hidden" appear in many different ways in the KJB, but together they essentially mean "accessible," hence, knowable. Words that are hidden might be in a library or buried in some ruin or desert. These qualities ("not hidden," "nor far off") certainly give a tangible quality to the commandment, written down and available in writing. Words far off could be those for which there is no available copy. They could be found in a museum in a display box in one location where the only people who could see it would have to travel a great distance to do so. They could also just reside in heaven, which the text goes on to dismiss as a valid possibility. God-guaranteed access to the Words would not require passing over the sea. The negative section of vv. 11-13 overrules unavailability. Since hearing and doing is dependent on accessibility, the text promises that these Words will not be inaccessible." (Brandenburg, 88-89)

- In contrast, verse 14 is positive; it states what the word "is."

  - o "Positively, the Word is nigh. It is close. The sufficient proximity of people to the Word is revealed by the further description of ". . . in thy mouth, and in thy heart. . ." in v. 14. The promise is repeated in the New Testament passage mentioned earlier (cf. Romans 10:6-8). "Mouth" and "heart" express the closest proximity. They express intimacy. They leave no room for an argument against the truth of the availability of God's Words as a possible excuse for unbelief and disobedience. . . The reason for the availability or accessibility is that one ". . . may hear it, and do it" (vv. 12c, 13c), or that one ". . . mayest do it" (v. 14b)." (Brandenburg, 89-90)

- Deuteronomy 30:15-20 express the seriousness of why availability matters.

  - o "Life, good, and ability to please God are dependent upon it. The potential consequences of unavailability, cursing and loss of blessing, stress the necessity for availability. The expression of punishment adds to the guarantee that His Words will be accessible. God is holy and just. He is merciful. There is a clear intimation in the blessings and curses that a holy, just, and merciful God will make sure that, with so much dependent on accessibility of His Words, He will make sure that they are available." (Brandenburg, 90)

- From this we can see that Dr. Brandenburg deduces the following logical syllogism:
  - *Major Premise*: If it is necessary that His Words be available to every generation, then a holy and just God will ensure their availability.
  - *Minor Premise*: It is necessary.
  - *Conclusion*: God's Words are available to every generation. (Brandenburg, 90)

- It is consistent with a believing viewpoint to maintain the belief that God's word will be available to every generation.

- II Peter 3:2 — "That ye may be mindful of the words which were spoken before by the holy prophets, and of the commandment of us the apostles of the Lord and Saviour:"
  - Peter's readers cannot be mindful "of the words which were spoken before by the holy prophets" unless they were available and accessible to them. The call to remembrance assumes the availability of the Old Testament.

- Jude 17 — "But, beloved, remember ye the words which were spoken before of the apostles of our Lord Jesus Christ;"
  - "The words of the Apostles, spoken before Jude wrote, are not part of the written record... This not only strongly implies that Jude has the Words of the apostles (the New Testament writings completed at that point in time), but also unequivocally states

that believers to which he writes also had these words available."
(La More in *Thou Shalt Keep Them*, 93-94)

- Dr. Gary E. La More concludes his chapter in *Thou Shalt Keep Them* on the availability of scripture with the following paragraph:
  - "The apostles, in quoting the Old Testament, never questioned whether they had available the true Word of God. The apostles acknowledged that what others had written in the New Testament was also God's Word. At the time of 2 Peter and Jude, the New Testament authors were not looking to verify what they had of the Old Testament as the true Word of God. Like all believers, they gladly received it. They were not looking for a lost Bible. God in His providence has seen to it that His Word was passed on from one generation to the next. The apostles received as authentic what they read and quoted from the Old Testament prophets as it had been passed on to them. True believers today should do the same thing. The correct and obvious interpretation of these texts and the implied belief of the apostles was that they had every Word God preserved and available to them. Based upon legitimate application of the text, the Lord's true churches today have available to them not only the Words of the Old Testament prophets but also the Words of the New Testament apostles and other New Testament writers. The teaching of the availability of every Word of Scripture has been and continues to be a strong basis for opposing the attacks on the teaching of the Scripture by the apostles." (La More, 94)

- For those who pay attention to the details, it is clear that God chose to preserve His word in a manner, i.e. copies, that allowed access to God's word by the common man. Consequently, the musings of Combs on the subject of "public availability" and preservation appear to be designed to serve the position that he has already determined is the correct one.

- Availability and access to the scriptures are a logical conclusion of the process of preservation outlined in scripture. God's word was preserved through the dynamic of people handling it, not in one copy sitting on a bookshelf for 500 or 1000 years. That is not the way God preserves His word. He preserves His word by it being in the hands of Bible-believing people, and those people are charged with the responsibility to execute God's purpose.

WORKS CITED

Brandenburg, Kent. "It Is Not Hidden, Neither Is It Far Off: Deuteronomy 30:11-13" in *Thou Shalt Keep Them: A Biblical Theology of the Perfect Preservation of Scripture*. El Sobrante, CA: Pillar & Ground Publishing, 2003.

Burgon, John William. *The Traditional Text of the Holy Gospels*. 1896.

Combs, William W. "The Preservation of Scripture?" in *Detroit Baptist Seminary Journal*. Fall 2000.

Hills, Edward F. *The King James Version Defended*. Des Moines: IA, Christian Research Press, 1956.

La More, Gary. "Be Mindful of the Words: 2 Peter 3:2 and Jude 17" in *Thou Shalt Keep Them: A Biblical Theology of the Perfect Preservation of Scripture*. El Sobrante, CA: Pillar & Ground Publishing, 2003.

Wallace, Daniel B. "Inspiration, Preservation, And New Testament Textual Criticism" in *Grace Theological Journal*. 1992.

Wallace, Daniel B. "The Majority-Text Theory: History, Methods, and Critique" in *Journal of the Evangelical Theological Society*. June 1994.

PUBLIC ACCESSIBILITY OF A PURE TEXT IS A THEOLOGICAL NECESSITY

"We have touched on this to some degree already - at least by way of analogy. But the argument is also contradicted by direct evidence. Pickering believes that "God *has* preserved the text of the New Testament in a very pure form and it has been readily available to His followers in every age throughout 1900 years. There are two fundamental problems with this view.

First, assuming that the majority text (as opposed to the TR) is the original, then this pure form of text has become available only since 1982. The *Textus Receptus* differs from it in almost 2,000 places and in fact has several readings which have "never been found in any known Greek manuscript," and scores, perhaps hundreds, of readings which depend on only a handful of very late manuscripts. Many of these passages are theologically significant texts. Yet virtually no one had access to any other text from 1516 to 1881, a period of over 350 years. In light of this, it is difficult to understand what Pickering means when he says that this pure text "has been readily available to [God's] followers in every age throughout 1900 years." Purity, it seems, has to be a relative term - and, if so, it certainly cannot be marshaled as a theological argument.

Second, again, assuming that the majority text is the original, and that it has been readily available to Christians for 1900 years, then it must have been readily available to Christians in Egypt in the first four centuries. But this is demonstrably not true, as we have already shown. Pickering speaks of our early Alexandrian witnesses as "polluted" and as coming from a "sewer pipe." Now if these manuscripts are really that defective, and if this is all Egypt had in the first three or four centuries, then this peculiar doctrine of preservation is in serious jeopardy, for those ancient Egyptian Christians had no access to the pure stream of the majority text. Therefore, if one were to define preservation in terms of the majority text, he would end up with a view which speaks very poorly of God's sovereign care of the text in ancient Egypt."

Wallace, Daniel B. "Inspiration, Preservation, And New Testament Textual Criticism" in *Grace Theological Journal*. 1992.

CONCLUDING THOUGHTS ON PRESERVATION

INTRODUCTION

- This morning we are going to conclude our nine-month study of the doctrine/promise of preservation. In order to accomplish this task, I would like to review the highlights of our study together as well as offer some concluding thoughts before we take a break for the summer.

- Please note that any [bracketed] text was added by me.

SUMMATIVE THOUGHTS ON PRESERVATION

- Our job as believers is not to **reconstruct the text** as though it has been lost. Rather our job is to allow the scriptures to be our guide in identifying the text God has preserved from generation to generation.

- In Lesson 2, I set forth the following list of Biblical presuppositions that would govern this study.

    o God exists. (Psalm 14:1)

    o God has magnified His word above His own name. (Psalms 138:2)

    o God's word is eternally settled in heaven. (Psalms 119:89)

    o God, through the process of inspiration, has communicated His word to mankind. (II Timothy 3:16 and II Peter 1:21)

    o God's words were written down so that they could be made eternally available to men. (Isaiah 30:8 and I Peter 1:23)

    o God promised to preserve that which He inspired. (Psalms 12:6-7)

- The entire second term of this course has been about establishing the validity of the sixth presupposition that "God promised to preserve that which He inspired." In order to accomplish this task we considered the following:

    o *Introduction* to Preservation (Lessons 28-29)

    o *Views* of Preservation (Lesson 30)

    o *Promise* of Preservation (Lessons 31-39)

    o *Importance* of Preservation (Lesson 40)

    o *Extent* of Preservation (Lessons 41-46)

    o *Method* of Preservation (Lesson 47)

    o *Process* of Preservation (Lessons 48-56)

- The following thoughts regarding why preservation matters are taken from Dr. Jim Taylor's 2016 book *In Defense of the Textus Receptus: God's Preserved Word to Every Generation.*

    o "If all we had were the principles of inspiration, we would not have enough information to make a sound choice concerning the Greek (or Hebrew for that matter) texts. Thankfully, the doctrine of inspiration does not stand alone for it has as its companion several other important and relevant truths by which we can make logical, biblically based choices concerning which text is to be preferred above others. Depending on your understanding and application of these two important doctrines, you will be led to definite conclusions concerning the Greek and Hebrew texts.

    The whole issue concerning Bible texts, and by extension, translations, hinges on the doctrine of preservation. Either God preserved his word or he did not. If he did not, then it does not matter which textual family you prefer and we cannot be sure if we have the uncorrupted Word of God. If he did not, then God did not keep his promises to preserve his word.

    But since we believe that God **most certainly did** preserve his word, then we must now define what exactly we mean by preservation. Did God preserve the exact words that he gave? Or did he merely preserve the ideas or main gist of what he gave? Since we have already clearly stated our belief in verbal-plenary inspiration, we can logically assume that God would preserve his exact words. [I agree with Taylor that God did preserve His words, not merely the idea or the gist of his words. As we have seen throughout this term, this does not mean "verbatim identicality" of wording.] Beyond this, there is ample Scriptural evidence pointing to this very fact!

    So how we define "preservation" will determine, in a large part, how we will respond to the subject of textual criticism. This will in turn define our position on the texts themselves which will then also greatly affect how we view translations.

    The subject of textual criticism itself is really nothing more than a determination of "if" or "how" to apply the principles of preservation to the extant manuscripts. This is why it is so crucial to have a biblical understanding of this doctrine." (Taylor, 43)

- In the next section Dr. Taylor offers a very common-sense approach to why a "faith-based approach" (fideistic approach) is a necessary Biblical prerequisite to textual criticism.

  o "Many, if not most, modern textual critics have approached the issue of textual criticism from a purely historical or academic perspective. This makes the foundation of their decisions either personal education or logic. Therefore, many have come to conclusions which may appear to be rational or academically sound, but are not really balanced because, in order to correctly approach any issue concerning the word of God, we must begin with the foundation of faith—what we believe about what the Bible says concerning itself. If there is a contradiction between our belief and the scriptures, then we are to conclude that the biblical principles are right, and all other opinions are wrong. Biblical principles always take precedence over human logic and understanding.

  Why must this be our approach? This must be our approach because the Bible is not like any other book. It claims to be the message from God and therefore is a book to be approached from the aspect of faith. It saddens me to see how some Bible teachers ridicule others for taking a faith-based approach to the textual issue. In one case, a certain textual critic who even supports the *Textus Receptus* from a logical and academic standpoint somewhat ridicules another because his approach is faith-based. But in reality, a faith-based approach does not negate the other. Provided that the academic and logical approach does not violate scripture, it is a valid argument and should be used in stating our case. However, it cannot be the main argument.

  Any approach that either rules out or contradicts a faith-based approach to the textual issue must be rejected on the grounds that it is humanistic. . . Let's stop and think about this for a moment. Our faith is the whole reason why we discuss the manuscripts at all! If the Bible were simply an ancient book of stories and anecdotes, then word-for-word transmission would cease to be so important.

If the Bible is just another book, then who really cares whether there are differences? Who cares if something was added or something was mistakenly edited out as long as the general ideas of the writer is kept intact? What makes one man's opinions any better than another man's opinions? But if the Bible is truly from God, then it really matters! And we better make sure we have it right!

Much of the disagreement today, tends to be more semantic than concrete. Where two people can both agree in the end result, how they arrived at their conclusions could be, and in many cases are, very different. For example, some refer to the King James Version as "the inspired Word of God," while others would rather say "The Preserved Word of God." Others would simply say that the King James is a faithful and accurate translation. Then there are yet others who would argue that all three statements are simultaneously true.

There are also many different arguments concerning the nature of preservation. Does God preserve his word? Does God preserve his Word in only one manuscript? Does God preserve every word or just the main ideas? Does preservation demand accessibility to what God has given? These questions, and many others boggle our minds day-in and day-out! But these questions have been answered by God himself in his Word. Additionally, theologians and scholarly men have written abundantly (especially in recent years) upon this very issue.

But we do not follow Dr. So-and-So. We must base our beliefs concerning God's Word on the Word itself. This is a faith-based approach. In the course of this book, history and science will be used to support our conclusions. But ultimately, these are merely supporting evidences that what the Bible says about itself is true. So it all comes down to an issue of faith. Do we believe that God can do and did do what he promised? As we shall see, God has amply promised to preserve his Word and clearly did just that!

As we speak of preservation, what we are really speaking of is the divine safeguarding of the manuscripts, and manuscript evidence. As we study preservation, we are unavoidably drawn into a discussion of the thousands of extant documents, where they came from, who wrote them, how old they are, how readable or trustworthy they are, and so on.

And if you will think about it for a few minutes, the answers to many of these questions will ultimately fall upon decisions of "textual critics." Most of us don't know enough about history, geography, or biblical languages to enter into a discussion of such magnitude. Does this mean my faith in God's Word must now rest in the hands of other men? No, because the promises of preservation are placed in the hands of all men to believe. God keeps his promises. All we need to determine is exactly what God promised, to what does his promise apply, and whether or not we are willing to believe Him!

Bible preservation refers to the biblical doctrine and historical process by which God has kept his word pure from corruption after he gave it by inspiration to man. Therefore, if we are to truly understand the extent of preservation, we must also consider doctrinal and historical principles." (Taylor, 43-45)

SUMMATIVE OBSERVATIONS REGARDING PRESERVATION

- Whatever one believes about preservation must take into account the following facts:

  o Fact 1 — the original autographs are not extant i.e., they no longer exist.

  o Fact 2 — no two Greek manuscripts are exactly the same.

- Fact 3 — no two printed editions of the Greek New Testament are exactly the same.
- Fact 4 — no two editions of the King James Bible are exactly the same.
- Fact 5 — the King James differs from modern versions.
- Fact 6 — no two modern versions read exactly the same.
- Summary Statement:
  - "If the preservation of the Word of God depends upon **exact** preservation of the words of the original documents, then the situation is dire. No two manuscripts contain exactly the same words. No two editions of the Masoretic Text contain exactly the same words. No two editions of the *Textus Receptus* contain exactly the same words. No two modifications of the King James Version contain exactly the same words and the Bible nowhere tells us which edition, if any, does contain the exact words of the originals. These are not speculations, these are plain facts." (Bauder, 155)

- Given the Biblical data as well as the historical and textual FACTS, the following points are inescapable:
  - God promised to preserve His word.
    - Psalms 12:6-7; 105:5; 119:89, 111, 152, 160; Isaiah 30:8; 40:8; Matthew 24:35; I Peter 1:23-25
  - God did not see fit to preserve His word by preserving the original autographs.
    - This is self-evident because the originals no longer exist.
  - God did not supernaturally over-take the pen of every scribe, copyist, or typesetter who ever handled the text to ensure that no differences of any kind entered the text.
    - Differences exist at every level of this discussion.

- o If the standard for preservation is "plenary," "pristine," or "*verbatim*" identicality why did God not just preserve the originals and thereby remove all doubt?
    - The reason is that God wants people to walk by faith in their view of the Biblical text.

- I believe in "perfect preservation" if, by "perfect," one means the existence of a pure text that does not report information about God, His nature or character, His doctrine, His dispensational dealings with mankind, history, archeology, or science that is false. In short, God's promise to preserve His word assures the existence of a text that has not been altered in its "character" or "doctrinal content" despite not being preserved in a state of *verbatim identicality*.

- Once again, our job as believers is not to **reconstruct the text** as though it has been lost. Rather our job is to allow the scriptures to be our guide in identifying the text God has preserved from generation to generation.

- The following scriptural principles will assist the believer in identifying the preserved text:

    - o *Multiplicity of Copies* — God's design was to preserve His word in a multiplicity of accurate reliable copies that were just as authoritative as the originals. Therefore, we ought to be able to observe in history a collection of manuscripts that are plenteous and in substantive agreement with each other regarding doctrinal content despite not possessing "verbatim" wording.

    - o *Available/Accessible* — the Preserved Text would not only exist in a multiplicity of copies but these copies would be available to God's people to possess, study, believe, and preach from. They would not be hidden under a rock, in the sand, or in an inaccessible library.

    - o *In Use* — a third Biblical mark of the Preserved Text would be use by God's people for generations. God's word was preserved through the dynamic of people handling it, not in one copy sitting on a bookshelf for 500 or 1000 years. That is not the way God preserves His word. He preserves His word by it being

- When these three Biblical principles are applied to the historical and textual facts, they point toward the *Textus Receptus* (*TR*), the text of the Protestant Reformation, as being the printed form of the Preserved Text. The *TR* is supported by the vast majority of extant Greek manuscripts (*multiplicity of copies*). Moreover, it represents a text that was clearly available, accessible, and in use by Bible-believing people throughout the history of the dispensation of grace.

- In stark contrast, the Critical Text supporting Modern Versions fails on all three counts to pass the tests of scripture: 1) it has few manuscript witnesses, that substantively disagree with each other, 2) its principal manuscripts were not accessible or available to believers throughout the dispensation of grace, and 3) given their lack of availability, they certainly were not used by Bible-believing people during the church age.

    o "Now, the crux of the matter is based upon the premise that God has divinely preserved every word that he gave. If we do not believe this, then any discussion concerning the two texts becomes a matter of personal preference based upon man's intellect or will. But since we firmly believe that God has preserved, not just the basic truths, not just the general ideas, not just the basic thoughts, but even the very words themselves, we must conclude that one text or the other has been corrupted." (Taylor, 56)

IMPLICATIONS OF PRESERVATION

- Consider the following implications of preservation outlined by Dr. Taylor:

- ". . . along with the doctrine of inspiration, the doctrine of preservation becomes an important key to choosing the right text. It is unfortunate that so many good people misunderstand the doctrine of preservation. And because of this, the terms "preservation," "preserved," etc. are often misapplied or simply misused. It is not uncommon to hear good men speak of translations being "preserved." But in a strict biblical sense, preservation only applies to what God has given by inspiration, and not what has been accomplished by translation. The past 2,000 years have seen many translations come and go—some translations were good, some not so good. But the fact is, none of them were preserved.

  Some would argue that the King James Version is over 400 years old so it MUST be preserved. I would simply make two observations on this thought. First, the fact that the King James Version is over 400 years old is a testimony to its beauty, accuracy, and influence. No one can take away from that. God's people would not have used it for so long if they felt it was not trustworthy. So its age becomes a great witness to its superiority as a translation. . .

  But let's not lose sight of the fact that languages are "containers" of that which has been eternally settled in heaven. It does not matter whether the "container" is in the form of a faithful translation, or the original languages themselves—the truth has not lost its identity or power in any way. Insofar as a translation is a faithful and accurate representation of the exact message God gave, it can be called God's inspired and preserved word.

  Yet we must understand that as we make this statement, we are not referring to the containers themselves but to the truth of God within the containers, as revealed to man. What we are discussing is how we choose the container. Or, to put it another way, we are discussing the condition of the container and whether or not it has effectively preserved its contents (the truth) [Daniel 10:21 affirms this notation. The scriptures by definition do not report information that is false.]. Personally, I want to drink my spiritual drink from the container that has ALL the truth and ONLY the truth. Thus, I stand upon the *Textus Receptus*, and by extension of its faithfulness and accuracy to the *Textus Receptus*, the King James Version.

[Recall from Lesson 40 the words of Louis Gaussen's seminal 1840 work *Theopneustia* (*The Divine Inspiration of the Bible*) about the word being incarnated in human language through inspiration and translation changing its dress.].

Some would argue that the King James Version has not "come and gone" like so many other translations, which proves it has been inspired or preserved. Although this is true, we should at least be honest enough to admit that if Jesus tarries his coming, English like the Greek language spoken by the whole Roman Empire in the first century could become a dead language...

[Therefore] Let's be reminded of what the biblical definition of preservation is. We define preservation as the act of God whereby He protects His text from any possible corruption from its very inception forevermore... So when we speak of preservation, we are not referring to a translation but to the Greek and Hebrew texts.

[Taylor seems to make contradictory statements in this section of his book. On the one hand he states, "preservation only applies to what God has given by inspiration, and not what has been accomplished by translation." Later he writes, "insofar as a translation is a faithful and accurate representation of the exact message God gave, it can be called God's inspired and preserved word." Then he says, "when we speak of preservation, we are not referring to a translation but to the Greek and Hebrew texts." While I appreciate Taylor very much for his evenhanded tone, these comments are not helpful and are confusing. I believe that the Process of Preservation includes both original language texts as well as translations thereof. This is the only way that access to God's word can be assured to every generation. Given the fact that early translations are vital to the *Textus Receptus* position, it seems strange that Dr. Taylor would make seemingly contradictory statements on this matter.]

Biblically, we must limit preservation in the strictest sense to the Greek and Hebrew manuscripts because those were the languages and words that God chose to deliver his message to man. As we apply the doctrine of preservation to the Greek manuscripts, several questions must logically and biblically be answered. Namely, "if a text had fallen out of use, does it still meet the criteria of "preservation"? Can we reasonably claim to have the pure Word of God if we do not know what the originals looked like? These questions and others should be answered.

As we seek to keep a balanced view, we should objectively examine both the *Textus Receptus* and the Critical Text with the same criteria." (Taylor, 57-59)

- In the next volume we will turn our attention to these considerations.

WORKS CITED

Bauder, Kevin T. "An Appeal to Scripture" in *One Bible Only? Examining the Exclusive Claims for the King James Bible*. Grand Rapids, MI: Kregel Publications, 2001.

Taylor, Jim. *In Defense of the Textus Receptus*. Cleveland, GA: Old Path Publications, 2016.

Trust Publishers House,
the trusted name in quality Christian books.

Trust House Publishers
PO Box 3181
Taos, NM 87571

TrustHousePublishers.com